"Somebody's Gotta Be Me"

"Somebody's Gotta Be Me"

The Wide, Wide World of the One and Only Charles Barkley

By David Casstevens

The Arizona Republic

ANDREWS AND McMEEL

A Universal Press Syndicate Company

Kansas City

Additional copies of this book may be ordered by calling (800) 642-6480.

Cataloging–in–Publication Data
Casstevens, David.
    "Somebody's gotta be me" : the wide, wide world of the one and only Charles Barkley / by David Casstevens.
    p.   cm.
    ISBN 0-8362-8074-1
    1. Barkley, Charles, 1963–   2. Basketball players—United States—Biography.   I. Title.
    GV884.B28C37   1994
    796.323'092—dc20
    [B]   94-35180
                                                                            CIP
Cover photograph: Rob Schumacher
Book design: Barrie Maguire

CONTENTS

ACKNOWLEDGMENTS

Many people helped in many ways to make this book possible. A special thanks to Jeff Dozbaba, assistant managing editor of *The Arizona Republic*, for his ideas and advice and the hours he spent editing the book and working with the publisher.

Thanks also to:

Rob Schumacher, *Republic* photographer, for following Charles Barkley through the rain in Munich and for the photo layout, which he designed.

Republic systems editor Bill Woodruff for convincing me my computer is my friend.

Republic sports editor Bill Hill for juggling schedules.

The *Republic* library staff, upon whom I relied from day one.

Thanks also to *Republic* executive editor John Oppedahl and managing editor Pam Johnson for their encouragement and support.

—D.C.

To Sharon, for believing in me, for showing me the possibilities and for always being there. To Amy, Anne and Casey. All I do, I do for you.

PROLOGUE

What's the best book you've ever read?

"*Days of Grace*, by Arthur Ashe."

Who is the sexiest woman in the world?

"The sexiest woman in the world ..." He looked off into the distance and thumbed through his global Rolodex of blondes, A to Z. Fifteen seconds passed. "Pamela Anderson," he said suddenly.

Pamela Anderson?

"She's an actress. On 'Baywatch.'"

If you were having a dinner party and could invite six people, living or dead, who would they be? "Malcolm X," Charles Barkley said. "Dr. Martin Luther King, Abe Lincoln. Colin Powell ... How many's that?"

Four.

"John F. Kennedy. And, Richard Nixon."

Sportswriters are a little like oil field workers. We search for interesting personalities. We dig for good quotes, as hopeful as wildcatters drilling for crude. Most athletes, I have found, don't yield much in the way of enlightening or entertaining conversation. Some speak in clichés. Some don't speak at all to the press, which is their prerogative. We hit a lot of dry holes in this business.

Now and then we get lucky. In early summer 1992, the Philadelphia 76ers traded Barkley to Phoenix. I knew only a little about him. He grew up in Leeds, Ala. He played at Auburn. He spent eight seasons with the Sixers in a city where he was loved and despised and never ignored. Barkley, it seemed, always was doing *something*. Always making news.

The trade was a stroke of good fortune for the Suns. For a writer, it was like hitting a gusher. Barkley is funny, charming, crude, opinionated, outspoken, brash, profane, thoughtful, contradictory, moody, honest, impulsive, playful, self-centered, kind-hearted, arrogant, gruff, gentle, optimistic, fiercely competitive and delightfully quotable. Like a producing oil well, he pumps out quips and quotes by the barrel. There isn't a question he won't answer—in some way. The challenge is thinking of questions he hasn't been asked.

Barkley has played two seasons for the Suns. That's two lifetimes.

An NBA campaign, if you count preseason and the playoffs, begins in October and ends in June, and spans Halloween, Thanksgiving, Christmas, New Year's, the Super Bowl, Martin Luther King, Jr., Day, Lincoln's Birthday, Washington's Birthday, my birthday, Valentine's Day, Groundhog Day, St. Patrick's Day, baseball spring training, Passover, Easter, the NFL draft, two dozen PGA Tour tournaments, Mother's Day and Memorial Day. The season stretches out like a trackless desert. Barkley is a canteen of cool water. The pause that refreshes.

This book, which spans the 1993–94 Suns season, is about the Charles Barkley I know and have observed, on stage and backstage. What's he like? I put that question, which I am often asked, to Ian Whittell, a reporter for *The Sun*, a London tabloid. Ian interviewed Barkley when the Suns were in Dallas in April 1994 to play the Mavericks.

"After all the press I had read about him I expected some kind of three-headed ogre," Whittell said. "But I didn't find him that way. Not at all. He is delightful. Very personable."

Ian smiled. "He does have this inability to keep quiet, doesn't he?"

Well said.

1

Dream Land

Charles is the NBA ambassador. I could not succeed him.
I could not crack all those jokes.
　—Hakeem Olajuwon, 1994 NBA Most Valuable Player

They sat at a long table, on display like our first space heroes, the *Mercury* astronauts. The names were as famous as Cooper, Carpenter, Shepard and Glenn, if not more so.

Jordan, Johnson, Ewing, Robinson, Stockton, Pippen, Drexler, Bird, Malone, Mullin and Charles Barkley, plus a kid, Laettner, thrown in. America's finest. The 1992 U.S. Olympic basketball team. The Dream Team. As strobes flashed, illuminating their faces in white light, the greatest collection of basketball talent ever assembled traded grins and sidelong glances and listened through earphones as questions were translated into English.

From Japan, for Michael Jordan: "Mr. Jordan, can you tell me how it feels to be called a god?"

Jordan looked at his smirking teammates. "I've never seen a god. So I don't know how a god would act. I take it as a compliment."

The journalist nodded appreciatively.

From Sweden, for Magic Johnson. "Do you hold any grudge against the Australian team because their captain said he was reluctant to play against you because you are HIV positive?"

"No, it doesn't matter," Magic said airily. "Like I've said, we'll win by 50 points with me, or by 60 without me." Quizzed about his stamina, his voice took on a hard edge. "I'll answer all your other questions when I hit the court. You'll find out real soon."

For Patrick Ewing: "All we hear about the American team is money. I wonder, is your heart really in it?"

"Our what?" The New York Knicks center turned his ear toward the throng of international journalists, and squinted into the lights.

"Heart," Jordan whispered.

"If our heart wasn't in it, we would have stayed in the U.S.A.," Ewing assured. "Come tomorrow, you'll see our heart."

The BBC, for John Stockton. "You say the Olympic Village is nice, and yet your team isn't staying there. How about the Olympic spirit?"

"To me," Stockton replied, "the Olympic spirit is about going out and beating other athletes, not living with them."

Another journalist stepped to the microphone. "Mr. Barkley . . ."

"There's your man," a colleague seated next to me whispered. *My man?* Charles Barkley and I had not met, formally. On June 17, 1992, the Philadelphia 76ers traded their discontented star to Phoenix. In exchange for Barkley, the Suns gave up Jeff Hornacek, the team's leading scorer and one of its most popular players, along with Tim Perry and Andrew Lang.

Barkley learned of the trade while at the airport in Milwaukee, where earlier in the day he was acquitted of battery and disorderly conduct for punching a man outside a local tavern. "I had a premonition that day I was going to get traded," Barkley said. "It sounds flaky, I know. But it happens to me, sometimes. It's a true story, I swear to God. I was at the airport, waiting to get on the plane, and something in my mind said I should call Philadelphia. There was no reason for me to call the Sixers. No reason. I called Jimmy Lynam, the Sixers general manager. He said, 'Call me right back. We may have a deal.' I called back 10 minutes later and Jimmy said, 'You're playing for the Phoenix Suns now.' "

When Jerry Colangelo hung up the phone, the deal done, he did not dance around his office, high-fiving with his staff. But the Suns owner was excited.

"We knew Charles had run his course in Philadelphia. He needed a change. He wanted out in the worst way," Colangelo said. "He wanted to come here, and the feeling was that we were going to catch him on a rebound. And we were going to catch him at exactly the right time. It was a deal we felt would get us to another level.

"You've got to be willing to roll the dice. You have to be willing to spend the money. You have to be willing to do things that maybe others are too conservative to do. I wasn't frightened by Charles Barkley's persona, his reputation or anything like that. I often hear people talk about talent in the following way: 'He can't do this and he can't do that.' I want to talk about the positives. What he can do. So, in my mind, the deal was a slam dunk. To go out and get a Charles Barkley, pay the price that we did, to give us that opportunity to take a shot at it, it was worth it.

"After the trade was consummated, issues were raised regarding Charles Barkley and his personal problems and all those things. We very quickly said you accept the whole package. The pluses so far outweighed the minuses that it was a no-brainer to go forward, especially when we believed we were going to catch him at the right time."

The trade wasn't three-for-one. It was three-for-three. The Suns received an All-Star scorer and rebounder, the most colorful personality in basketball, and a whole new attitude, rolled into one.

Barkley arrived in Phoenix two days later. As the media awaited his arrival at a press conference at America West Arena—"Elvis is in the building," Al McCoy, TV and radio voice of the Suns, assured—fans outside the team's new home peered in, hoping to glimpse the newest Sun, their noses pressed against the glass doors like children looking through a storefront window at Christmas.

"That first day was really the first time I had spoken with Charles," Colangelo said. "I had never had a conversation with him. It was my first exposure to him. One story I would tell. I remember sitting home reading the newspaper and watching a college basketball game on TV. Auburn was playing. I looked over my glasses and saw this roly-poly kid named Charles Barkley do something that kind of stunned me. He got the ball off the boards, dribbled down the court, dribbled behind his back, made a sensational pass to someone cutting to the hoop, who missed the shot, and Charles went up and jammed the rebound.

"I couldn't believe a guy that size did all those things in one sequence and had so much agility, speed and quickness. I mean, in just one *whooosh*, one play, he did it all. The only other time I had seen anything else like that was the first time I saw Larry Bird, in a college game. He had about 40 in the first half and put on a clinic like you wouldn't believe. What I saw Charles do in that one play made me realize that this guy is some kind of talent. I mean how can you pack that kind of talent in a six-foot-four frame?"

He is shorter than I envisioned. Listed at 6-6, he stands 6-4½. He doesn't look tall enough to play power forward in the NBA. But as the newest Phoenix Sun said, that first day, "Height is overrated. I've played with a lot of bad tall players."

His shoulders are broad. They looked capable of carrying the Suns to the NBA Finals, maybe even to the championship, which is why the team got him. That day Cotton Fitzsimmons, senior executive vice president and former Suns coach, gave Barkley a tour of the team's new $89 million home. Fitzsimmons took Barkley to the top of the balcony. "You see these seats," Cotton said, looking out at the 19,000 purple chairs. "They're all sold. Nobody is buying a ticket because you're here. See the mortar in this building? You didn't put down one block." In the eerie silence, Fitzsimmons pointed to the rafters. Up there, Charles. Barkley lifted his eyes. It didn't take an interior decorator to point out what the palace needed, what was missing. "There's not an NBA championship banner up there. That's all you can bring to us. Anything less and you haven't done it."

His torso is as thick as *Webster's Unabridged.* At Auburn, he played at 280 pounds. Fans nicknamed him Food World, after a grocery chain. The Round Mound of Rebound. Boy Gorge. The Leaning Tower of Pizza. But that was then. He put a palm to his 36-inch waist. "I might go 250, 255."

His hands aren't large, by NBA standards. He performs most of his dunks two-handed. But they are strong hands, sure hands.

His legs are hitching posts. As a kid he burned off energy by jumping back and forth over a fence behind his home in tiny Leeds, Ala. The exercise strengthened his legs, which are the source of his explosiveness and power.

His rear end is ample. The syndicated cartoon "In The Bleachers" pictures a group of children sprawled on the ground alongside a parked school bus. In the background, a mother, hands on hips, is complaining, "Well, there goes that Barkley kid again. Using his big rump to clear out a position in line." The caption: "Charles Barkley—the formative years." Mychal Thompson, the ex-Laker, said of Barkley, "You can't shove him because he's got such a low center of gravity. And by low center of gravity, I mean he's got a big butt. He's definitely got a butt that could win any butt contest he enters."

The sockless feet inside the suede loafers are made for someone else. His foot speed is remarkable for his body type.

"The Phoenix Suns have made me very, very happy," he said, and his smile was genuine. Ironically, he was leaving Philadelphia, a city he labeled "racist" and moving to a state where voters had rejected a paid state holiday honoring the late Martin Luther King, Jr., one of Barkley's heroes. But Barkley said labeling Arizona as a racist state was unfair. He refused to pass judgment on a place he hadn't lived.

A fresh start. A new beginning. "I can't tell you how much I owe you," he told Colangelo in private. "You got me out of purgatory." He was leaving a losing team and joining one where he could win, and a chance to win was all he ever wanted.

"I think it's going to rejuvenate me," Barkley said of the trade. "I think I died a little bit inside last year. It's no fun going to work every night and getting your brains beat out. I'm not going to sit here and guarantee us a championship, but I think we've got a shot at it, and that's all anybody can ask."

Philadelphia. Phoenix. Now, five weeks later in this whirlwind summer Barkley was in Barcelona, on the world stage. As a Phoenix Sun, he was my responsibility, my man, so to speak. Everything Barkley said and did would be big news, especially in Arizona. Maybe, hopefully, Barkley would play the role of diplomat.

"Mr. Barkley, what do you know about your team's first opponent, Angola?"

"I don't know anything about Angola," Barkley replied. "But Angola's in *trouble*."

The room exploded in laughter.

Voice of America: "Mr. Barkley, how did you feel when the Soviet Union beat the U.S. basketball team in the gold-medal game in 1972?"

"Well, I had just flunked my entrance exam into kindergarten back then. But I think it was a travesty. We'll remember that. None of those foreign athletes will admit it—they don't like Americans. But we're gonna get it done, and we're gonna have a little revenge in our hearts."

Barkley looked down the row at David Robinson, center for the San Antonio Spurs. "David can't say that because he's a Christian, but I think we feel some revenge for '72 and '88."

Mexico TV. For Mr. Barkley. "How do you feel about your team not staying in the Olympic Village with the other athletes?"

"I think it's a little unfair to ask us to stay in the village because of the magnitude of Michael and Magic and Larry Bird. We got god on our team. We couldn't stay in the village. We're gonna stay where god wants us to stay." Barkley looked at Jordan. "Ain't that right, Michael?"

From Russian TV. "Mr. Barkley, how do you feel about NBA playing in Olympic Games?"

"Well, you can't please everybody, number one. And I don't think the criticism is fair. Why is it such a big deal when we use pros and those teams have been using pros for years? Why is it such a big deal now? Why don't they take their ass-whippin' like people and go home?"

Jordan covered his mouth with both hands. Other members of the Dream Team bowed their heads, hiding grins.

The Dream Team hadn't played a game and already Barkley was the center of attention. Next day, when the U.S. beat Angola 116–48 and Barkley elbowed a skinny Angolan in the chest and afterward refused to apologize—"We're here to win the gold medal. If people don't like it, then turn the TV off"—Barkley began to upstage everyone.

"The only reason they came up with the Dream Team was to make basketball popular around the world. That and to make money," Barkley said, looking back on the experience. "From a money standpoint, we were just pawns in a big game. Anybody that tells you differently is lying.

"But the players had fun. Playing in the Olympics was one of the highlights of my life. It was like a reward. I had never won an NBA championship. Being on the team was like a thank you for playing hard and busting my ass for all those years in Philadelphia.

"It was like a big fraternity party, being with those guys. Patrick and Larry didn't like each other. So we called Patrick 'Harry' and had these T-shirts made up that said 'Larry and Harry.' Those two became good friends. I became close to Chris Mullin. His baby kept me up every night. It got to be a joke between us.

"There was so much pressure. We couldn't lose. And the security was so tight it was unreal. Every time you walked out of the hotel there was a guy standing there with a semi-automatic rifle. You'd go up to the pool on the roof and there were guys with rifles. You'd go to practice and there would be four police cars in front of the bus, four cars in back, two guys on each side with rifles, and a helicopter was flying overhead. It made you realize the enormity of the whole situation.

"The games were easy. I wish people could have gone to our practices. They were a lot more entertaining than the games. The best basketball I've ever seen or been around was those practices. I had never been in a situation like that, and never will again. We had me and Karl Malone trying to prove who was the best power forward. We had Michael and Clyde trying to prove who was the best shooting guard. Scottie was guarding Magic. We had David and Patrick trying to kill each other. We had Larry and Chris going at it. It was so intense. Every game in practice went down to the last moment, the last shot.

"People talk about egos, how it might be hard to get along. That's a misconception. You don't get to be really, really great unless you're a good guy. You never get to that next level unless you're a team player who will do whatever it takes to win. All great players are concerned about is winning."

As predicted, the Dream Team rolled through the bracket unchallenged. The Americans shattered the previous Olympic scoring record and became the first team to score at least 100 points in every game. They won by an average of 43.8 points.

Barkley referred to himself as just one of the fellas on the bus, and there was no mistaking what bus it was that sped away from the Palau D' Esports after the U.S. Olympic team beat Croatia, 117–85, to win the gold medal. Lights flashed and sirens wailed as the Dream Team headed toward the airport, escorted by six motorcycle policemen, vans of armed soldiers, an ambulance, and a fire truck in tow.

But Barkley was being modest, which he rarely is. On the world stage, the NBA star grew in stature. *Sports Illustrated* featured him in a Dream Team story titled "Wild Bull of Las Ramblas." Barkley led the U.S. Olympians in scoring, averaging 18 points. In the championship game, with the U.S. trailing 25–23, Barkley took over. He swished a shot from behind the three-point line. Next time down the court he stole the ball, dribbled behind his back and whipped a pass to Clyde Drexler, racing to the basket. A Barkley dunk. Then another. A Barkley tip-in. The suspense, and the game, were over.

"The Olympics showed that when I play with good players I was even better. The game was so easy for me over there. When you play with good players the game is simple. The game is only hard when you play with bad players. I believe that.

"I think the Olympics took me to the next level. My popularity hit a new peak," Barkley said, thinking back to that glorious night he stepped up on the medal stand, washed in cheers. He blew kisses to the crowd. He and Magic Johnson wrapped their arms around each other and laughed like schoolboys as they shared the once-in-a-lifetime moment.

"Bark-ley! Bark-ley!" fans chanted from the arena's upper deck. Barkley turned in the direction of the cheers, smiled and snapped off a crisp military salute.

As Barkley left the court, his work done, a TV reporter from Milan called out frantically, "Charles, Charles! Can you please say something to the people of Italy?"

"Hello, little Italian people," Barkley said, daintily wiggling his fingers at the camera. "Keep making that good spaghetti!"

As the cheers finally died, and the arena emptied, Barkley walked into the interview area, still wearing his sweaty uniform, and plopped down in a chair. "You guys step back," he instructed the media. "I got body odor."

Charles, what are you going to do with your gold medal?

"I'm gonna put it on a big gold chain, get myself a boom box and play rap music all day."

No, seriously?

Barkley lifted the shiny medallion from his chest and looked down at it, inspecting it for the first time. His voice softened. "I may give it to my daughter. I might send it to my high school. I want them to know that a little fat kid from a small Southern town can make it somewhere. Maybe someday, they'll have a hundred medals just like this one. But this is the first one. For me, this is a thrill."

Then he went off again, lecturing the media, as he did after every game. Why do y'all keep asking about the village? What does it matter who slept where? He hit an Angolan. What's the big deal? You guys try to make a controversy out of everything. You never let up. Always stirring things up.

"I'm tired of you guys. Eighty percent of the media are ass wipes." The newest Phoenix Sun lifted his eyes. He spotted *The Arizona Republic* printed on the laminated credential hanging from the stranger's neck. "My man from Arizona here," he said, "he's in the 20 percent."

That's how I met Charles Barkley.

2

Welcome Home

Aug. 21, 1993

When she told him about the idea, he shook his head. "Mama, I'm gonna be so busy this summer . . . I need some time for myself." Charcey Glenn waved her hand. "Charles went on and on and on. I told him, 'All right, baby, I guess we'll just have to go ahead and set a date then.' "

"Mama, don't do that."

"We'll look for you to show up."

It was a busy summer, and too short, he thought, as he drove along the interstate out of Birmingham, headed east. Where had the time gone? The 1993 NBA season ended in late June, only two months ago. Every day since the Suns walked off the court in America West Arena, in stunned silence, he had thought about Game 6. Every day he replayed the dramatic finish over and over in his mind. Every day he second-guessed himself. Every day he thought of what he would have done differently. The last minute haunted him.

There are only three or four guys in the world who can make plays down the stretch. I don't care what anybody says. Look at the Lakers, the Celtics, the Bulls. Every time the Bulls needed a play Michael made it. Every time the Celtics needed a play Larry Bird made it. The same with the Lakers, and Magic. It's no coincidence that all the teams that win championships have a super guy on their team. I had the ball. They made me pass it three straight times.

He saw it all, in slow motion, like an underwater ballet. The clock ticked down . . . :05 . . . :04 . . . :03. John Paxson, the Chicago sharp-shooter, spotted up behind the three-point line. Paxson, wide open with the ball . . .

We could have won. We should have won. I'm paid to make the plays. I didn't do it.

8

He pulled off the interstate and crossed the Cahaba River. What he saw made him smile. A full-length picture of himself, wearing his U.S. Olympic uniform, grinned down from a giant billboard that welcomed motorists to Leeds, Ala., pop. 10,006. "My Hometown," the towering likeness of Charles Barkley proclaimed.

Home. He was coming home. Home to his mother and grandmother who raised him. Home to two younger brothers he took care of as a teenager while his mother did domestic work, cleaning white folks' homes for $15 a day. Home to boyhood friends, many of whom still live there. Leeds reached out to him, arms open wide.

The sign outside Old Smokey Bar-B-Q said, "Welcome Home Charles. BBQ plate, drink $4.99." Whitfield's Pawn Shop: "Welcome Home Charles!" On another sign an arrow pointed to the office of Dr. Alan Walch, chiropractor. "Welcome Home, Sir Charles!" the sign read. "Need Adjustment?"

Mayor Lynn Maxey officially proclaimed this as Charles Barkley Day in Leeds. The event, which had been in the planning since Barkley returned from the '92 Barcelona Olympics, was bigger than the annual spring Creek Bank Festival and the March of Dimes Walk-a-Thon. It was even bigger than the town landmark, a giant triple-dip ice-cream cone that towers above the rooftop of Spruiell's Dairy. "This is the biggest thing I can ever remember happening here," said Mayor Maxey, 47, who was born and raised in Leeds.

The headline in *The Leeds News* read, "5,000 Expected to Meet Barkley." The front-page story upstaged all other local and area news, including the arrest of a male stripper at a nightclub in nearby Moody. According to the newspaper account, during the raid "a chorus of obscenities coupled with obscene gestures were hurled at police and press, with a number of threats of violence shouted by females of the audience."

In its news briefs, Barkley's hometown paper urged residents to put their best foot forward on Charles Barkley Day. "National media will be on hand in Leeds Friday and Saturday. . . . They will be interviewing citizens, city officials, merchants and maybe even the family dog. This is your chance to 'Say Something Good About Leeds!' And don't forget to smile for the cameras. NBA and ESPN Sports will be on hand to tape footage for a sports special in the fall. Leeds will be featured on national TV."

Barkley was born in Leeds. "Six pounds, 12 ounces. Can you believe it?" said his mom, who helped arrange the town celebration. Charcey Glenn never doubted for a moment that once they set a date, her son would come.

As a child, Barkley lived with his mother and grandmother in a one-bedroom housing project across the railroad tracks in a neighborhood known as Moton. They later moved into a home nearby. Barkley's mom and 67-year-old grandmother, Johnnie Mickens, have lived there for 18 years, surrounded by Barkley's plaques and trophies and awards.

"My mother and grandmother fight over them," Barkley said of his basketball hardware. He keeps few of his trophies, for a reason. "I don't want to sit around and think about what I've accomplished." He doesn't want to grow complacent. "Yesterday, I won the MVP," Barkley said before the Suns played Seattle in the 1993 Western Conference finals. "Today the Seattle SuperSonics don't give a shit."

Charcey Glenn and her mother don't fight over Barkley's basketball awards. Barkley's grandmother gets first pick. "My mother's got a much better collection than I do, or Charles does. She's got so much stuff she's run out of room for it all. She's Charles' biggest critic, and biggest fan. If he's playing, she's sitting in front of the TV. Never misses a game."

In a way, all the plaques and honors are a repayment to Ms. Mickens for the high spirit and speak-your-mindedness she instilled in her grandson. "She's his granny, all right," Charcey Glenn said with a laugh. "Anyone who knows my mother and Charles will say they're the same way. She won't bite her tongue. If she wants to tell you something she will. She'll say, 'If I hurt your feelings, I'm sorry, but I meant what I said.' I know Charles is my child. But he is so much like his grandmother it's unreal."

The brick home is Barkley's haven when he visits Leeds, and a source of family pride. He paid to have his mother's home remodeled, and enlarged.

"When Charles was in junior high he would tell me that when he got into the NBA I could have anything I wanted," Ms. Glenn said. "I told him, 'Well, honey, the first thing Mama wants you to do when you get into the NBA is for her to have her own bathroom.' When I raised Charles and his brothers we had just the one. I told him the second thing I wanted was a dishwasher.

"One Christmas when he was at Auburn, he came home for the holidays. Charles would always buy a card on Mother's Day and special occasions. He would write his own sayings. That Christmas he bought me this beautiful card, and in his own way, in his own writing, he said, 'One of these days I'm gonna give you everything you ever wanted because you're the best mama in the world.'" Charcey Glenn glanced around the living room of her home, which now has a playroom, another bedroom, a three-car garage and that extra bathroom she once dreamed about. "I got that card here somewhere. It meant so much to me. I remember we had a house full of people that Christmas. I was so proud of it, I read it in front of everybody. It brought tears to my eyes."

Everything was ready. The main street was blocked off. The Leeds Police and Fire and Rescue departments were on hand. The Charles Barkley Day Committee had arranged for free hot dogs and soft drinks. But where was he? An elderly man from Birmingham looked across the street at the boy, who was standing near the front of the line, holding a basketball. "That child's been worrin' me to death," the man said. "He kept asking, 'Grandpa, when are we leaving? When are we gonna see Charles?'"

At 10 A.M. the line stretched from the little downtown park all the way down Parkway Drive, past the painted windows of Carl Ann Florist and Leeds Beauty School and $3 Dollar Bill's. The line extended to the public library, and turned the corner onto Eighth Street.

"I'm big everywhere," Barkley said as he walked from the town depot to the gazebo. "But I'm *really* big in Leeds."

It hasn't changed a lot. Leeds looks much the same as it did when he left it and as he remembers it, his memories packed away like old clothes in an attic. As a kid Barkley and some of his friends stole a supply of ballpoint pens from a drugstore.

"I was bored and stupid," he recalled. "More stupid than bored."

On Sunday nights, Barkley and his friends hid outside a grocery store. After the bakery truck made its delivery and drove away, they snatched the sugary goods and devoured the evidence, stuffing cake after cake into their mouths with their fingers. One night he almost got caught. He still can see the squad car, headlights shining. Heart trip-hammering in his chest, he fled, running blindly into the nearby woods, police in pursuit. In the darkness he ran into a tree and almost knocked himself out.

Hiding, scared, the young fugitive thought, "This is not for me. This is not what I want to do with my life."

Basketball was his ticket out of Leeds. It took him to college and became his rocket ship to wealth and worldwide fame. From Barcelona to Tokyo he is Charles Barkley, or Sir Charles, but in his hometown folks know him as just plain Charles, or Wade, his middle name.

"People in Leeds know Charles more for who he is than who they see on a basketball court or in commercials," Mayor Maxey said. "People have a different image of him than the person we know. He's like an actor. We see him on TV battling Godzilla, but that's an image. We see Charles like he is in real life. He's a very caring person."

As the Leeds High School band played and majorettes twirled their batons, Barkley sat beneath the steepled shingled roof in his place of honor. One by one, like kids waiting to meet a shopping-mall Santa, Barkley's fans stepped up to meet him, get his autograph, snap a picture, shake his hand.

As in any community, a few took a sour view of the celebration. Why all the fuss? What had Charles Barkley ever done for Leeds? Not more than 100 yards from the gazebo, Southern Flag and Novelty was opening for business. The store sells bumper stickers that read "American By Birth. Southern By the Grace of God" and "Secession: The Right Thing To Do." The message on a black T-shirt, with the Confederate flag superimposed: "If I Had Known This I Would Have Picked My Own Cotton." Times have changed, but Leeds isn't color-blind. No place is.

"Racism exists in Leeds, and it will always exist there," Barkley said. "I think it's just hidden better now. But there are a lot of good people, white and black, in Leeds. You can't judge the town by what a few people do. It's like Phoenix, when the state voted down Martin Luther King Day. People say Arizona is a racist state. That isn't fair."

For one day he was royalty. King for a day in his hometown. Kalyn Chapman, the first black Miss Alabama, sat at Barkley's side, a rhinestone tiara in her hair. Leeds-Unity Funeral Home, formerly the town Pizza Hut, provided the guest of honor with transportation, a black Cadillac. Disc jockey Spider Williams played music from the WENN radio broadcast van. The Leeds Water Works Board provided ice water in free commemorative Barkley Day water bottles.

He signed autographs for two hours. He saw old friends and met new ones, like 5-year-old Glen Wade. Eight months earlier, the boy was trapped in a house fire. The child suffered burns over 50 percent of his body. He spent four months in the hospital. A clear plastic shield covered his scarred face.

"Charles is all he talks about," said Glen's mother, Vivian. "We'd drive by Charles' grandmother's house and he'd ask, 'Is Charles home? Is Charles home?' This is a dream come true."

Raylene Sparks remembered Barkley. "Years ago, we had a makeshift roller-skating rink here. Concrete floor," she said, smiling at the memory. "Charles was a teenager, but he was big even then. He'd fall on those roller skates, and hon, it was like dominoes." Raylene's voice softened. "I'll always have a warm place in my heart for what he did for Bryan."

Last year, Bryan Kirkland, Raylene's 22-year-old nephew, crashed his motorcycle. The accident left him crippled. Barkley helped with medical expenses. Bryan rolled his wheelchair to the gazebo and held out his hand. He wanted to say hello and thanks.

There is no Hyatt Regency in Leeds. No Ritz Carlton. At the end of his special day, after the autographs and the "Old Timers Game" and a formal program that evening, Barkley fell into bed in the spare bedroom in the brick house that overlooks a sandlot baseball field.

"I think it was his second year in the NBA," Charcey Glenn said. "Charles came home around Christmas time. He was here for one night. He had to leave the next day because he had a game. We were still remodeling and it was *c-o-o-l-d* in this house! But we were so happy and so thankful. We covered up and bundled up and stayed right here that Christmas.

"This is where it all started. Right here. My mother let me build onto her house after she worked so hard to get this piece of property. There are a lot of influential neighborhoods here in Leeds. If we wanted to move Charles said he would buy us a house anywhere we wanted. But we're satisfied right here. We are simple, down-to-earth people. We enjoy what we have. God has blessed us. We don't want to go anywhere else.

"This is home."

3

Barney's Friend

*Under the new Clinton health plan, First Lady Hillary Clinton
may finally have her Rodham removed.*
—Kevin Nealon, "Saturday Night Live" news anchor man

The group got an unexpected surprise halfway through the $8.25
tour of the NBC Studio, one of several offered each day at 30 Rock-
efeller Plaza in New York City. "There's Charles Barkley!" a woman
in the group called out.

"Where?"

"Down there."

"I don't see . . ."

"There. There he is!"

The tour group, on the building's ninth floor, pressed against the
glass partition. A youngster laughed. "He's wearing a dress!" It was
Barkley, all right. He was on the eighth floor, on the set at Studio 8H,
rehearsing a skit. Barkley glanced up and spotted the strangers. He
returned their smiles and gave a little wave.

He dressed in drag. He played a cop. He was A.J. Jamaal, host of
a TV game show, "What's That?," in which contestants guessed
(unsuccessfully) people's gender. As proprietor of Charles Barkley's
Big, Tall and Black Men's Stores, he displayed a line of garish clothing in sizes long, double long and "Jabbar." At Charles Barkley's
Donkey Basketball Camp, campers played basketball while riding
burros. "I'm going to tell you again," Coach Barkley said as he sat
atop a skittish donkey, "I don't care if you're the greatest player in the
world . . . unless you and your donkey are in the game mentally, the
rest doesn't mean a thing."

"Saturday Night Live" is funny, irreverent, sassy, topical, unpredictable, outrageous and popular. The same description fits the guest
host of SNL's Sept. 25 season-opening show.

"It's been a fun week," Barkley said, smiling into the lights during
his opening monologue. "Working with the cast. Watching Nirvana
rehearse." (Six months later, Kurt Cobain, lead singer of the rock

14

band, committed suicide.) "I even got to play a little basketball. You see, awhile back, I played basketball with Godzilla. Everyone here, and myself, thought it would be fun to have a rematch. You know. Rent a gym. Play a little one-on-one. And give the profits to charity . . ."

The scene switches to a gymnasium. Barkley continued the narrative. "We ran into a problem. At the last minute, Godzilla canceled. We were incredibly lucky to find a worthy replacement. Barney."

The studio audience roared.

"Hey, Barney," Barkley told the irrepressibly cheerful dinosaur of children's TV. "Thanks for doing this on such a short notice."

"That's okay, Charles," Barney replied. "That's what caring and sharing are all about."

Barkley proceeded to humiliate the lovable character with a bullying display of his basketball superiority. Barkley stole the ball and dunked it. Barkley threw an elbow, knocking Barney to the floor. He ran over him and talked trash. "Had enough, Barney? Huh? Huh?" The game over, Barkley and Barney walked off the court, arm in arm. Barney's tail was bent. One eyeball dangled from its socket.

The host delivered his lines. He made the quick wardrobe changes with no problem. When his donkey decided it wanted to leave the set, Barkley couldn't read the cue cards, so he ad-libbed. His biggest challenge—and one failing—was trying to keep a straight face in the company of comedian Al Franken, the star of a regular SNL skit titled "Daily Affirmation With Stuart Smalley."

Smalley is described as a caring nurturer, a member of several 12-step programs but not a licensed therapist. His daily affirmation is to look into the mirror and recite his mantra. "I'm good enough, I'm smart enough and doggone it, people *like* me."

"We have a terrific show today," Smalley said, "because my guest is a professional basketball player, Charles B., who plays for the Phoenix S's. We're going to maintain your anonymity, Charles." Smalley, wearing a cardigan sweater and a blond hairpiece, turned to the guest seated beside him. "Now Charles, have you seen the show?"

"No."

"Well, basically, I am the child of an alcoholic. I weighed nearly 300 pounds until I got into Overeaters Anonymous, and I do this show as part of my recovery, and also to help people."

Barkley: "So you're really messed up."

Smalley: "Yes, but I am *owning* my dysfunction."

Barkley: "Well, own it away from me."

Smalley: "Okay. Well, Charles, tell us your story. Charles, are you happy?"

Barkley: "Yeah, I'm happy. I've got millions of adoring fans. I travel all over the world. I play golf in Hawaii. Get paid unreal money to do commercials for Nike and perspiration sticks. I'm a multimillionaire and I'm set for life."

Smalley: Uh huh. And that . . . that really makes you happy?"

Barkley: "Yeah. And the fact I'm the best basketball player in the world. There is nobody better than me."

(applause)

Smalley: "So, I guess, you know, you're the best basketball player in the world, then I guess you've won a lot of championships."

(laughter)

Barkley: "Well, actually, I've never won a championship."

Smalley: "And Charles, how do you . . . *feel* . . . about not having won a championship?"

Barkley: "It's not a big deal."

"Uh huh." Smalley, knees together, hands folded primly in his lap, turned away from Barkley and looked into the camera. "I guess Cleopatra isn't the only queen of denial . . ."

4

Home Remedies

Dear Charles," he said, putting voice to the words of the letter in his hand. "I can't believe I'm writing you. You are my favorite player. I heard about your back . . ."

Barkley stopped in mid-sentence and bounded from his chair. "My back! EVERYBODY wants to know about my BACK!!!"

He wasn't angry. He couldn't be angry with people who care about him and wish him well. People only wanted to help. He appreciated their concern. Even so . . .

"You wouldn't believe the stuff I get. I've got every back magazine in the world. I've got every back book in the world. Chiropractors. Exercises. Everybody has a cure." Barkley held up a canister. "See this?" The can contained a powdered protein supplement used by weightlifters. "Some lady sent me these milkshakes. For my BACK!"

Two weeks after his appearance on "Saturday Night Live," Barkley was racing rookie Byron Wilson after practice at the Suns' training camp in Flagstaff, Ariz., when he collapsed. Teammates thought he was clowning around. "Heart attack!" Danny Ainge called out. "Mouth-to-mouth!"

But the gym fell silent when teammates realized Barkley wasn't joking. He complained his left leg felt numb, and he remained on the ground until the team physician, Dr. Richard Emerson, arrived. In August, doctors had discovered a bulging disk in Barkley's lower back after the Suns forward complained that a sore hamstring had not responded to rest.

Emerson later said he thought Barkley's collapse was due to "muscle and respiratory fatigue." Barkley reported to camp out of shape. He tired out. As a precaution, he returned to Phoenix for tests, which showed no change in his back condition.

Next morning, newspaper headlines blared, "BARKLEY COLLAPSES." Tom Friend, a reporter for *The New York Times*, was in the pressbox at the LA Coliseum when his editor called. Forget the Jets-Raiders game. Get on a plane. Find Barkley. Write the story. Friend left before the kickoff. He flew to Phoenix and camped out at a hospital, along with other reporters, hoping for some news. He never saw

Barkley, or talked to him.

The training camp incident set a negative tone for the season. Every day for the next seven months Barkley heard the same questions, over and over again. How do you feel? Are you serious about retirement? Is this season really your last? Do you think you can hold up? Have you tried this? How about that?

Everybody wanted to help. A doctor in Wisconsin wrote Barkley and recommended he consult Dr. Jacques Theron, an interventional neuroradiologist in France. A woman suggested Barkley visit a chiropractor in Sedona, Ariz., and undergo something called a directional non-force technique adjustment, which was developed in the 1920s by the late Dr. Richard Van Rumpt. She included a pamphlet that pictured a young Dr. Rumpt, his hair parted in the middle and plastered to his head. He wore a Charlie Chaplin mustache.

A physical therapist sent a reprint of the McKenzie Program, an individualized series of progressive exercises designed to relieve acute and chronic back pain. In one illustration, a man is sitting on a stool, legs apart, hands resting on his knees. In the next photo, he is slumped over, hands touching the floor. He looks like a drunk who passed out.

Most letters were addressed to Dr. Emerson. Someone sent an article printed in the *New Zealand Medical Journal* titled, "Prophylaxis in Recurrent Low Back Pain." Another, "Manual Correction of Sciatic Scoliosis."

The C.C. Pollen Company sent a fax. "We have a product called Bee Pain Free which has been fed to 1,200-pound thoroughbred race horses who have been in excruciating pain. The Bee Pain Free has eliminated their pain, time and time again.

"The same thing is true of humans. . . . The least Sir Charles Barkley should do is take the Bee Pain Free as we instruct for 30 days. He will be pain free before the 30 days are over."

One Suns fan claimed Barkley could find relief by hanging upside down in a doorway, like a bat. Another said the answer was a flexonic galvanic stimulator, an apparatus that produces a high-voltage, low-amperage square wave which relieves muscle cramps and reduces swelling by the osmotic effect. Other remedies: friction massage therapy, and a cervical pillow with bio magnets. Barkley received a book titled *No Milk: A Revolutionary Solution For Neck Pain, Back Pain and Headaches.*

Hundreds of people called the Suns' office offering help, but no one was more persistent than Dean Kashiwagi, an engineer and faculty member at Arizona State University's School of Construction. "I have the solution," Kashiwagi wrote in one of numerous faxes he sent to the Suns during the season. Kashiwagi said he once suffered from lower back pain. He developed a non-medical treatment he said is based on engineering principles. He claimed to have relieved his own pain and offered to do the same for Barkley, in exchange for a $5,000 research grant, plus two tickets to Suns home games for as long as Barkley played.

The Suns thanked Kashiwagi for his interest and filed his correspondence in a thick binder, along with testimonials for Swedish Sports Rub and a gravity inversion bench.

I thought about telling Dr. Emerson about Fuzzy Zoeller. The pro golfer battled back pain for years. He tried everything. Exercises. Acupuncture. Massage. Pain pills. Nothing worked. "Finally, I went to this doctor who gave me two shots of woo koo juice," Zoeller said. "I have no idea what it was. It might have been straight vodka, but I haven't had a pain in two years."

Hallelujah.

5

Munich

If you win by 20, people say it should have been more. If you win by 30 or 40, then you're rubbing it in. We probably could have won by 40 . . . but that wouldn't prove anything. This isn't life or death. Life and death begins in two weeks when the regular season begins.

Oct. 21, 1993

Joe Kleine doesn't speak German but he knows how to drink beer. On his first night in Munich, the Suns center found himself in good company as he sat with locals in the Hofbrauhaus, the famous beer hall. Gathered around a wooden table, they lifted their steins. They sang along to the festive music of a Bavarian oompah band.

Kleine spotted a familiar face at the door. In a conspiratorial whisper, he instructed a German who spoke English to tell the others seated at the table about his plan. Okay? Understand? Got it? Heads nodded. Good.

Charles Barkley walked over. A grinning Kleine hoisted his mug and together, he and his new friends greeted his teammate with that old German cheer. "Au-burn SUCKS! Au-burn SUCKS!"

The name of the October event is the McDonald's Open. The NBA might as well have called it "Charles Barkley Visits Germany." Barkley was the headliner of the three-day tournament that featured national championship teams from Germany, Spain, France, Italy and Brazil, plus the Phoenix Suns.

Barkley's slam-dunking likeness appeared on the game program and the official poster. I mentioned that if the Suns won the tournament—they would play two games—the team would receive first-place prize money of $50,000.

"We will?" Barkley's grin said this was news to him, but it took him only a split second to determine a way to divide the windfall in a manner that would be equitable to all. "I'll give (each teammate) $1,000 and keep the rest myself."

The $50,000 was more like an appearance fee paid to the Suns in exchange for their filling the Olympiahalle and putting on a good show. The *International Herald Tribune* compared the other teams sharing the spotlight with Barkley with "those extras who leap out behind buildings and get shot by Schwarzenegger or Rambo . . . from their perspective, they're just happy to be in the movie."

It was a long, tiring trip and a disruption in the Suns' preseason routine. Players had to deal with time changes and jet lag and odd schedules and different food. Kleine walked around Munich repeating the same question, over and over. "Ver iz zee app-el stroooooooooooo-del?"

Barkley said he ate Bavarian food—hot dogs—while growing up in Alabama. "We *thought* we were German," he joked.

The Suns won the tournament and spared themselves the embarrassment of becoming the first NBA team to lose a game in the six-year history of the event. No one got arrested. No one got lost (miss the subway stop at Donnersbergerbrucke and you could end up at Germering-Unterpfaffenhofen). In four days of interviews with the German media, Barkley mentioned Adolph Hitler only once.

"Mr. Barkley," a German TV reporter asked, "what do you think of when you think of Bavaria?"

The crush of media pressed in tighter around the American Ambassador of Basketball, eager to hear his answer. "When you think about Germany," Barkley said, "you think about the Olympics, Jesse Owens. Obviously, you've got to think somewhat about Adolf Hitler."

Barkley also thought somewhat about the World Series, which was being played back home, but wasn't on German TV. "Charles," Danny Ainge asked, one eye shut as he aimed his video camera at his teammate, "what do you think about a country that doesn't have the World Series on TV?"

"I think it's a total disgrace," Barkley replied. "We were up all night last night trying to get the World Series and we couldn't find it." Barkley made several calls home to get the latest score. "They call it the *World* Series. It ought to be on *someplace* over here."

"It's not the World Series if it's not on TV in Germany," Ainge said, egging Barkley on.

"You're right," Charles said. "It shouldn't be called the World Series if everybody can't watch it. Maybe they should call it the Almost World Series."

Someone suggested they could listen to the Series on the Armed Forces network. "First of all," Barkley said, "you've got to be a total nitwit to listen to any sporting event on the radio. You can't watch it.

We want to *see* it. Isn't it on *anywhere* around here?"

The Series was on in Great Britain.

Barkley frowned. "Maybe we ought to move this there then."

Barkley's spirits brightened when he and his teammates conducted a basketball clinic for a group of German schoolchildren. For half an hour the Suns showed the youngsters how to dribble, shoot free throws and pass the ball behind their backs. "Hey, Ced," Barkley called out to Cedric Ceballos, the Suns forward who had a new five-year, $9 million contract. "Tell these kids you can make a lot more money scoring than you can if you pass and play defense. Remember," Barkley told the group, waiting for the translator to catch up, "offense is the key."

Barkley smiled at one German lad. "One thing you'll learn before you leave here today, and that's how to say, 'Gimme five, homeboy!'"

Paul Westphal faced a challenge. He had to convince the Suns they weren't on vacation. They had a job to do. The start of the regular season was two weeks away. The coach expected his players to be focused and ready to go, which was asking a lot of the group that congregated in the hotel lobby the morning after their first night out in the German city, famous for its sausages and beer.

Westphal put the Suns through a demanding practice. "Quit dinkin' around!" he shouted. He slammed the ball to the floor. "C'mon, let's go! We're playing like a bunch of wimps! I bet we get beat in one of these games!"

The Suns knew there was little chance of that. During Barkley's first meeting with the media he was asked how wide the gap is between the NBA brand of basketball and the European professional game. Barkley picked out a diminutive reporter and said, "About the same as the difference in my height and yours."

"Is the gap closing?"

"No," Barkley replied, and took another bite from his Big Mac.

After rolling past Real Madrid, 145–115, the Suns beat Buckler Bologna of Italy 112–90 in the championship game. Asked which Italian players impressed him, Barkley said, "Number 5, number 11, number 14." He sounded like a guy announcing the winning lottery numbers. Barkley scored 28 points, with eight rebounds, four assists and four steals and was awarded the Drazen Petrovic Most Valuable Player Trophy, named after the NBA All-Star for the New Jersey Nets who had died the previous summer in an auto crash.

Petrovic's parents visited Barkley in his hotel room. Through an interpreter, they told him that he was their son's idol as a player. Petrovic's mother wept. "I was kind of in shock, actually," Barkley said. "She kept crying. I just told her, over and over, 'Thank you, thank you, thank you' . . . . I didn't know what else to say."

Barkley received another visitor in Munich, NBA commissioner David Stern. "He told me that since Michael (Jordan) had retired I was the man now. He said if I thought what I said and did was big before, it would be even bigger now. It really meant a lot to me. It was a respect thing."

But was Barkley the Man? "I think people have looked at me as number two for the last few years. Basketball ain't like the presidency, where the president dies and the vice president moves in. I don't want to inherit the presidency. I want to earn it. I want to prove to people how good I am."

In Munich, Barkley looked like a presidential candidate on the campaign trail. He signed autographs. Ignoring a cold rain, he hopped off the team bus at the City Hall square and hoisted a blond, apple-cheeked child dressed in Bavarian costume into his arms, as strobes flashed and shutters clicked. He dined with the U.S. ambassador to Germany.

The media followed him everywhere. Please, he was asked after practice, could you please read this for German TV? Barkley looked at the foreign words printed on a card. He shook his head no. The bus was waiting. He glanced toward the exit door.

Please?

Barkley said, "I don't even know what this means." Please? He looked at the card again. Over his own protest, he read the promo anyway, sounding out the strange gutteral syllables as best he could.

For four days, they pulled at him, like salt-water taffy. The Suns. The NBA. NBC. Nike. McDonald's. After the championship game he sat in the emptying locker room at the Olympiahalle, the last Suns player out of the shower, the last to dress.

"I'm going home," he said softly. "I've done my duty here."

He was tired. His back ached after playing back-to-back games. To ease the pain, before tipoff he received an anti-inflammatory injection in the hamstring muscle of his left leg. Barkley wouldn't have played had this been just another preseason game. He played because the game was televised live on NBC to the United States and "television runs the show."

Finally, it was over. Barkley felt a crushing tiredness as he dressed. "It's like I have two full-time jobs now," he said, reflecting on the demands upon his time. His teammates had returned to the hotel. Outside the locker room fans waited, hoping to see the Suns star, maybe snap his picture and get his autograph.

Barkley shook his head and sighed. "Michael, *please* come back."

6

Deadly Game

River Phoenix's death was accidental and a homicide investigation is closed. The 23-year-old actor died of the same lethal mix that killed John Belushi—a heroin and cocaine "speedball," the L.A. county coroner's office said.

Toxicological tests conducted on Phoenix, who died outside a Sunset Boulevard nightclub Oct. 31...
   —USA Today

Charles Barkley looked up from the pages of the newspaper. "I don't understand it," he said. "Don't people ever learn?"

He smoked marijuana in college. During his NBA career he has been offered cocaine. He considered trying it. "Once. One time. Just to see what's so powerful about the stuff." But using drugs, he knows, is a losing game. The roll call of those who have died or ruined their careers because of drug use is a long one, and Barkley isn't so foolish as to risk everything to satisfy a curiosity.

Len Bias, the Boston Celtics' No. 1 draft choice in 1986, dropped dead from an overdose of coke. River Phoenix, gone at 23. "People who use drugs must not have a TV and see the news. You lose your wife, your family, most important, your life. Cocaine," Barkley said as he thought of Darryl, "is a time bomb."

Five years ago, Barkley's younger brother suffered a mild stroke which doctors said was caused by cocaine use. At the time, Darryl was 21.

"Twenty something, and partially paralyzed on one side of his body," Barkley said. "Darryl risked his life to use drugs. He seems to be doing okay now. He's done a good job of getting his life straightened out. I've talked to him a lot about it. But it's tough. It's a tough situation. . . ."

If Barkley were NBA commissioner, "the first thing I would do is mandatory drug testing. I would test every player." Barkley believes the league needs a tougher drug policy. I've never heard him express much sympathy for professional athletes who throw away their careers because they made the wrong choices.

The Suns selected Richard Dumas in the second round of the 1991 draft. He spent his rookie season on suspension for substance abuse. After being reinstated, Dumas started 32 games during the 1992–93 season and helped the Suns reach the NBA Finals. The Suns rewarded him with a five-year, $9 million contract. Two months later, Dumas took a drug test and later was suspended without pay for violating rules of his after-care program. The 6-foot-7 forward returned to a Houston drug abuse center, where he had been cared for in the past by the clinic's founder, John Lucas, the former San Antonio Spurs coach and now coach of the Philadelphia 76ers.

Lucas is an inspiring story. In 1976, the Houston Rockets selected him with the No. 1 pick in the draft. He later turned to drugs and alcohol. Eight years ago his life bottomed out after he failed a drug test. The Rockets released him. He went on a cocaine binge. Lucas awakened the next morning, shoeless, lying on a street in downtown Houston. Fortunately, he turned his life around, and his center is helping others do the same.

"I've worked too hard to snort my money up my nose," Barkley said. "I just can't see myself giving away my paycheck. John Lucas told me that if a person is an addict and you put him in a room with a pound of cocaine and $100,000, he would take the cocaine. Not me. The cocaine would be there, and the cash would be gone.

"People say a lot of things about me. But you'll never hear I'm on something. Never. I'm not going to let nothing happen to the Chuckster. I'm one of my favorite people."

7

Heaven & Hell

I've enjoyed my life. I've accomplished everything I've wanted to accomplish, except winning a championship. I've done that. If I die tomorrow, I'll be at peace.

Nov. 5, 1993

Opening night. L.A. The Great Western Forum. Jack Nicholson. Dyan Cannon. The Laker Girls. "Anybody need tickets?" Charles Barkley shouted as he breezed into the locker room.

He was upbeat, excited. He had looked forward to this night since the end of the 1992-93 season, when he stood on the balcony at America West Arena after a downtown parade and told a cheering crowd of 300,000 what it wanted to hear—that the Suns had the greatest fans in the world, that the Western Conference champions would be back, that he would do everything in his power to bring the NBA championship to Phoenix in 1994.

"Gonna be a *good* day, Scotty," Barkley assured Scotty Robertson, the Suns assistant coach. Barkley glanced around the small room. Kevin Johnson listened to music, a stereo headset covering his ears. Dan Majerle lay on the floor, doing situps. Other players watched video of the Lakers. Vitamins, aspirin, chewing gum and jock-itch spray lay on a table. The message on the chalkboard read: "Don't get beat off the dribble. Expect help from your teammates."

Another NBA game was in progress on TV. "HOW 'BOUT A CHARGE?!" Barkley shouted at the screen.

He placed his palm against his solar plexus and frowned, like a guy suffering a gastric attack in an antacid commercial. "I'll be glad when 7:30 gets here. Man, my stomach's tight as a drum."

Barkley was beginning his 10th NBA season. The grind, the nightly wear-and-tear on his body has not diminished his enthusiasm for the game. Barkley is the circus horse who still smells the sawdust. "I don't sleep much during the season. I don't sleep much period.

I never sleep the night before a game. I get too excited. Too hyper to play. Any athlete who says he sleeps before games, big games, is lying."

On game days, Barkley takes an afternoon nap. He also thinks about his opponent, assessing his strengths and weaknesses. "I look at a guy's mental makeup. Sometimes, you can jump on a guy quick and he thinks, 'Damn, I *am* playing against Charles Barkley,' and he goes downhill." Barkley thought of Antonio Harvey. The Lakers' rookie free agent played at Pfeiffer College, a small school in Misenheimer, N.C.

"I don't think he saw anything like me in the NAIA," Barkley said, and flashed his 1,000-watt smile. "I wasn't on the curriculum."

"HEY, CAN I GET MY ANKLES TAPED!?"

Joe Proski pretended not to hear. The Suns' veteran trainer was busy, bent over a rubbing table, his fingers kneading the muscles in A.C. Green's lower back. Green was stretched out, like a boxer, arms folded beneath his chin.

"A.C.'s never played a game here!" Barkley shouted. "How come HE gets special treatment! A.C., tell 'em how you hated it here."

Barkley was joking, as he often does, as the wall clock ticks down to game time. Green and the Lakers were synonymous. A.C. played eight years wearing Lakers purple and gold—756 games—and earned two NBA championship rings. Green is an iron man.

An unrestricted free agent, Green spent the summer weighing his options. The Suns wanted him, needed him, but he was in no hurry to make a decision, which irritated Barkley. "A.C.'s waiting for God to lead him the right way," he groused. "I told A.C. I've talked to God, too. He said He is a Suns fan."

They are an odd couple, Barkley and Green. Barkley is loud, earthy, ribald, at times shockingly profane. A.C., a lay minister, is soft-spoken and well mannered. He plays the game the way he lives his life, with purpose, quiet dignity, class. Barkley spews four-letter words. Green doesn't curse, and his trash talk is G-rated. "Nice try," A.C. will chide an opponent who tries and fails to block his shot. "After we beat you, perhaps you and I could go out and have sundaes or something."

Barkley frequents nightclubs. Green's idea of self-indulgence is a trip to an ice-cream parlor for a frozen yogurt. Green walks the straight and narrow. Barkley strolls the main streets and the side streets of life. He is a boulevardier, as the French say.

Both talk to God, in different ways. "I release my pressure to Jesus," Green says. Barkley says, "Pressure is when I get to the Pearly Gates and God says to me, 'Oops, sorry, you're going to hell.'"

Barkley is a night owl. "A.C." said Barkley, "goes to bed at 10 o'clock." Most of their conversations are on the basketball court, although one day they engaged in a lively locker-room discussion about television evangelists. "Charles didn't like a particular preacher. I took the opposite position, just to get him riled up," Green said. "It worked. We went back and forth for a couple of days . . ."

"People will believe anything," Barkley said. "If some of these guys on TV are as religious as they say they are they shouldn't be driving Rolls Royces and living in big mansions. They should be pumping money back into the community. When I was growing up, we watched Rev. Ernest Angley. He's a faith healer. He came on TV every Saturday night, right before wrestling. We'd be getting ready for wrestling and there was Angley."

"What did he do?" I asked.

"They would bring people to him, and he'd reach out like this," Barkley said, arms extended, fingers spread. "He'd grab 'em by the head and squeeze their forehead, and he'd say, 'Let the *e*-vil spirit come OUUUUUUUUT!' Then he'd push 'em over backward, and they'd be healed."

"He sort of zapped 'em?"

"Yeah," Barkley said. "It was great."

Unlike Green, Barkley isn't a churchgoer, but he grew up attending Sunday services at the Macedonia Baptist Church in Leeds. Barkley says he believes in God and prays regularly, but he doesn't use religion as a rabbit's foot. He doesn't pray for the Suns to beat the Lakers, or any other team. "A.C's very religious, but I respect him because he doesn't try to force it on other people. He doesn't walk around with a Bible in his hand talking about it. He's not like some religious fanatics. What bothers me about some Christian people is they forget the verse about not judging others. They block abortion clinics and go on TV and talk about other people. If they want to be true Christians they wouldn't judge other people.

"Number one," Barkley said, "we all sin. So they're no better than me, if they want to be technically honest. I believe God gave me special skills. I believe that. I'm not cocky enough to think I did it all by myself. I feel like God is the only person in the world who has been there for me through the good times and the bad."

"Do you believe in heaven and hell?" I asked.

"I don't know if there is a heaven or hell," Barkley said. "But I've been to Philadelphia. Hell can't be no worse than Philly. Phoenix might be as close to heaven as I ever get, so I'm gonna enjoy it."

Contrary to his avowed dislike for the media, Barkley enjoys holding court and sparring with reporters. He conducts a press conference before every game. "You know, it's kind of funky playing the Lakers.

You think of the Lakers and you think of Kareem and Magic and A.C. Green. I don't know any of their players now."

"How's the back, Charles?"

"I'm not going to lie on the floor anymore." During the exhibition season whenever Barkley came out of the game he stretched out in front of the bench on his stomach, like a salamander. "I'm not going to let everybody know I'm in pain. Let me correct that. I'm not going to let 'em *see* me in pain. It's psychological warfare."

"Can Phoenix win it all?"

"No. I don't think we can beat Seattle," Barkley said with a straight face. "Seattle. Portland. New York. They all have better teams than we do." Reporters scribbled down his words. "In fact, I think it'll take a miracle for us to beat those teams. I think we'll sneak into the playoffs, and hope for the best. Isn't that right, Scotty?"

Robertson, seated nearby, smiled at Barkley's musings.

Tom Friend, the *Times* reporter, related his story about trying to track down Barkley in Phoenix the day after Charles collapsed at training camp. "Where *were* you?" Friend asked. He had spent all day at the hospital.

"Did you try the strip bars?" Barkley asked. "That's the best place to find me."

That night, Green and James Worthy, former teammates, engaged in a private war. LA fans booed the turncoat unmercifully as the Lakers embarrassed the Suns, 116–108. Barkley scored 38 points, but he accepted full responsibility for the loss. "This is one you can definitely pin on me. I blew this one. I was terrible . . . I don't know what was wrong. I'm not a psychiatrist. It's one thing to miss shots with players around you. But when you're alone at the line and can't throw it in the ocean . . ." Barkley missed 10 of 18 free throws.

Next night, before the Suns' home opener in which they redeemed themselves at the expense of the Sacramento Kings, Barkley peeled the foil wrapper from an energy snack called a PowerBar.

"What's that for?" someone asked.

"It helps your free-throwing shooting," Barkley said.

"In that case," I suggested, "have two."

No. 34 laughed and took another bite.

8

Radio Days

The Arizona Republic invites readers to call and express their opinions about local and national sports. The responses are printed on the sports pages in a feature titled, "It's Your Call."

"Listen to this," Barkley said. Nose buried in the gray pages of his morning paper, he read one of the caller's opinions aloud. " 'I'm a big Dallas Cowboys fan. If the Cardinals want to improve their team they should keep Joe Bugel and trade Garrison Hearst. Look what the Cowboys did with the Herschel Walker trade.' "

Barkley put down the paper. "First of all," Barkley said, in rebuttal, "the guy in Minnesota who made that Herschel Walker deal, they threw his ass out. How can you compare Herschel Walker with Garrison Hearst? Garrison Hearst is a rookie. He's hurt." Barkley shook his head. "Fans are idiots."

"Chuck, that's why we need to have our own radio show," Danny Ainge said.

"You know what?" Barkley said. "I had my own show in Philadelphia. I did it for a year. The fans were such assholes I couldn't take it anymore. They'd call in and they'd say this guy sucks or this guy ought to be playing. I always defended my teammates, if they tried hard. The bottom line is people don't know. Fans think because they watch basketball they know what's going on. But they don't know.

"I didn't mind people asking questions, but I'd get some guy call and say 'you suck and your teammates suck.' It would ruin the whole hour for me. I'd get pissed off. It was verbal warfare."

"How did you keep your composure on the air?" I asked.

"It was hard. They could bleep out curse words on the radio, but they did the show at a restaurant and the place was packed with people. A lot of them in the audience were little kids. They were right there, looking at you. The show seemed like a good idea at the time. They told me all I had to do was go there once a week and talk to the fans. That was it. They offered a fortune. It sounded good. But after about two weeks it was like, 'Oh, man, what have I done?'

"When you were winning it wasn't bad. But if you got on a losing streak or you had a bad game it was horrible. The show was on Monday night. If I had a bad game on Saturday and the team had lost three or four in a row, I started worrying about it all day Sunday. I thought about it all that day. All the next day. On Monday I told myself, 'I do NOT want to go there.' I dreaded it. I think the show lasted two hours. It seemed more like 10 hours when you were losing. The worst night ever was after the spitting incident."

On March 28, 1991, Barkley spit at a heckler seated near courtside during the fourth quarter of a road game against the New Jersey Nets. He hit an 8-year-old girl. The NBA suspended Barkley for one game, without pay, and fined him $10,000.

"That whole time was the worst two weeks in my life. I couldn't run away from it. All day, before the show, I felt like I was on death row. Walking into the restaurant that night I felt like I was going in for my last supper. Usually when I got there the people cheered and went crazy. But that night, it was quiet. They didn't know how to react."

"How did you handle it?"

"I just bit the bullet. There wasn't really anything I could say. I was wrong. I made a mistake. I had to take the heat from there on. Ninety percent of the calls were great. The other 10 percent said I should be thrown out of the league. Some people said I should have gotten a 10-game suspension. Three or four said I should be suspended for the rest of the year. People were arguing over how many games I should be suspended. I let the co-host handle the arguments. I couldn't really say anything. If I said a one-game suspension was enough it would have turned some people off. There was really no fair number of games. If they had suspended me for five games that would be fair. Ten games would have been fair. One game seemed like an eternity, but there was no answer to the question."

"Were you ever threatened?"

"No. But after the incident a guy spit in my wife's face. He called her a nigger lover. I was crazy during that time. When I found out I went ballistic. I went back to the place looking for the guy.

"In Philly, they crucify athletes. I love it there, but they love me and they hate me. I never thought they really appreciated me in Philadelphia. There was only one year they saw me play great on a great team, when I was the man. We were great my first couple of years but there was still Doc (Julius Erving) and Moses (Malone). The year we won the Atlantic Division was the first year they saw how great I was.

"Mitch Williams couldn't go back to the Phillies after the World Series. There's no way. And the Phillies knew that. The guy's no bum. He was saving 40 games a year. He's a helluva player, obviously. He could go back to Philly and save 50 games for the next five years, but they'll never forgive him because he lost the World Series."

"Will Philadelphia forgive you?" I asked.

Barkley thought a moment, reflecting on his eight stormy seasons with the 76ers. "I think the people there can forgive me because they see I wasn't the problem. The 76ers organization was. I didn't get along with the organization because they tried to say I was one of the reasons they were losing. So they traded me to the Suns, and we immediately went to the NBA Finals. Number two, all those guys I said couldn't play they got rid of. I think people in Philly realize that maybe Charles was right. It's no coincidence that my first year on a good team I got to the Finals. I didn't get good overnight. People in Phoenix think I played great last year when I was the MVP. But they ain't seen nothing. I just wish I could have been traded to Phoenix three years sooner, when I could *really* play . . ."

9

Jason

Nov. 10, 1993

The San Antonio Spurs were waiting, but there was something he had to do first. Charles Barkley asked a ball boy for a felt-tipped pen. In large letters he blacked in the initials "JS" on a white elastic band and placed it around the biceps of his left arm.

"What's that for?" someone asked.

Barkley said it was private. Personal.

Jason Silva loved the Phoenix Suns. The 10-year-old Glendale, Ariz., boy collected trading cards of all the Suns players, but his favorite, his hero, was Charles Barkley. When chemotherapy caused Jason to lose his hair, his school friends jokingly told him he looked like Sir Charles. The fifth-grader took it as a compliment.

Suns. Suns. Suns. That's all Jason talked about. Earlier in the year, when Jason was hospitalized in Tucson, where he underwent a bone-marrow transplant, the walls of his room were covered with purple and orange posters, honoring his favorite team. "The Suns were the one thing in his life that always put a smile on his face," said Linda Silva, Jason's mother. "His whole world revolved around the team."

Jason's dream was to meet Barkley. The previous Christmas the Suns star was visiting the hospital where Jason was a patient. The boy was in line to get Barkley's autograph—Jason had a special Barkley card he wanted Charles to sign—when he grew faint and was carried back to his room with a high fever. Barkley never saw him. "It's not fair," Jason told his mom.

If life were fair, Jason would have beaten Hodgkin's disease. But his condition worsened. The day before the Suns-Spurs game he asked his mother to tell him the truth, the bottom line. "Until then, we had always been so hopeful," his mother said.

Mother and son talked. Then Jason asked his mom to call Hannah.

Hannah Glouberman works with the Make-a-Wish Foundation. Jason knew her as his "fairy godmother." Linda Silva dialed the number. To her relief, Hannah answered on the first ring, and she recog-

33

nized the small voice immediately.

"Hannah, I just got some terrible news . . ."

"Jason, what can I do for you?"

"Hannah, I want to get to meet Charles Barkley."

Hannah called the Suns and shared the story. Was it possible . . . was there any way . . . no, we don't have that long. . .

Next day, at 2:45 P.M., the door opened in the room at Phoenix Children's Hospital. The nurse told Jason he had a visitor. "I couldn't believe it," Linda said. Barkley walked into the room and went to her son's bedside.

Charles and Jason visited. They made a deal and sealed it with a handshake. Before he left, Barkley signed Jason's Charles Barkley card.

That night, Jason's last, Barkley scored 16 points in the first quarter and finished with 35 in his best game of the season.

Jason didn't see the game. But he listened to it on the radio, eyes closed. Afterward, the family turned on the 10 P.M. news. A film clip showed Barkley running up and down the court. "Jason," his mother called to him. She lifted her son's head so he could see the screen. "Look. On his arm. He wore 'JS.' Charles Barkley dedicated the game to you."

10

Liquid Courage

He cut a bite of teriyaki chicken. As he lifted the fork to his mouth a stranger appeared at the table, as if out of thin air. "Excuse me, could I have your autograph?"

Barkley put down his fork. The woman offered him a pen. He scribbled his signature on the paper napkin and handed it to her with a nod. "That bugs me," he said, after the woman walked away.

"Signing autographs?" I asked.

"When I'm eating. I don't like it when I'm eating."

Seconds later, a child approached, shy as a rabbit. "Can you sign this?"

"You're very pretty," Barkley told the girl, trying to put her at ease. He signed his name. The child returned his smile and headed back to her table in the small Japanese restaurant where her parents, who had sent her over, were watching, observing them both, with interest.

"Sign one and they line up."

"Tell 'em no," I said.

"Then I'm an asshole."

Everywhere he goes, they flock to him. "Excuse me, I hope I'm not bothering you . . ." "Would you mind . . ." "Ohhhhhhh, Charles, my son would just KILL me if I don't get your autograph . . ."

Barkley loves being a celebrity, as few who are will admit. "I have charm, personality, charisma," he often reminds his teammates. Being hounded for his autograph is one small price he pays for his fame.

As a rule, he won't sign trading cards, or anything bearing his picture. He doesn't want dealers to sell the items and profit from his signature. Barkley can't imagine appearing at card shows and charging money for his autograph as many athletes and former athletes do.

Barkley earns millions from Nike, but he bristled one day when he was asked to sign 50 Nike posters that he was told were to be sold on a TV home shopping show.

"You're going to *sell* this stuff?" Barkley stared at his glowering likeness on the poster. "The poster is fine, but I'm not happy with this. I'm not happy with this at all. I'm not into athletes selling stuff.

This is the same thing as charging for autographs." Reluctantly, he began scratching his name, in gold ink, the first of 50 times. "I never charge for autographs. Tell them I'm not doing this anymore. This really disappoints me. I ain't lying. This goes against everything I believe . . ."

On April 18, 1993, he was dining at Dutch John's, a sports bar, with teammate Frank Johnson when a Scottsdale woman approached. She asked him to sign five napkins, which she wanted to give to residents of a nursing home where she worked. Barkley's policy is one autograph per fan, and he told her so. He signed one napkin. The woman pressed him for more. He said no. They exchanged words.

"This is what I think of your autograph," she said. The woman tore up the napkin and dropped it on Barkley's table. Barkley poured a beer over her head.

Early in the new season, Jerry Colangelo picked up his morning newspaper. The headline jumped off the front page. "BARKLEY HIT ME, FAN CLAIMS." The Suns owner can't stand negative publicity, but when he traded for Barkley he understood that there might be days like this. "Charles is who he is. I never thought for a moment that we were going to change him in any way. He's not an instigator. He doesn't go looking for trouble. But if I had my druthers, I wish he wouldn't go into certain places where he is apt to put himself in a position where trouble can find him."

Barkley isn't hard to find after dark. One of his hangouts in Phoenix is Stixx, an upscale pool hall/bar. Barkley was in Stixx the night a woman approached him and complained that he had refused to sign an autograph for her at last year's Phoenix Open golf tournament.

"I told her to get out of my face," Barkley said.

A local vitamin salesman stepped in. By his account, the man confronted Barkley and delivered a line right out of a Cary Grant movie. "That's not the way you treat a lady." He said the two exchanged words before Barkley charged him and hit him in the face. The man filed an assault complaint.

He later told reporters he would forget the incident if Barkley gave his 5-year-old daughter an autograph and apologized. Informed of the offer, Barkley said he had no problem with the autograph.

"Will you apologize?"

"I'd rather go to a (Ku Klux) Klan meeting wearing a Malcolm X hat than apologize," Barkley said defiantly. Mark West, who was stretching on the floor of the clubhouse, heard the remark and laughed. Barkley was serious. "I won't apologize because I didn't do anything wrong. Every time I go out someone wants to start something. I told the guy, 'When people get in my face, something bad is gonna happen.' He said, 'Oh, yeah, I'll get in your face.' They had to hold him and they had to hold me. I don't ever want to fight. But I get at least two people a night who do.

"The other night, I had a guy come over. He said to me, 'Nice to meet you.' His date, standing behind him, said, 'That's not what you told me. You told me he's a jerk and he's wearing the worst-looking suit you've ever seen.' I thought, 'Uh oh, well, here we go . . .'

"It's liquid courage. People want to make a scene. They can say, 'I punched Charles Barkley in the face, or Charles Barkley punched me.' I cannot win, ever. But I'm not going to stay in the house all the time like a moron. Majerle has been in a couple of brushes. Guys get jealous of other guys."

"I never had that problem," Frank Johnson piped up.

"You're not famous," Barkley said.

"They pay me a lot of money to keep Chuck out of trouble," Johnson, who is 6-foot-1, 180 pounds, joked. "If Chuck is going out he's supposed to call me."

No charges were filed, but the Stixx incident upset Barkley. Around the country, people would read a line or two in the newspaper that he had been involved in another fight and think the worst. Barkley says he doesn't care what people think about him, but he does.

Eight days later, at the same club, a California man claimed Barkley punched him and chipped one of his front teeth. He didn't press charges. Barkley was growing tired of the hassles. Phoenix police were spending an inordinate amount of time interviewing bartenders and bouncers. Although neither asked for my assistance, I wrote a column in *The Arizona Republic* offering a list of do's and don'ts for people who find themselves in Barkley's company:

Do not pet Barkley.

Do NOT attempt to feed Charles by tossing beer nuts at him.

No flash photography!

Do not introduce yourself to Barkley at the bar by saying, "Hey, Slick, you're in my seat."

If you must introduce yourself, address Barkley in a friendly manner. Example: "Charles" or, if you prefer, "Mr. Barkley . . . my name is (state name). I hope I'm not bothering you. I just wanted to (state reason for meeting him)." Then politely walk away.

If Barkley extends his hand, smile, shake it twice and let go. Do NOT attempt to hold Charles' hand for more than six seconds, particularly if you are male.

Do take no for an answer.

Do not mention John Paxson.

If you insist upon provoking a confrontation, wear a mouthpiece.

Do not say, "Mr. Hagler, can I have your autograph?"

Do not say, "Chuck, you don't know me, but I'm a friend of Bill Laimbeer."

Do not get into a four-letter-word-off with Barkley. You will l-o-s-e.

Do not attempt to write your telephone number on Barkley's forehead.

No smirking.

No mooning.

"You know, it bothers me when people ask me for my autograph, and they say, joking, 'You're not gonna hit me, are you?' I hate that. I just want people to treat me like a person first, and an athlete second. I don't want to fight, but I'm going to defend myself verbally and physically. Just because I'm Charles Barkley I don't have to take crap off people.

"People say I have a reputation to uphold because I represent the Suns. Well, if somebody wants to kick my ass am I supposed to say, 'Oh, go on and kick my ass because I don't want to embarrass Jerry Colangelo?' That's bullshit. I'm not taking no ass-kicking for the team. Hey, I don't want to embarrass the Suns. I don't want to embarrass Phoenix. But I don't think they pay me enough money to get my ass whupped.

"We can negotiate that."

11

Mail Call

Charles Barkley held up an unopened envelope, like Johnny Carson doing Carnak on the old "Tonight" show. "That's a fine," he announced. Barkley opened the letter. The dispatch from the National Basketball Association confirmed he had been docked $100 for unsportsmanlike conduct in the Portland game.

He held up another envelope. "Another fine." Right again. Technical foul against Utah. He tossed it, alongside the other, on the clubhouse floor.

"I don't care about fines," Barkley said airily. He has been docked more than $35,000 some years. "I quit worrying about 'em when I found out they're tax deductible."

Barkley was opening his mail. He gets stacks of it, bags of it, boxes and boxes of mail, some of which he never sees. Steve Evans, an executive staff assistant for the Suns, sorts through the hundreds of cards and letters that arrive each week addressed to the star player. The trading cards, jerseys, the basketballs which people send, asking Barkley to autograph, are forwarded to Charles Barkley Enterprises in Birmingham, Ala.

Barkley's mail piles up. Fan letters. Invitations to play in golf pro-ams. Requests for a pair of sneakers for a charity auction. Letters from golfers asking Barkley to bankroll them on the pro tour. "They're going to pay me back when they make it big. I probably get 10 of those a week." Students and parents write asking for financial aid. "Everybody," Barkley said, "wants me to put them through school."

Barkley opened a letter. Inside was a color snapshot of a large-breasted woman wearing a string bikini. In a flowery cursive hand, she wrote, "Dear Charles, the next time you're in L.A. I would like to invite you to lunch or dinner." Barkley had never seen or spoken with the woman. Just another admiring fan.

The National Association for the Advancement of Colored People asked Barkley to make a donation to the National Civil Rights Museum. Enclosed was a small block of cream-colored brick, a piece of the Lorraine Hotel in Memphis, Tenn., where civil rights leader Dr. Martin Luther King, Jr., was slain.

Fans send gifts. Caps. T-shirts. Pillows. A sleeve of "Slick Willie" golf balls, bearing the likeness of President Bill Clinton and the promise, "A Good Lie Guaranteed." A wood carving of a Nike shoe. A lawn chair in Suns colors. A hand-knit Charles Barkley doll, wearing a Suns uniform.

One day, an object titled "White Buffalo Kachina" arrived at the Suns clubhouse. The kachina, an Indian representation of spiritual thanksgiving, was a gift to Barkley "from your Arizona friends." Greyson Armstrong, an Arizona artist, fashioned the kachina from a log. The buffalo dancer, seven feet tall and 300 pounds, remained in the Suns clubhouse all season. Players touched the bull horns, or the raven feathers or the hank of horsehair for good luck.

Business offers pour in. Real estate deals. Investment opportunities. Barkley has received at least 20 offers to open a restaurant. Dan Majerle is part owner of Majerle's Sports Grill, a popular spot in downtown Phoenix. The menu, printed in Suns colors, purple and orange, features items such as KJ's Kajun Caesar Salad, McCoy's Chicken and Ham "Shazam"—in honor of Suns' broadcaster Al McCoy—and Danny Ainge's Three-Pointer Burger. There's also Sir Charles Chicken, a grilled chicken breast with peppers, onions and mozzarella cheese, for $6.25.

"I'll have a bowl of clam chowder, and the barbecued chicken breast, extra well done," Barkley told the waitress one day at lunch.

"You don't eat the Sir Charles Chicken?" I asked Sir Charles.

"Nope. Don't like peppers and onions."

Barkley looked over the list of appetizers. One item, Joe Courtney's Nachos, brought a smile. "Majerle's gotta quit naming nachos after players." Courtney, a 6-foot-9 second-year forward, no longer was with the Suns. "Know what Courtney's Nachos used to be?" Barkley asked. "Negele Knight's Nachos." The Suns traded Knight to San Antonio in November.

A trendy restaurant named "Barkley's" would do well in Phoenix. But Barkley is no more interested in owning a restaurant than he is in buying an ostrich ranch or becoming a local distributor for Amway. "If you've got a restaurant, you've got to serve alcohol and I'm not going to do that," he said, thumbing through another stack of letters, some with postmarks as far away as Tokyo, Japan. "People don't have good sense to start with. Give them alcohol on top of it and you're asking for trouble."

Barkley grew impatient. He tossed his unopened mail in his cubicle. He would look at it later. As an afterthought, he picked up the photo of the female admirer in the bikini and studied it in thoughtful silence, the way he would a box score after a big game. He shook his head. A grin spread across his face.

"Those *can't* be real."

12

Painful Conversation

Larry Bird said I should give it up. I don't think he meant right away. I think he meant at the end of the season. But he said everything I'm going through, he went through. He said it only gets worse.

The Suns pocket schedule is the color of a desert sunset. Home games appear in orange; away games in purple.

"Got a good stretch coming up," Barkley announced as he looked over the dates of upcoming games. The Suns would play on successive nights only once during late December and early January. When he was younger, when he could run and jump and never seem to tire, he never worried about back-to-back games. He felt invincible. Indestructible.

The NBA life is a grindstone. For 10 seasons Barkley has played what he calls "kamikaze" basketball, pushing, shoving, banging. Fighting nightly territorial wars in the paint. If he could trade his body in on a new model he would. But he can't. Like miles on a car, the wear and tear have taken their toll.

Every morning Barkley has the same conversation with himself. His mind says, "Get up." His body says, "Whoa, not so fast." Some mornings, his wife, Maureen, has to help him out of bed. When he sits up and swings his feet onto the floor, his body groans. His joints crackle and pop, like breakfast cereal. He is stiff and sore. He hurts all over. He routinely takes several aspirin a day for chronic aches and pains.

"My body's disintegrating. I know that," he said. "My back is just part of the problem. I've got arthritis in my knees, ankles. Look at these."

Barkley held out his hands. The knuckles are swollen and knobbed, like ginger root. His fingers are bent, the result of repeated dislocations. "This one," he said, lifting one finger, "used to be straight. Now it's angling off." Like a child playing Ten Little Indians, a counting game, he pointed to another finger, and the one next to it.

"I just hope I never get as bad as Train. Ever seen his fingers?"

Barkley shouted, "Hey, Train. Come over here."

Lionel "Train" Hollins played 10 NBA seasons with Portland, Philadelphia, San Diego, Detroit and Houston before retiring in 1985. His left hand is wincing testimony to the physical price professional basketball players pay.

The Suns assistant coach held out his hand for inspection. The last two fingers are bent at grotesque angles. His pinkie makes an abrupt turn. Almost 90 degrees. It looks like a broken twig.

"It started jumping out on me," Hollins said of his little finger. "I would dislocate it, and put it back. Then one night Maurice Cheeks threw a little pass behind me on the break and I reached back to get it and . . ."

"Yep," Barkley said, with an understanding nod.

"And I tore the ligament. Ripped it. Completely apart. I had it fixed once. Then it happened again. I'm on a fastbreak and Norm Nixon is trying to catch up and I'm trying to cut him off and he trips me. I go down and fall on my hand and both fingers go right out to the side. The doctors say all they can do is put in a false joint. Forget that. After my first surgery, it took almost two years to get all the strength back in my hand."

Barkley held out his hands, fingers spread. "My fingers are turning, but I don't know how bad they're gonna turn."

"That's what happens when they keep getting jammed," Hollins warned. "When they're jammed the ligament is susceptible to tearing because the swelling and the fluid is in the joint. It restricts me some when I play golf because of my grip. I used to play tennis. The lower part of my body is screwed up at age 40. When I get older, I'm sure the upper part will go, too. My knees, man, they're shot."

"See," Barkley said, "that's the thing that bugs me. I feel like my knees are shot."

"My knees," Hollins said. "My feet, my back. . ."

"He's right," Barkley said. "That's exactly what I feel like. When I get up in the morning you can hear shit go pop, pop, pop-pop."

Hollins smiled. "You know in that movie *North Dallas Forty*, when Nick Nolte, who played a football player, gets out of bed real slow. Sometimes my feet touch the floor and I think 'Ohhh, I don't want to get up.' I just want to sit there awhile and make sure everything is working."

Barkley laughed.

Hollins said, "When I watch myself on film, sitting on the bench, it sure takes me a *long* time to get up."

"Hey, when you're in the NBA something *always* hurts," Barkley said. "Your feet, your ankles, your knees and your back. All the time.

My shoulder hurts all the time, too."

"Chuck," Hollins said, "when I got through playing, I went to a doctor to have a physical and I was telling him all this stuff that was hurting. This was two years after I quit. The doctor said, 'Son, your body is coming back to tell you what you used to do to it. You didn't treat it right.' You know how you run into picks sometimes, and hurt your shoulder. . ."

"Yeah, you just shake it off," Barkley said. "You just consider pain part of the game. There's not a guy on our team that doesn't have something wrong with him. But you play with it. No matter what you do, whether you're a lawyer, a teacher or whatever, there are going to be days when your back hurts, or you've got a headache, and you still go to work. Just because you're sick don't mean you stay home from work. If people didn't go to work because something hurts, man, the world would be standing still. I think you're supposed to play in pain. But I know this is going to get me. Sooner or later it's going to get me."

Hollins nodded. "That's why I look at those football players and I really respect them. Last night, I was watching TV and they were talking about the 49ers starting offensive line still being in the game. Guys on that big old line go out there for 16 years and lay it on the line, every stinking game, and don't get a whole lot of credit for it. I read about Jim Otto. Guy had bone on bone on both knees."

In any discussion about pain, and the courage to play through it, Barkley thinks about Derek Smith, a former teammate in Philadelphia. "Derek is the toughest guy I ever played with. The toughest. Watching him get ready for a game was the most incredible thing. He got to the gym four hours early. He had no cartilage in either knee. It was bone on bone. He was 30 years old."

Barkley's toenails are badly discolored. The nails on his big toes looked as if someone had dropped an anvil on them.

"They're dying," Barkley said, with a shrug. "I guess it's from playing basketball for so many years. They stay black all the time. When somebody steps on your foot in a game, that is THE worst feeling. Talk about *pain*. If you've got bad toes that's the worst pain in the world. And it happens at least once a game. For about 15 seconds it's the worst pain you can imagine. You can't breathe it hurts so much."

Barkley looked at his toes as if seeing them for the first time. "Look at that. They're all black. I'll tell you, though, Michael Jordan's got the worst. His toes are a lot worse than mine."

Paul Westphal calls Barkley a warrior. The Suns head coach has no higher praise for a player. The description fits. Barkley's arms bear a crisscross of scratches and scars. Battle scars. "They're from little guards," Barkley said, inspecting his forearms and biceps. "Little guards are always reaching in. They're always in the way. I got a couple of these from the Portland Trail Blazers." He pointed to one scar. "This is a bad one." He fingered another. "That's a bad one, too. Guards don't want to get in there and get hit, so they're always reaching in."

Barkley injured his shoulder midway through the 1988–89 season. He played though the pain. During the 1990 playoffs between the Sixers and the Cleveland Cavaliers, Craig Ehlo "jumped" on Barkley's tender shoulder. Next game, Barkley retaliated. "That's when I tried to separate Ehlo's ribcage from his body. It led to the Barkley Rule." (For unnecessary and excessive contact, automatic ejection and a fine.)

Barkley had surgery after the season. He began rehab the next morning, lifting a light weight. C'mon, the therapist told him. Lift. Lift. He couldn't. His arm shook from the exertion. Pain? "I was screaming at the top of my lungs."

Today his shoulder talks to him regularly. "My shoulder's never going to be the same. Any doctor who tells you surgery is good for you is lying. Any time they cut you open it's bad. You're never going to be 100 percent again."

Stress fractures. Tendinitis. Second-degree sprains. A bruised spleen. Over time, Barkley has come to feel like that armored knight in *Monty Python and the Holy Grail,* indestructible, but diminished little by little as he is hacked away at, piece by piece, an arm, and a leg at a time. His back is the latest body part to tell him what he already knows. His days as a basketball player are numbered.

"I've never been through anything like this. The thing about my back is that it makes my legs go numb when I'm sitting around. It's messing up my hamstrings and my groin. Your body is a great machine. When one part of it isn't working the other parts will overcompensate. Your body will try and protect itself. I figure I've gotten about everything I can out of mine."

Barkley thought of the months that lay ahead. January. February. March. April. "You know the thing that scares me more than anything else? We've only played about 25 games. We've got 80 more to go, counting the playoffs. Can I hold up? I dunno. It's gonna be a long long grind . . ."

13

Shaq

Dec. 18, 1993

The morning after the Suns' first home loss, Barkley was alone in the clubhouse when a visitor appeared in the doorway. A giant man, he wore a furry little black cap. It lay flat atop his head, at a slight angle, like a beret. A gold ring dangled from one ear. He looked like a bebop musician, or a very hip pirate.

"Shaq!" Barkley said with surprise. "What's up, big fella?"

Shaquille O'Neal flashed a lopsided grin. O'Neal's disarming smile is part of the gentle-giant persona of the 22-year-old basketball player/rapper/movie star who, according to *Forbes*, earns more than $15 million a year from his various business interests, a third more than Barkley pulls in.

"Can I use your whirlpool?" Shaq asked.

"Go ahead," Barkley said.

As O'Neal ambled off, Barkley called out to him, "Switch is on the wall . . ."

Barkley doesn't appear in TV commercials for spas and hot tubs, but he would be an ideal pitchman. To relieve soreness and stiffness in his joints and back, he often spends 30 minutes a day in the whirlpool. Barkley enjoys lounging in the warm churning waters. Semi-submerged, he reads the sports page, or occasionally conducts an interview, which is a trick for the person asking the questions. For whirlpool interviews, I sat on the edge of the tiled tub, leaning out over the water, holding a pocket tape recorder at arm's length. Barkley, neck deep, waded over. I felt like I was at Sea World, feeding Shamu.

Barkley likes O'Neal. The kid has charisma, what Barkley calls "it." He also respects Shaq's talents. One day Barkley and Danny Ainge were discussing who they considered the true stars in the NBA. "I would say Shaq," Ainge said. O'Neal topped Ainge's list.

"I guess he is," Barkley said. "He's so damn *big*, and he dunks."

"You can't stop him," Ainge said. "He dominates a game. Shaq.

Patrick Ewing. David Robinson. Hakeem (Olajuwon). Chuck."

"I'm not a star," Barkley corrected. "I'm a SUPERstar."

O'Neal is a superstar too. His future is ahead of him, as the sports cliche goes, which is where one's future should be. The previous night, the Orlando center scored 36 points and grabbed 15 rebounds. His fifth blocked shot—he rejected Kevin Johnson's layup attempt, with eight seconds left—was the play of the game in the Magic's 104–101 victory over the Suns.

The Suns' Gorilla paid tribute to O'Neal's strength and power in a pregame skit. Dressed in coveralls, like a maintenance worker, the mascot inspected the backboard support beneath one goal in America West Arena. Finding the support insufficient, the Gorilla added fake boulders to anchor it.

Darryl Dawkins may have been the first NBA player to name his dunks, the way parents name their offspring. His repertoire included the Go-rilla, the Cuff, the Hammer of Thor, the Dunk You Very Much, and the Sexophonic Turbo Delight. These were exotic dunks, but they paled in comparison with the basket O'Neal made in his first visit to Phoenix on Feb. 7, 1993.

Shaq became the first NBA player to execute successfully the Oh-My-Gosh-Look-Out-Get-Back-It's-Coming-Down-Hello, 911?-Untamed-Delay-Of-Game-Hope-Nobody-Was-Maimed-Call-A-Welder-I-Don't-Care-If-It-Is-Sunday Dunkeroo Supreme.

When he witnessed it, Suns owner Jerry Colangelo rose from his seat in alarm. "I've seen the glass shattered. I've seen rims torn down. But I've never seen the *whole thing* go . . ."

Early in the first quarter, O'Neal grabbed an offensive rebound and scored on a ferocious dunk. He didn't swing from the rim, the way some players do. O'Neal just hung from the side of the hoop. Like a guy who had one too many, the $15,000 backboard support system suddenly tipped forward, as if in slow motion. The angular structure rocked back and began to sag. Slowly, down it came, all in one piece, backboard, rim, struts and all, heaving a mechanical sigh. It was like watching a brontosaurus die. O'Neal's weight caused a weld on a lower support bar to snap, crippling the structure.

As the sellout crowd looked on, mesmerized, Shaq retreated to the Magic bench, like a fighter who had just delivered a knockdown punch and was sent to a neutral corner. The rookie gazed at the deflated structure, took a sip of water and grinned. During the 37-minute delay, the teams relaxed in their dressing rooms.

"You didn't dunk it *that* hard, did you?" one of O'Neal's teammates asked.

"I dunk 'em all hard," Shaq replied.

Replay of the spectacle was shown over and over on national TV.

It was fascinating to watch, like slow-mo footage of an abandoned high rise imploding and collapsing, floor on top of floor, after being detonated by a team of explosives experts. Shaq's dunk irritated Barkley. The kid had upstaged the Suns on their new home court. Barkley dismissed the dunk as a "distraction" and the delay a waste of time.

But Barkley knows a fellow showman when he sees him. He recognizes O'Neal's marquee value to the NBA. Shaq is the present and future. The night the Suns lost to the Magic, Barkley slid into the whirlpool after the game. When he came out, someone handed him a sheet of paper. He scanned the box score in unhappy silence, then wadded it into a ball and fired it into the trash. Later, he went out to dinner. Shaq was his guest.

"Ever since I've been in the league we've had this thing where the top guys look after each other. They are friendly to each other. It's sort of an unwritten rule. We're like a fraternity. It's important that the veterans teach the young guys the ropes. Michael took me under his wing. Early in my career, Doctor J did, a little. So did Moses Malone.

"Last night, I heard a couple guys on our team joking around. I don't like that. You shouldn't talk loud or joke around after a loss. I played with a lot of guys who it didn't bother them to lose."

Barkley looked toward the whirlpool. "That's one of the things I talked to Shaq about last night. You know, we assume that everyone wants to win, but that's not true. A lot of players just want to get a check and that's it. I think that's true everywhere. Few people in our society want to do their job really well. I'd say only about 30 percent really want to excel in what they do . . ."

14

Merry Widow

Only one person gets to be Charles Barkley.
—Paul Westphal

Dec. 22, 1993

He was in bra heaven. Push-up bras. Full-figure bras. Lace demi bras. Bras in satin jacquard edged with embroidered stretch tulle. Bras with scalloped underwire uplift. Bras with crocheted lace. Bras with floral print. Accent bows. Faux pearl trim. Some bras even had names. The Carolina bra. The Kimberley bra. The Samantha bra. The Lauren bra.

And panties. Cotton panties. Silk panties, in every color. Gold, ivory, champagne, black, peach, periwinkle, teal, taupe, sage, coral, cream. Buy one pair, get one pair free!

Gowns. Camisoles. Slips. Teddies.

"What's this?" Barkley pointed to a red lacy undergarment.

"It's called the Merry Widow," the saleswoman at Victoria's Secret said.

"Hmmmmm." Barkley's eyes slid down the front of the outfit. "That would make *me* merry," he said with a lecherous grin.

With the afternoon off in Seattle, Barkley went Christmas shopping. He wanted to buy something for the flight attendants who travel with the Suns on their America West charter. "Every thing I say people take seriously," Barkley said as he looked around the store. "Remember when we lost to Chicago and I said something about the flight attendants?"

After the Bulls game, reporters asked Barkley his opinion of the Suns' 19-point loss. He shrugged off the early-season defeat. "Everybody played bad," Barkley said. The loss was a team effort. "The coaches coached bad. The trainers trained bad." Jokingly, he added, "Even the flight attendants did a bad job on the plane." Barkley's quote appeared in the newspaper. Some readers took his comment seriously and phoned the airlines to complain.

The saleswoman led Barkley to another wing in the Louvre of lingerie. With her help, he selected an assortment of silky negligees and pajamas. As he waited for the merchandise to be boxed, shoppers pressed in around him, surrounding him. Men reached out and shook his hand. Women pawed through their purses, looking for pens and scraps of paper, holding up anything he could sign.

Everywhere he goes in public, he is recognized. When Barkley walked through the mall, shoppers fell in behind him, like children behind the Pied Piper. Some followed him out onto the downtown streets.

"Barkley! Barkley!"

"Hey, Charles! What are you doing here?"

"We play the Sonics tonight."

"Too bad you're gonna lose."

Barkley wasn't so sure. "You make them guys think," he said of the Suns' division rivals, "and they get a headache."

"Charles! Charles!" A scruffy fellow, unshaven, dressed in rags, huddled beneath a blanket on the chilly pavement, a dog at his side. The crude lettering on his cardboard sign read, "Need food, or dog food." Barkley leaned down and handed the man a couple of folded bills. "Merry Christmas, Charles!"

Barkley stopped at a corner. While he waited for the light to change, a young man on a bicycle pedaled through the intersection and held out his right palm. Barkley gave him a high five as he sped by.

Barkley walked past a jewelry store. He stopped and peered in the window. On a whim, he went inside.

"Hello, Charles." The salesman shook Barkley's hand, as if they were old friends.

"Charles, I want to show you something."

The salesman stepped behind the counter. He produced a rectangular wooden box, polished to a high shine, and opened the lid. Inside was a gold watch. A Rolex Daytona Chronograph. He removed the watch from its velvet bed and handed it to the customer for his inspection.

"Handsome, isn't it?"

Barkley looked at the watch in silence. The heavy gold band gleamed under the fluorescent lights. The salesman said the watch was the finest in the store. He only had one, and Charles was holding it, turning it over in his hands, hefting it, impressed by its considerable weight.

"How much?" Barkley asked.

"Eighteen."

"Eighteen what?" Barkley said.

"Eighteen thousand."

Barkley took a shambling step backward, as if he had been elbowed in the chest by Shawn Kemp, the Sonics forward. "EIGHTEEN THOUSAND! OH MY GOD!" Around the store, heads turned.

"Charles," the salesman said in his level cultured voice, "this is a special timepiece."

"No shit," Barkley said, grinning.

The salesman, Terry, explained the features. This Rolex came equipped with everything but a 24-second shot clock. Like a car salesman who opens the car door and invites the prospective buyer to slide in behind the wheel, Terry unlocked the clasp and urged Barkley to try it on. See how it felt. How it looked on his wrist.

Barkley wears a Rolex, a beauty. The dial is ringed with sparkling diamonds. The year before, after a game against the Lakers, Barkley left his watch in the locker room at the Forum. He discovered he wasn't wearing it just before the bus pulled away from the arena. Barkley looked at his diamond Rolex with affection. "Terry, I need another watch like I need a hole in the head."

"Charles, you can have two watches. Go on, try it on." Barkley slipped the link band over his hand. He held out his wrist at eye level. He studied it carefully. It was tempting. "It is a sweet watch."

The salesman agreed. "You deserve it."

"Fifteen thousand," Barkley deadpanned.

"Eighteen, Charles," the salesman said gently, refreshing his memory.

This was a game, one-on-one, and the opponents on each side of the display case were enjoying the sparring immensely. Barkley suddenly disappeared from view. The salesman peered over the countertop. Barkley had dropped into a squat, like a Russian folk dancer. His back hurt. A moment later he popped up.

"Eighteen thousand," Barkley said. He cocked his head and squinted, and did some arithmetic. "Terry, do you realize I'd have to play two quarters to make enough to buy that watch?" Charles laughed. It was true. Barkley's $3 million salary, divided by 82, the number of regular-season games, equals more than $36,000 a game, or $9,000 per quarter. Barkley could afford the watch. He could buy every watch in the store if he wanted.

Barkley shook his head. "I can't do it, Terry. I don't need a watch. Do you think I rumble up and down the court just so I can buy jewelry?"

"Charles, let me tell you something. If you buy this watch you will not regret it. In fact, you will thank me for it, Charles. This watch is an investment."

"No," Barkley corrected. "My Mercedes is an investment."

"Go on, Charles. Do it."

Barkley looked at the watch.

The salesman tried another tack. "Benoit (Benjamin) was in here." Benjamin is a former Sonics player. "He bought nine watches. Not like this watch. But he bought nine."

"Benoit's an idiot," Barkley said.

Undaunted, the salesman produced a small pamphlet from the wooden box. "Damn, the thing comes with a *book!*" Barkley said in a loud voice. He gave the salesman an admiring smile. "I like you, Terry."

"I like you, too, Charles."

"You're good. You're real good."

"Thank you."

"But Terry, you don't seem to understand. I don't *need* a watch."

As silence fell between them, Barkley looked out the store window. Outside, people were peering in, noses pressed to the glass, waving at him. He waved back. Across the street shoppers stood in line at an automatic teller machine. "See that," Barkley said. "That's what people think I am. A money machine."

"Charles, we only have this one."

"Yeah," Barkley replied, "and you'll still have it the next time I come back."

"Do it, Charles," the salesman cooed, giving him a verbal nudge. "Go on. Make the decision. You make decisions every time you run up and down the court."

He didn't buy the Rolex. Instead he purchased a Cartier watch with a sporty sharkskin band. Excellent choice, very nice, Terry assured, as he handed the customer his credit card and wished him happy holidays.

"I can't believe you just spent $9,000 for a watch," I told him after we left the store.

"Charles! Charles!" Strangers called to him and waved.

"Hey, *somebody's* gotta be me," he said with a grin, as he crossed the street, shopping bags swinging at his side.

15

Season's Greetings

Dec. 23, 1993

In the biggest game of the young season, the Phoenix Suns beat Seattle, the hottest team in the NBA, by one point, on the Sonics' home court. Forty-five minutes later, the Suns players began filing out of the Seattle Center Coliseum. A bus waited to take them to the airport, for the flight home.

Outside, a crowd of Sonics fans had gathered. They watched and waited, their angry faces pressed against a chain-link fence.

Where is he?

Has he come out yet?

The mood of the crowd brought to mind the old Westerns where a lynch mob gathers outside the jail and demands that the sheriff turn the prisoner over to them. Barkley had infuriated Sonics fans with his play and his cockiness. He answered the boos by flashing his best 18-points-18-rebounds-go-to-hell grin, which made the locals even madder. Sonics fans hadn't been this riled up since Game 3 of the 1993 Western Conference finals, when Barkley left the court escorted by police.

Oh, how they had loathed him *that* night. Angered by an abusive fan, Barkley mouthed obscenities. He pretended to scratch his head, but Sonics fans knew what he was doing. He was giving them the finger. When he stepped to the free-throw line, the sellout crowd erupted. "Bark-ley sucks! Bark-ley sucks!"

As the chant grew louder, Barkley waved his arms, like an orchestra conductor, egging the crowd on. Outraged, one Sonics fan pointed the tip of her green umbrella at the bald lout and furiously began opening and closing it, opening and closing it, as if she were spraying him with pesticide.

It was all an act. A ploy. Show biz. Before the start of the second half, Barkley sat alone on the Suns' bench, arms folded across his chest. Fans were hurling insults, shaking their fists. "This is better than the World Wrestling Federation," I told him. Barkley threw back his head and laughed.

Barkley loves being booed. "Booing is the same as cheering," he said one day. "They don't boo you on the road unless you're a great player. Danny Ainge must be the greatest player who ever played the game." Barkley liked the line so much he shared it with his teammate.

"Hey, Danny?"

"What?" Ainge said. The former Celtic sat nearby, tying the laces of his sneakers.

"I said they only boo the great players. You gotta be the greatest player in *history!*"

The day before the game, the skies were gray, but Barkley was Mr. Sunshine as he waded through autograph seekers outside the hotel and stepped aboard the bus for the ride to the arena for the team's shoot-around. As he walked down the aisle, Cotton Fitzsimmons grabbed the sleeve of his turquoise warmup jacket.

"Don't touch me," Barkley said and jerked his arm away.

"Oh, I forget you're a star," Fitzsimmons said sarcastically.

"See what I got to put up with?" Barkley announced. He plopped his wide body into the seat next to Fitzsimmons, pinning Cotton against the window. Fitzsimmons is the one person in the Suns organization who can out-talk Barkley. When they are together on "Suns Jam Session with Charles Barkley," a weekly show on KPNX, the NBC affiliate in Phoenix, the repartee is the verbal equivalent of Agassi and Sampras trading serves on Centre Court at Wimbledon.

Fitzsimmons interviews Barkley, and vice versa. One day Cotton was late for the taping. No problem, Barkley said. He would do the show himself. Roll camera.

"Ladies and gentlemen. After numerous complaints from my audience, I have fired Cotton Fitzsimmons. It just got to the point where I could not carry him anymore and make him look respectable on camera. I can't fool you people out there. I get all these letters from fans saying what an idiot he is. That he's only in the way on the show. I totally agree with you, 100 percent. So Cotton is fired." With the freewheeling spontaneity of an improvisational comic, Barkley, seated on a sofa, began a conversation with his invisible co-host. "Cotton, the show's much better now without you."

Barkley stood, moved to the other end of the couch, sat down and crossed his legs. "No Charles," he said, pretending to be Fitzsimmons. "The show is not as successful without me."

Barkley got up, moved to his end of the couch. "Cotton, now that you have no job and, basically, have no life, what do you do?" Back to the far end of the couch. "Well, Chuck, I really do have a life. I play golf. I kiss up to Jerry (Colangelo) all the time . . ."

As the Suns' bus rolled away from the curb, Barkley asked if the team got Christmas off.

"You took *last* night off," Fitzsimmons said, zinging him with an ace. The night before, Barkley, hobbled by a sprained ankle, played a season-low 20 minutes and scored 12 points in a 121–95 loss at Denver.

"Most guys couldn't have played," Barkley shot back, which was true. The Suns forward probably should have rested. As Barkley often reminds, the NBA season is a marathon, not a sprint. But he played anyway, because he wanted to, because few road games are winnable without him. He also felt an obligation to the ticket buyers.

Joe Kleine sat near the back of the bus. Phoenix signed the 7-foot center as an insurance policy. The former Celtic gives the team another big body, a banger, six more fouls at playoff time. Kleine and Barkley became friends at the U.S. Olympic trials in 1984. "We sort of connected from the start," Kleine said. "I like his sense of humor. He likes mine. At the trials, he would make wisecracks in front of Bobby Knight that nobody else would laugh at, but I thought were funny as hell. When I came to the Suns it was a dream come true. Initially, I didn't know if I was happy because I was going to a team that I thought could win it all, or if I was happy because I was finally going to get to play with Charles. After a day or two, as I had time to think about it, I thought 'Man, this is great. I'm going to get to do both.' The guy hasn't changed. I loved him back then, and I love him now."

Kleine and Barkley torment each other. When the Suns played host to Orlando, tipoff for the home game was moved from 7 P.M. to 8:30 to accommodate television. Barkley, a creature of habit, loudly complained about the change, cursing TV for running sports. The time change irritated him. "I don't even know what time I'm supposed to eat today."

Kleine overheard the comment and couldn't resist. "Charles," Kleine said, and his hoarse voice took on this soft patient tone, like that of a teacher instructing a slow child, "I know they didn't teach you this at Auburn, but it's really not that difficult. Say, we play all our home games at 7 o'clock. Are you with me so far? Now, for one game they move the start from 7 o'clock to 8:30. So, Charles, you tell me, what time do you eat?"

Barkley told Kleine to go have sex with himself.

As the bus approached the arena entrance, about 50 fans were waiting. "Hit 'em!" Barkley shouted at the bus driver. "We'll say it was an accident. I'll be a character witness."

Shoot-arounds are closed to the media, although little if anything goes on during the brief sessions to warrant secrecy. The players loosen up, reacquainting themselves with the floor, the lighting, the baskets. The mood is playful. The 20-minute workout over, Barkley announced he was going to take, and make, a shot from behind the 3-point line. Anybody want to bet against him? Duane Cooper, a reserve guard, eagerly fished into his pocket. So did Ainge. Dan Majerle chipped in. Oliver Miller, too. The money went to Lionel Hollins, who they trusted wouldn't run off with it.

All the balls stopped bouncing. Barkley, who had been sitting at courtside, in kingly repose, milked the moment for all it was worth. Slowly rising from his chair, he removed his warmup jacket and placed it in the seat beside him. He picked up a ball and turned it over in his hand. He bounced it lightly in his palm. Eyes turned to the basket, he delicately pushed the ball off his fingertips, once, twice, catching it each time.

"C'mon!" someone said impatiently.

"I'm checking the rotation," Barkley said, unable to hide his amusement. Again, he asked for quiet. Feet together, he toed the 3-point line. He lifted his brown eyes to the basket. Filling his lungs with air, he took aim and let the ball fly in a high, lazy arc. Swish!

With the speed of a purse snatcher, Barkley grabbed $420 in bills from Hollins' hand and took off dancing toward the exit, grinning, laughing all the way.

Twelve hours later Barkley was still smiling as he walked out of Seattle Coliseum, a travel bag slung over his shoulder. When they saw him, the knot of angry fans came to life. "Hey, jerk!" "Barkley! You're an asshole!" They screamed at him and rattled the chain-link fence.

Barkley ignored the crowd. He stepped onto the darkened bus. Halfway down the aisle, he stopped, turned around and stuck his head out the open door. "We came! We beat your ass! We're going home! MER-RY CHRISTMAS!!"

16

The Yes Man

*One doesn't forget the rounded wonder in the eyes of a boy as
he comes bursting upstairs on Christmas morning and finds the
two-wheeler or the fire truck of which for weeks he scarcely dared
dream.*
—Max Lerner, *The Unfinished Country*

Christmas Day. Suns 111, Rockets 91. The game over, Charles
Barkley tore off the shiny wrapping paper and red ribbon and
removed the present from its box.

"Here, Daddy!" Barkley handed Mark West his Christmas gift.
Barkley, who had scored 38 points, grinned with delicious anticipation as he waited for his teammate's reaction.

West, a soft-spoken, serious fellow, looked at the object and
blinked. It was a plastic bust of a man dressed in a coat and tie, arms
folded, a big boot-licking grin on his face. The gag gift, called the
Executive Yes Man, is battery powered and voice activated and programmed to respond affirmatively to any statement.

Barkley snatched the gift from West's hand and held the toy
brown-noser aloft, showing it off to his teammates. "Charles Barkley
is one handsome brother!" Charles declared.

"I couldn't agree with you more," a tinny voice replied.

Barkley nearly fell down laughing.

West is not a good free-throw shooter. His career average from the
line is 58.1 percent. "Mark West is a great foul shooter," Barkley told
The Yes Man. The Yes Man replied, "You're absolutely right!"

The Suns weren't sure what to expect when Barkley came to
Phoenix. Gone was Jeff Hornacek, a Boy Scout, friendly, polite, a guy
who played hard every night and did his job well, without fanfare, and
who everybody on the team respected and liked.

Barkley? He was brash. Outspoken. Irreverent. Controversial. In
Philadelphia, Barkley challenged his coach's authority in front of his
teammates. He insulted the owner. "This team is bad. The whole
damn team," he said after one particularly frustrating loss.

Barkley brought a new attitude to the Suns' locker room. It was an attitude that said, "We're supposed to win and something is wrong if we don't." But how well would he relate to his teammates, and vice versa? No one knew what to expect when Barkley stepped onto the court at training camp two years ago, but they didn't have to wait long to find out.

Cedric Ceballos was leading a fast break. Barkley, irritated because Ceballos had blocked his shot at the other end, put on a burst of speed and mugged the Suns forward as he put up a layup.

"It was a bad foul," Paul Westphal said. "A flagrant two, for sure. If it had been a real game, he probably would have been ejected. The rest of the team told Charles they didn't appreciate what he did to Ced. Charles had gone over the line. He had taken a chance of really hurting a teammate, basically because he was mad."

Kevin Johnson was particularly upset. As a 76er Barkley had once hammered Johnson in a similar manner during a game. KJ hadn't forgotten, or forgiven. "It was a cheap shot," Johnson recalled. "I took it personally. Ever since it happened, I told myself, 'I owe him one.' "

Barkley didn't back down when his new teammates confronted him, but he respected them for standing up to him and coming to Ceballos' defense. He was testing them. They passed.

On Christmas Day, Barkley looked around the happy clubhouse. He saw a family. There was KJ, or "Franchise, Jr." as Barkley called him. West, the stoic professional whose work ethic reminds Barkley of Bobby Jones and Maurice Cheeks, two of his former teammates in Philadelphia. Dan Majerle, competitor, friend and restaurateur. "If you're gonna get poisoned, might as well be by a teammate," Barkley joked one day over lunch at Majerle's Sports Grill. A.C. Green, Christian soldier. Ceballos, the moody and explosive scorer. Frank Johnson, friend, and "pound for pound as tough as anybody in the league." Oliver Miller, great talent, but still a question mark. Joe Kleine, battler. Danny Ainge . . .

Ainge and Barkley are kindred spirits. They golf together. They have a running debate over who knows more sports trivia.

Ainge: "Chuck, who hit .361 in 1961?"

Barkley: "Rod Carew."

Ainge: "Wrong. Norm Cash."

They argue. They scream at each other on the court because 1) they share a mutual respect, and 2) each knows the other can take it. Both players are near the end of their careers. Both understand fame is fleeting, a temporary thing.

"Have you seen the Brooks Robinson commercial?" Ainge said. "Brooks is wearing a suit, and he's watching some kids playing baseball. One of the kids says, 'Want to play with us?' Robinson joins them and he makes this play and the kid says 'Hey, didn't you used to be Brooks Robinson?' Charles and I are like that. I'll tell him, 'Hey, didn't you used to be Charles Barkley?' and Charles will tell me, 'Didn't you used to be Danny Ainge?' "

Ainge, perhaps better than anyone, appreciates Barkley's talent. A 13-year NBA veteran, he played on two NBA championship teams in Boston. He understands completely when Barkley talks about the pressure he feels to perform at a high level game after game, to be "Charles Barkley every night."

"I have all the sympathy in the world for what superstar athletes go through," Ainge said. "It amazes me, not only what they go through physically, and what Charles goes through physically is 10 times more than what I go through. But emotionally. Having to do it every night. People pay to see Charles Barkley and Michael Jordan play. Those guys have to do it every night. That's why Michael Jordan retires at age 30. That's why Charles is talking about retiring before he's 32. I totally understand . . ."

Barkley said if he were in a foxhole he would want Ainge with him. And Frank Johnson. And Mark West, too.

"Merry Christmas," Barkley told West.

"Merry Christmas," West said.

"I couldn't have said it better myself!" squawked Daddy's toy.

17

Hey, Ball Boy!

Bill Russell, the former Boston Celtics great, speaks from a sign above the Suns clubhouse door. "The game is scheduled. We have to play it. We might as well win."

From a sign on the clubhouse wall, God asks, "Where were you when I laid the foundation of the Earth?" Proverbs 12.1 says, "Whoever loves discipline loves knowledge, but he who hates correction is stupid."

Go into the bathroom. There is the spirit of Mark Twain, hovering over the urinals. "Always do right," Twain advises. "It will gratify some people and astonish the rest."

On New Year's Eve day, Suns ball boy Jae Staats heard a voice in the empty locker room. He knew it wasn't Russell or Twain or The Lord Almighty, although the voice did make him jump. "HEY CHUMPY! GET IN HERE!"

Staats, a 20-year-old student at Arizona State University, doesn't know why Charles Barkley calls him Chumpy, but he doesn't mind the nickname. Staats has been called worse.

"Hey, c'mere you little fucker!" Barkley said one day. Staats dutifully obeyed. "You know why I like to call you that?" Barkley asked.

"No," Jae replied.

Barkley draped an arm around the kid's shoulder and smiled. "Because," he said, "there's nothing you can do about it."

Staats and Randy Gaspar, who work in the Suns' clubhouse, take Barkley's ribbing in the playful spirit in which it is intended. "That's just Charles. That's the way he is," Staats said. "He started joking with us the first game. I like someone who kids around a lot better than someone who ignores us. One day Charles said to me, 'Hey, you ugly something.' His wife was there. She said, 'Charles, don't call him that.' Charles came over to me and said, 'You know I'm just joking with you.' "

Barkley is their favorite. He gives the ball boys T-shirts. Caps. Flowers fans send him. Boxes of food. Barkley can't possibly eat all the baked goods. "Here," he tells the ball boys, handing them cookies or a Christmas ham. "Take this home to your family."

They do favors for him in return. The ball boys park his car near the clubhouse door after games. They take his Mercedes to the car wash. One day Barkley discovered he didn't have his game shoes. He had left them at his home, in the garage. The Suns were leaving that day for a road trip.

"Hey, do you know how to drive?" he asked Staats. He knew Staats did.

"Yes."

"Do you have a license?"

"Yes."

Barkley pitched Staats the keys to his brand-new Mercedes. "Drive over to my house and get my shoes. And Chumpy, if you wreck it, I will *kill* you . . ."

On New Year's Eve morning the ball boy was summoned again, in full voice. Staats found Barkley sitting in front of the mirror, shaving his head. "You ever shaved someone's head before?" he asked.

"No," Staats said.

He handed the kid his electric clippers. "Well, shave mine."

As Staats nervously ran the shears back and forth, Barkley engaged the young barber in conversation. How's your family? Do you have a girlfriend? "Do you want to come to my party tonight?" Barkley asked suddenly. Barkley was having a New Year's Eve bash.

Staats said he didn't think he would fit in.

"Sure you would," Barkley said. "Drop by. You are 21 aren't you?"

"No," the ball boy said.

"That's okay. We'll have pop there."

"So, did you?" I asked. "Did you go to the party?"

"No," Staats said. "It was for the players and coaches. It would have been kind of weird. I would have felt out of place. But I thought it was pretty cool that he invited me."

18

A Role Model?

The director clapped his hands twice, like a grade school teacher at the start of class. "All right everybody. Quiet on the set! . . . Ready? . . . Roll camera . . . action . . ."

Charles Barkley has just finished playing in a pickup basketball game. He reaches for the door of his new car. "Sonata. By Hyundai?" the voiceover asks.

Barkley looks over his shoulder. The camera zooms in. Glowering, Barkley says, "You got a problem with that?"

"CUT!"

The rehearsal was going well. Bill Halladay, creative director for Bates USA, an advertising agency in Irvine, Calif., stood near the set in Studio 15 at Sony Studios in Los Angeles, where Barkley was filming a 30-second TV spot for Hyundai, the Korean car company. Halladay served as the commercial's art director. Between takes, he conferred with Jim Jolliffe, his associate.

"Charles is a unique combination," Halladay said. "He's a tough guy, a tell-it-straight guy. At the same time, he has a lovability, if you can use that word with Charles Barkley. The genesis of the commercial was the line, 'Do you have a problem with that?' We felt Charles was the perfect person for the ad."

Barkley had his own idea for the Hyundai car commercial. "My teammates and I can't all get in, so I open the door and tear out the front seat." It wasn't quite what the ad agency, or the car company, which paid Barkley half a million dollars, had in mind.

Turn on TV. There he is. Floating through space in a McDonald's commercial. Playing a talk-show host in a Nike ad. In Egypt, selling underarm deodorant sticks.

"Oh, I haven't seen this!" Barkley said one day, interrupting a conversation. He jumped up and stood in front of the giant TV screen in the Suns clubhouse. In the Nike ad, Barkley tells a group of kids that wearing his shoes won't make them as good-looking as he is.

"Good," a youngster replies.

"I love that," Barkley said, grinning at the screen.

Brian Murphy is publisher of the *Sports Marketing Letter*. The

Westport, Conn.–based publication annually ranks endorsement income of athletes. In Murphy's 1994 list of "Ten Most Wanted" spokesmen, Michael Jordan is ranked No. 1, with $31 million in off-the-court earnings. Shaquille O'Neal is No. 2, with $13.5 million. Murphy projects Barkley's endorsement income at $5 million a year, ranking him No. 8.

"Barkley is an advertising treasure," said David Burns, founder of the Burns Sports Celebrity Service in Chicago. "Five years ago there is no way we would be seeing some of the commercials he has done. The CEOs of companies who make the decisions about who they use as spokesmen are stuffy, very conservative. Barkley is a bit anti-establishment. He's the only outspoken athlete able to do what he has done commercially. People like him because he speaks the truth. What he's done is a real breakthrough."

"Barkley," Burns said, "is the most quotable sports celebrity today."

"Who is number two?" I asked.

"Probably Lou Holtz."

"Lou Holtz really pisses me off," Barkley said. He was listening to Holtz on TV the day the final college football polls were announced. Florida State (12–1) which beat Nebraska in the Orange Bowl, was voted No. 1. Notre Dame (11–1) finished No. 2. Holtz, the Notre Dame coach, argued the Fighting Irish should have won the national championship because his team defeated the Seminoles, 31–24, in South Bend, Ind., and both teams finished with one loss. On TV, Holtz said, "I've never hurt so much for a team as I do for this one."

"Lou," Barkley shouted, "take some Pepto Bismol!"

Nike and McDonald's are Barkley's cash cows. His best-known commercial is the Nike role-model message. Barkley says he is not a role model just because he plays basketball.

The commercial sparked a lively national debate over the role of athletes in society.

Donald Kaul of *The Des Moines Register* wrote: "The thing is, if Sir Charles is no role model, then why do corporations pay him millions—yes, millions—to wear their shoes, drink their soft drinks, extol their cars? They do it precisely because he is a role model, one whose actions are emulated by others, particularly the young. He's earning something on the order of 10 mill a year for being a role model; now he's telling us 'never mind'?

"If Charles wants to stop being a role model, he should stop endorsing products and earn all of his money, rather than just a fraction of it, wreaking havoc on the basketball floor. He's being a hypocrite wanting it both ways."

E.J. Dionne of *The Washington Post*: "Effectively, Nike is using both Barkley and the Chicago Bulls' Michael Jordan as the fric and frak of their ad campaign. Jordan is the role model, Barkley is the anti-role model. Nike sells shoes coming and going, and Jordan and Barkley get richer."

Mike Royko, *Chicago Tribune*: "I agree with Barkley. The ability to jump high and slam-dunk a basketball has entertainment value and pays well, but compared with other skills — such as collecting garbage — it really doesn't make the world a better place to live. Think about that. Let us say that tomorrow nobody in the United States jumped high and slam-dunked a basketball. So what? Would it affect your life? Of course not.

"But if nobody in the United States picked up the garbage, we would really have a stinking mess, with flies and rodents and pestilence and all sorts of unpleasantness. . ."

Dale Turner, *The Seattle Times*: "Barkley's claim is a valid one. Parents cannot place their own responsibilities onto the shoulders of others. Yet parents depend on the help of others to support the ideals they would have their children reveal. Barkley and other athletic heroes know how star athletes are adulated and imitated by the young. Many great athletes were undoubtedly inspired in their younger days by the athletes they admired."

Scott Bernarde, *Atlanta Constitution*: "Apparently Sir Charles, as he is inappropriately named, feels he can have his cake and eat it, too. The reality of fame and fortune hasn't hit Barkley yet. Everything has a price, Charles, and one that comes with being a superstar athlete is the adulation of millions of people, most of whom are children. It comes with the territory, Bud, so deal with it."

Bruce Lowitt, *St. Petersburg Times*: "What Barkley says is very much his view. He has said it for years, not just when he was getting paid to say it. Then again, if he weren't a role model, would Nike be paying him megabucks to wear its products and to say he isn't a role model? And if he weren't a role model, would anyone be listening? It is a paradox."

Karl Malone, the Utah Jazz star, offered his view in a *Sports Illustrated* essay titled, "One Role Model to Another": "I don't think we can accept all the glory, and the money that comes with being a famous athlete and not accept the responsibility of being a role model, of knowing that kids and even some adults are watching us and looking for us to set an example. I mean, why do we get endorsements in the first place? Because there are people who follow our lead and buy a certain sneaker or cereal because we use it . . . Charles, you can deny being a role model all you want, but I don't think it's your decision to make. We don't choose to be role models, we are chosen."

Barkley is proud of the commercial. "It's the best thing I've done since I came into sports. Most of the mail I've received about it is positive. I'm a role model, but I'm a secondary role model, and that was what I was saying. The number one role model should be parents. They're the ones who raise you."

For Kevin Johnson, it finally happened. Twice jilted, the Suns guard was named to Dream Team II, which represented the United States at the World Championships in Toronto in August. So Charles, how would Dream Team II fare against Dream Team I?

"We'd kick their ass," Barkley said. "We'd spank 'em good." Barkley appeared offended that anyone would think otherwise. "C'mon," said the Hyundai spokesman, "you don't compare no Hyundai to no Rolls-Royce."

19

Bogey Golf

Five feet. Slightly downhill. No break. As a hush fell over the other members of the foursome, Charles Barkley took a deep breath to steel himself. Not a sound now, except for a bird singing in a nearby tree. Carefully, he placed the blade of his putter behind the ball. He looked at the hole, then at his ball, then at the hole again, his eyes darting back and forth, measuring the distance, gauging the speed. Time passed. He wanted this one. He needed it for par.

Click. The dimpled sphere began to roll. The ball rolled . . .

. . . and rolled . . .

. . . and . . .

"Fuck!"

Barkley's first love is basketball, but his passion is golf. The game is his getaway from the spotlight and the demands of being an NBA superstar. On the course, there are no referees. No media. No crowds. For Barkley, the freedom to play golf whenever and wherever he wants, like his pal Michael Jordan, makes the prospect of retirement inviting.

After an early-season home game, Barkley came out of the shower, a towel tied around his waist. Settling into a golf stance, he wiggled his toes in the clubhouse carpet. He addressed an imaginary ball with an imaginary wedge and looked at a rolling green only he could see, beyond the team's whirlpool.

Barkley swung. "Perfect! Eighty-five yards!" he cried, his eyes tracking the ball's flight. Barkley turned to Frank Johnson, perhaps his closest friend on the Suns team, and raised his right hand, as if taking an oath. "Frank," he said, solemnly, "I swear to God this is the last year I'm playing basketball."

Andrew Toney introduced Barkley to golf six years ago. The game became his escape hatch from the maddening frustration he felt trying to carry the dead weight of a bad team on his shoulders. On the golf course, Barkley didn't have to depend upon Charles Shackleford to select the right club for him, or Armon Gilliam to bail him out of trouble from a bad lie. "That's why I started playing golf. In Philly I had so many guys who wouldn't go to war with me all the time that it was nice to be able to control everything. In golf, if you screw up, you screw up. You can't blame anyone else.

"The golf course is probably the only place I can go and relax. It's very important in my life. I'm not that good at it, but it's fun to pretend Paul (Westphal) and Jerry (Colangelo) are on that little ball and hit it hard. That relaxes me."

"How about Howard Katz's ball?" someone asked, referring to the Philadelphia 76ers owner, with whom Barkley feuded.

"I *shot* his ball," Barkley said. Charles raised the barrel of an imaginary shotgun, and took aim, one eye closed, like a skeet shooter tracking a clay pigeon. "I put his picture on one of those little plates and shot it down."

Barkley loves to watch golf on television. He counts several PGA Tour pros among his friends. "There's my man Payne," Barkley will say, nodding at the TV image of Payne Stewart competing in some tournament on a course Barkley has played, or plans to, once he retires.

One day I found him sitting in front of the giant TV screen in the clubhouse. A sign above the set says, "Win Playoff Games," but Barkley wasn't thinking about the post-season, which was months away. He was watching the Johnnie Walker World Championship in Montego Bay, Jamaica. Barkley recognized every player in the international field.

Steve Elkington laced his drive down the middle of the fairway. "Look at that tempo!" Barkley said. "Beautiful. It's the same every time. That guy's got the best swing in golf."

Basketball players. Football players. Baseball players. Tennis stars. Pro golfers. They belong to a mutual admiration society. "We're all in a kind of fraternity," Barkley said. "We all have something in common. Before you get to the point you're really good, and you get on TV, there's all that work and dedication and sacrifice people never see. Elkington's golf swing is like my game of basketball. It took a long time to perfect. He didn't get good overnight. He's out hitting balls, just like I've run suicides, running, running all the time."

Barkley's golf handicap is the subject of good-natured debate. "Chuck's terrible," Danny Ainge said. "On TV they'll do an interview with him and he says he's a 12 handicap. Then you get out on the course with him and all of a sudden he's a 16. Chuck's more like an 18."

According to *Golf Digest*, Barkley has a 14 handicap. Mike LaBauve, a member of the *Golf Digest* schools staff, analyzed Barkley's swing in a story for the magazine. The teaching pro left Barkley with a lot to think about. "He waits a little too long to cock his wrists . . . Charles starts to lean left when he should be turning around his right leg . . . the weight in his left toe should be in his right heel . . . Charles needs to rotate his left arm more . . . He is 'holding on,' trying to stop the ball from hooking."

When shown the sequence photos of Barkley's swing, Dan Majerle turned his head and threw up his arms in a warding-off gesture. "I don't want to look at that. That swing's lost a lot of money."

Barkley loves golf so much he will play with almost anyone, even sports writers. The day before Game 5 of the 1993 Suns-Lakers play-off series Barkley spent the afternoon on the course with a group of duffers that included a Dallas writer, David Moore.

Moore met Barkley three years ago in Dallas. Charles was in his last season with Philadelphia. His calculated efforts to force the 76ers to trade him was the subject of Moore's column that appeared in the Dallas paper that morning. After the Sixers-Mavericks game, Barkley ran into Bob Ford of *The Philadelphia Inquirer* in the lobby bar at the Hyatt Regency Hotel. "Charles, do you know David Moore, of *The Dallas Morning News*?" Ford said, introducing his companion.

"Yeah," Barkley said, leveling his gaze at the reporter. "I know who you are. You're the guy who cut me up in the paper today."

Moore smiled and held his ground. "Charles, what other guy would cut you up in the paper, sit here and let you buy him drinks the rest of the night?"

Barkley laughed, and bought the next round.

Moore is a better writer than a golfer. Suffice to say no course records were set that afternoon. Next day the Suns beat the Lakers, 112–104, in overtime to win the first-round series, which was much tougher than anyone had anticipated. The Lakers won the first two games in Phoenix. The season on the brink, Suns coach Paul West-phal boldly predicted his resilient team would come back and win three in a row, and the series, which it did.

After Game 5, reporters went to Barkley. "Charles," someone asked, "what did you learn about the Lakers series?"

Barkley looked around the group. He nodded toward Moore, who was standing in the back of the pack. "I learned *that* son of a bitch can't play golf."

At 8 A.M. they began to arrive, wheeling their luxury cars into the parking lot of the Phoenix Country Club. Frank Johnson. Tim Kempton. Majerle. Ainge. Joe Kleine shook his head as he hoisted his golf bag from the trunk. He didn't appear too enthused. "I got suck-ered into this," Kleine said. His clubs clanked dully as he reluctantly trudged off toward the practice putting green.

As his teammates predicted, Barkley arrived last. He stepped out of his black Mercedes convertible and gulped in the cool morning air. His companion was Howard Eskin, a Philadelphia sportscaster who was spending the weekend in Phoenix as Barkley's house guest.

When Barkley spotted his waiting teammates, his face split into a huge grin. "The first annual Bragathon!" he announced loudly. Charles clapped his hands and rubbed them together with glee. "This is great. This is gonna be great!"

Barkley and Ainge had arranged the Suns' golf tournament. Each player was seeded, and given a handicap. On the first tee, Barkley divided the field into two groups, a foursome of the top seeds—Barkley, Ainge, Majerle and Kleine—and a threesome, made up of Johnson, Kempton and Eskin, who happily put in his $200 entry fee. Eskin plays lots of golf with Barkley, for fun and profit. Howard saw this as another can't-miss opportunity to fatten his wallet.

Barkley, the self-appointed starter, sent the threesome off first. Johnson's tee shot sailed wildly off to the right, headed out of bounds. Barkley followed the ball with upturned eyes and happily described its flight with the theatrical flair of a radio baseball announcer calling a game-winning home run. "It could be . . . it MIGHT be . . . it's GONE!"

Johnson's luck didn't improve. When he arrived at the first green the Suns point guard looked into his golf bag. "My putter? Where's my putter? It's gone. Somebody took my putter!" Frank looked back down the fairway and shouted, "Chuck, did you take my putter?" Barkley, eyes rounded in innocence, shook his head.

Eskin suggested Charles wasn't above pulling such a prank. He related a time he and Barkley played for $100 a hole. As they arrived at the green, Eskin said, Barkley stepped into a sand trap and, using his club head, nudged his ball out of a fried-egg lie.

"What are you doing?" Howard asked incredulously.

"The ball's not sitting up," Barkley said.

"You can't do that!"

"I can do anything I want," Barkley replied.

"I've never lost to him," Howard said, "and I've played some bad rounds, too. I probably won $2,000 from him last summer. Charles will play pretty well for a few holes. Then he'll blow up. He'll have an eight or a 10. Big holes kill him. He can't put it together. It all falls apart."

Eskin stepped out of the cart, and lined up his approach shot. *Whack.* His ball hit the top of a palm tree, rattling the fronds. "Goddammit, Howard!" he cried, berating himself. Eskin's ball came to rest an inch from a concrete ditch.

"I'll tell you the funniest thing I ever saw with Charles on a golf course," Eskin said. "We were playing in Philly with Lenny Dykstra of the Phillies and Nick Levya, who was managing the Phillies then. We got to the last hole and Charles was down $400 to both of them. Charles said, 'Let's go double or nothing.' I'll say one thing about Charles. He's always confident. One time we played at Merion.

68

Tough course. Charles said, 'I'm gonna shoot 85.' Eighty-five! There's no way in hell he can shoot 85 on that course. I said, 'Okay, you're on.' He shot 102. I won $150.

"Anyway, we get to the last hole. Charles hits his tee shot down the fairway, not real far but safe. Dykstra hits it in the water. So does Levya. Charles is thinking he's got them. Know what he did?" Eskin grinned at the memory. "He dribbled his next four shots down the fairway and lost the hole. Cost him $1,600."

"Was he mad?" I asked.

"Hell yes, he was mad. I told him, 'Charles, you choked.' He told me, 'You're right, I did. It's the only time I ever choked in my life.'"

Barkley, playing in the second group, shot 48 on the front nine. He was enjoying himself. What could be better than playing winter golf with friends under a bright desert sun?

"Lots of old money here," Barkley said, all smiles, as he strolled down the 10th fairway. "That's what I like about it. The members have more money than I do, so they're not impressed by me. Out here nobody bothers me. People leave you alone."

While Barkley delivered a running commentary on golf, basketball and the joy of being alive, Majerle toiled away quietly. "All I want to do is beat Chuck," he confided. About the only time Majerle spoke was to express his exasperation. "How do you take an eight?" Majerle asked, after doing so on one hole.

"Easy," Barkley told him. "You hit it seven times, and tap it in."

The remark brought to mind Seve Ballesteros' response when he was asked how he four-putted one hole at the Masters. "I mees the putt. I mees the putt. I mees the putt. I make the putt."

Rallying, Barkley shot 90. He finished behind Ainge, Majerle, Kempton and Eskin and ahead of Johnson, who never found his putter. He also beat Kleine, which was gratifying, since Kleine had delighted in heckling Charles throughout their round.

When Barkley knocked a tee shot into the water, Kleine broke into song. "Splash, splash I was takin' a bath . . ." Next hole, as Kleine teed his ball, Barkley pointed to two groundskeepers. Both wore hard hats. "Hey, Kleine, these guys must have seen you play!"

Kleine had the last word. Late in the round, Barkley stood over his ball, facing a treacherous downhill putt. Touch it. Just start the ball rolling. That's how fast it was. Barkley steadied himself. He milked the grip of his putter. Just before he drew back the blade, Kleine offered a word of advice. "Hit it firm, Chuck."

Barkley flinched. "You're going to hell, Kleine."

Kleine: "Well, at least I'll have somebody there I can beat in golf."

Ainge piped up, "There's no golf courses in hell."

"Yes there are," Kleine said. "And they're *hard*."

20

Hurt Again

Jan. 7, 1994

The voice of Al McCoy, the Suns' play-by-play announcer, crackled over radio station KTAR. "Majerle out front. Goes to Barkley on the left side. Tellis Frank playing him defensively for Minnesota. Barkley backing, backing down. He's in the lane. Here comes the shot. Won't get it. Rebound Mike Brown. Out it comes to J.R. Ryder, waiting . . ."

"Charles Barkley is gonna have to come out of the game, Al," said color commentator Cotton Fitzsimmons.

"He's limping," McCoy said. "He's limping right now. Barkley's gimping around in the lane . . . and Barkley is coming out . . . he's limping . . . going down to the end of the bench . . . he's headed for the locker room . . . we'll wait to get a report . . ."

Jan. 9, 1994

Barkley, dressed in a suit, limped into the Suns training room at America West Arena. Dr. Emerson was waiting. As public address announcer Jeff Munn introduced Barkley's teammates to the sellout crowd, "And now, coming onto the court, YOUR Phoenix Suns!" Emerson, glasses perched on his nose, re-examined Barkley's right leg. Barkley had suffered a small tear in the quadraceps tendon above the knee. The good news: no surgery. The bad news: the Suns' star forward was placed on the injured list. He would be sidelined "indefinitely."

Back. Hamstring. Groin. Elbow. Ankle. Now his knee. A week earlier, Barkley rang in the new year by proclaiming 1994 "The Year of the Chuckster!" Barkley thrust his fists into the air, like a prizefighter after scoring a knockout.

Now Barkley sat in glum silence, leg extended on a padded table as Emerson fitted him with a brace. *Maybe I should have listened. My body tried to tell me back in November. Maybe I should have quit then.*

In the third game of the season, against the Clippers in L.A., Barkley tried to block a shot by center Stanley Roberts. He fell, landing on his sore back. For several seconds, he lay motionless, like a marionette whose strings had been cut. "The floor is really hard here, too," Barkley joked after the game.

"Next morning, when I woke up, I was so sore I couldn't walk. I thought, 'This is ridiculous. I've had enough. It's not worth it anymore.' I talked to my wife and my agent. Both told me to do what I wanted to do."

Barkley started to pick up the phone. He was going to call Suns owner Jerry Colangelo. He had his speech prepared. "Jerry, I can't play anymore. It's too painful." But he didn't make the call. "I couldn't get the words out." Several times since then Barkley planned to tell Paul Westphal he couldn't play that night. Westphal would understand. But Barkley never followed through. He didn't forget his lines. He just couldn't deliver them.

"I'm here with Dr. Kevorkian . . . I mean, Dr. Emerson." Barkley was sitting in the training room, filming his weekly "Jam Session" TV show. The camera, and Barkley, were rolling. "And the first thing he's doing is putting on these plastic gloves and grabbing this jar of Vaseline . . ."

Joe Kleine stuck his face in front of the lens. "When a horse breaks his leg, whattaya do? You shoot him."

Emerson and Aaron Nelson, the Suns assistant trainer, looked at Barkley's bum leg. They were going to fit him with a new splint. "Is this the first time you ever did this?" Barkley asked.

Emerson lightly touched Barkley's leg, above the kneecap. "How does that feel?"

"OWWWWWW. That HURTS!!"

Barkley laughed. So did the doctor and the trainer. Barkley turned and looked directly into the camera, and spoke to his viewing audience. "You see, you think that's funny. Folks, why is it that doctors always push on the place that is hurting? That's one of the things you need to think about. I think if doctors didn't push on a spot that was hurting so often, you would heal a lot faster.

"Don't you think?"

21

Barbados Calling . . .

Jan. 19, 1994

The pilot of the small plane glanced over his shoulder. "Charles, we can't land in Santa Monica. You want to go to Van Nuys or LAX?"

Barkley peered out the oval window. Greater Los Angeles was shrouded in fog. It was like looking at the city through gauze. "LAX is fine. Can you call my driver at the other airport and have him meet us?"

"Will do," the pilot said.

As the plane descended, the rooftops of houses and apartments came into view. From the air, there were no signs of the massive destruction from the earthquake that 48 hours earlier had awakened Los Angeles with a terrifying jolt.

Barkley thought about his father. When he heard the news bulletin, he called L.A. He couldn't get through. He dialed the number a dozen times. All circuits were busy.

Frank Barkley and his wife separated when Charles was a year old. The boy grew up resenting his father, who moved to California. "Frank wasn't a part of Charles' life," said Barkley's mother, Charcey Glenn. "It wasn't just financially. He wasn't there for him in any way. I would tell Frank, 'Pick up the phone and call him every now and then. Write him a letter. Send him $5.' I always felt like a piece of daddy was better than no daddy at all.

"I never taught Charles against his father, but I could relate to how Charles felt because my father left my mother. I was raised by my mother, too. Charles had so much hostility toward his father as he grew up. He didn't see his father until he was 9 years old. That summer he went to California and visited Frank. Charles came back from that vacation and told me he didn't ever want to be with his father again."

As Barkley grew into manhood, Frank attempted to reach out to his son. He asked for Charles' telephone number. Charles told his mother not to give it to him.

"I told Frank he couldn't just push himself into Charles' life after all these years. Charles was a grown man and had to work this out for himself. He needed to try and forgive his father because it was only hurting him. I wasn't so concerned for Frank as I was for my child."

During Barkley's rookie season, the Philadelphia 76ers flew to Los Angeles to play the Lakers. Barkley's mother remembers every word of her conversation with her oldest son.

"Mama, Frank's probably going to go to the game. You know his phone number. Do you think I should call?"

"Honey, do you *want* to call him?"

"Tell me what you think, Mama."

"Honey, it's your decision. If you want to call your daddy and talk to him, then call him and talk to him. Invite him to the game if you want to. You need to do whatever is in your heart to do."

Barkley telephoned his father and left him tickets. Over time they began to establish a relationship. Frank visited his son in Phoenix at Thanksgiving in 1992. It was the first holiday they had spent together. "Frank was on cloud nine," Charles' mother said. "They enjoyed each other. They have a pretty good relationship now. I think Charles has forgiven his father, but he won't ever forget."

Barkley likens his relationship with his father to repairing a car tire. "I put a patch on it. I don't know if it'll ever ride smooth, but there's a patch on it now."

As the limo nosed through rush hour traffic, Barkley leaned back in the gray leather seats and smiled. He was in an upbeat mood. He looked forward to being a guest on the "Larry King Live" television show. The bigger the stage, the larger the audience, the better he likes it. Barkley is never at a loss for words. Arsenio. Letterman. Leno. Barkley has done them all.

Barkley unfolded his cellular telephone and happily began punching numbers on the dial. He was like a kid with a new toy. He called Phoenix and spoke with his wife and daughter. He dialed Salt Lake City, the home of Karl Malone.

Marc Perman met him at the CNN studios. Perman, a 37-year-old attorney, is a talent representative with J. Michael Bloom and Associates in New York. "Marc's great. He negotiates the way I play basketball," Barkley said by way of introduction. "Marc's very good at what he does."

Wendy, the makeup artist, seated Barkley in a swivel chair in front of a brightly lit mirror and draped a towel around his shoulders. Like an archeologist dusting some ancient artifact, she began delicately powdering Barkley's face and bald head using a fine bristle brush.

"Finished," she said.

Barkley opened his eyes and stared at his cosmetic reflection.

"Wendy," he said.

"Yes."

"After this is over, you're gonna take all this makeup off me, aren't you? I don't want to walk out of here looking like a fag." Barkley paused. "Not that I have anything against fags. I just don't want to be misconstrued."

Barkley joined his agent in the green room, which isn't green but brown. The King show was in progress. The host was interviewing the president of the Tonya Harding fan club. Barkley switched channels. He was more interested in the Los Angeles Clippers–Orlando Magic game. Magic guard Anfernee Hardaway pulled up and swished an 18-foot jump shot. "That kid can play," Barkley said. "He's going to be the best of all the rookies this year."

During a commercial break, Barkley took a seat in a darkened studio. An engineer wired him for sound. The show's host wasn't present. Larry King conducted the interview from Washington, D.C. Five, four, three, two . . .

Larry King: "Joining us from Los Angeles, where the Suns play tomorrow, but he will not because of an injury, is Charles Barkley. How goes the health?"

Barkley: "I'm getting better. I'm going to talk to the doctors and get them to let me play next week, Larry."

LK: "You weren't here for the earthquake, were you, Charles?"

CB: "No, I just got in today. It's a very sad situation. My prayers go out to everybody who lost their loved ones and everybody who lost their homes."

LK: "By the way, I hear the new Right Guard commercial comes out Feb. 1. Is this going to be a new breakthrough commercial, like the last one you did with Nike?"

CB: "Well, I tell you what, Larry. Every time I make a commercial I just want it to be funny and for people to have a good time watching it. . . . That's the most important thing."

LK: "Will you stand by that statement about role models? Were you misquoted, or would you change it . . ."

CB: "The best thing I've ever done in my career is the role model commercial, for two reasons, Larry. Number one, I think we put a big misconception out there to all our kids. They should be listening more to their parents than to someone who can dunk or can rush for 1,000 yards or a guy who can hit .300. They should listen to their parents, because their parents are with them every day. Secondly, I think we are making black kids especially feel like the only way they can be successful is through athletics. And that's wrong. We've got to make sure they get back to their family values and stop building up celebrityism, as I call it. Let them know they can be successful as doctors, lawyers, they can be policemen. They can be anything they want to be. The hardest thing, the thing they probably aren't going to be, are professional athletes."

LK: "But that does not mean that the professional athlete doesn't have some role in the life . . ."

CB: "No question. But they are secondary role models. I don't think you can say athletes play a more important role than their parents. The parents are far and away the major influence in a kid's life, whether the parents want that responsibility or not."

LK: "Is this a hang-it-up season, really?"

CB: "Larry, I'm in kind of a difficult situation. I'm in a lot of pain because of my back. And I don't want to become a bad player. I really love playing in Phoenix. And I want to keep playing in Phoenix. But I would never become a mediocre player, who just played for money. That's not in my system. So I'm looking if my health does not improve, and I don't have back surgery, I'm looking at this as my last season. But it's not because I don't love the game. It's because I don't want to become a bad player."

LK: "So if your health improves, you will play more?"

CB: "I think so. But I definitely think I'm going to have to have back surgery, regardless. My back is not going to get any better through exercise or rest."

LK: "Similarly, you and Larry Bird apparently go that same path. Bird left because of his back."

CB: "I had a good talk with Larry about a month ago. . . . He advised me that it would be in my best interest to retire."

LK: "So he advised you to retire?"

CB: "Yes."

LK: "And, of course, he apparently stays away from the limelight, which you won't do, right?"

CB: "Oh, I'll stay away from it. I just can't wait to be a retired millionaire and play golf every day. I want a talk show like you, though."

LK: "Oh, the Barkley show."

CB: "Ah, 'Charles Barkley Live'!"

LK: "Good name, Charles. How about 10 o'clock eastern on CNN. You follow us."

CB: "That would be a good lead-in show."

During a commercial break, Barkley's agent was beaming. Perman was monitoring the interview from a sound booth. Barkley was saying all the right things, especially about leaving the door open to play another year.

LK: "Currently, Charles Barkley is leading the NBA voting in the Western Conference for the All-Star Game in Minneapolis in mid-February. Orlando, Florida, as we go to calls for Sir Charles. Hello?"

Caller: "Hello, I'm calling from the land of the Shaq. I wanted to ask Charles if they're going to make it to the championship, meaning Phoenix, and who are they going to beat?"

CB: "Well, number one, thank you. Hopefully, that will come true. I think we are a lot better team this year than we were last year. The best team in the East is the New York Knicks. We're going to have a hard time getting out of the West. The three best teams in the NBA, and no disrespect to the Knicks or the Bulls or the Hawks, are the Seattle SuperSonics, the Phoenix Suns and the Houston Rockets."

LK: "Has Chicago surprised you, playing as well with the loss of Jordan?"

CB: "No. Not at all. They won't miss Michael Jordan until the playoffs. They've got some good players. But until you get into a close game in a pressure situation where Michael always made those plays, that's the only time they're going to miss him. They're going to miss Michael, and anyone who thinks they're not is crazy."

LK: "Ealing Park, Barbados. For Charles Barkley. Hello."

Caller: "Larry, Happy New Year. And ditto to your terrific guest. A twin question, Sir Charles. Have you ever thought of being a rock 'n' role model . . . with some slam dunk sounds?"

LK: "Not a bad idea."

Caller: "And the quick second question. How did you come to be called Sir Charles?"

CB: "Well, number one, I couldn't be a rock 'n' roll star because that's just too many people for me. I don't need all that."

LK: "How about Sir Charles?"

CB: "I don't know who gave me that nickname, Larry. I got so many nicknames in college, I don't know how I got them all. Larry, I'm really impressed. You must be really large if you're getting calls from Barbados."

LK: "We get calls from all over the world, Charles. This is the only live worldwide talk show. You're being seen in 162 countries."

CB: "Do all of 'em speak English?"

LK: "I assume the ones watching are speaking English. English is spoken in a lot of places."

CB: "Get me some commercials in Barbados."

LK: "You never stop, do you Charles?"

CB: "Hey, Larry. I'm here to have a good time. I'm not here to be here a long time . . ."

22

Purgatory Revisited

Jan. 27, 1994

Stan, a Philadelphia cabbie, glanced in the rear-view mirror. "How bad are they? They stink. You can't get a bet on the Sixers in this town. When they play a good team, people stay home. Watch it on cable. Why waste the money?

"When Barkley left, he said the Sixers would be lucky to win 30 games. What have they won? I dunno. I hate to say it, but Barkley knew what he was talking about."

"Did you like him?" I asked.

"Barkley? Yeah. He ran his mouth. But the thing about him is he produced, know what I mean? After Doctor J retired, this was his team. He could always get you 30 points, 15 rebounds, nine, 10 assists. Who we got can do that now?"

"How about Hornacek?"

"He's a good player. But Barkley, he brought some excitement. It's like L.A. When Magic played there, all of Hollywood was there. He had charisma. They talk about wantin' to rebuild with young players. Rebuild my ass. This town ain't gonna wait for that. I don't understand these front offices. We lose Barkley. Then we lose Reggie White. Guy wouldn't pay the money. You get what you pay for. You know?

"Barkley was controversial. So what? It's like Pete Rose. The guy had a hobby. Liked to gamble. Lots of people like to gamble. It was his money, wasn't it?

"Barkley, he wasn't perfect. He called guys lazy, and I guess they were." Stan looked into the mirror. "But he was good for this town. People who didn't like him came to see him get his butt whipped. People who liked him came to see him play. He's like Ali. He's got that personality . . ."

On the day of the NBA trade deadline in his final season with the Sixers, Barkley sat in the visitors locker room at The Summit in Houston. He was hoping, praying, watching the clock. "Telegram.

Telegram for Charles Barkley . . ."

"It was like something out of a George Raft movie," Bob Ford of *The Philadelphia Inquirer* recalled. "Nobody gets telegrams anymore."

This was it, Barkley hoped. The news he was waiting for. He had been traded. His ticket to freedom. Barkley tore open the envelope, his eyes scanned the brief message.

Barkley's face fell. "Awww. . ."

No trade. The telegram was a birthday greeting.

He wanted out. He was tired of playing on losing teams with players he believed didn't want to win. He criticized the owner, Harold Katz. Looking back, Barkley realizes that playing for the Sixers wasn't as bad as it seemed at the time. It was worse.

"I'll give you an idea of how cheap they were," Barkley was saying before the Suns made their one appearance of the year at the Spectrum. "One year they took all the alcohol out of the locker room. The Sixers decided they didn't want to pay for two cases of beer. So I went to Harold. Harold said, 'I don't want you guys drinking after a game and driving home.' I said, 'Harold, if you want to be like that, fine. But then don't sell beer in the stands. Because that's hypocritical. You don't want highly trained athletes drinking beer after running up and down the court for two hours, but it's all right to sell beer to a guy in the stands who has to drive his wife and kids home.' Harold was cheap. That's all it was . . ."

"I don't recall that ever happened," Katz said. "First of all, I've never taken beer out. Maybe that particular coach did. Maybe a coach didn't want beer, but I don't ever recall doing that. I don't recall Charles ever making that statement to me. I think he believes those things. He likes to be a statesman. I think he thinks he would like to have said that, but I can absolutely guarantee he never said it to me."

Question: What do you think of Barkley?

Katz: "I like him. He's a warm guy, totally different off the court than on the court. Off the court he's great. Very pleasant. Very cordial. When I'm with him I have fun with him. The only problem I had with Charles was his way of speaking to certain teammates. I've spoken to him various times about what happens in the locker room should be kept private, but that's about it. I've never had a serious confrontation with him."

Q: Did he dedicate himself to getting traded?

Katz: "I really didn't think so, although history may prove me wrong. About a month before the trade we met for two hours at my house. He let it be known that he wanted to have a much better supporting cast. I told him I would try. But it's not that simple in this league. I mean, because of the salary cap restrictions, making trades and so on. He never really said to me, 'Unless I get traded, I'm not going to play.' Nothing like that. It's frustrating for the owner, the coach, the players when you don't win. But there is only one champion each year. And even though Charles is with Phoenix, they still haven't won the championship. So it's very hard to get it. It's very elusive."

Q: Barkley's stock soared during the Dream Team summer. Hindsight is 20/20, but could you have gotten more for him if you had waited until after the Olympics to trade him?

Katz: "The real problem in this league is that there is a magic number. Once a guy turns 30 the value usually drops. When we were shopping around, that was the best offer that we had. There are teams that would say they would have paid more, but nobody offered more. The only team that stepped out and said they would make a trade was Phoenix. Yes, we would have liked more, but we felt we had no choice at that time, and Charles had to be traded, and from that standpoint they offered the most. What if we had held on? I don't know. I really don't know."

Q: When the trade was done, how did you feel? Happy? Sad? Relieved?

Katz: "It was everything. First of all, I didn't want to do it. Had Charles basically been the way I wanted him to be, supportive of his teammates and not asking to be traded through the media, I would have kept him. I would have preferred to keep him, to be honest with you. And so when the trade was made, I didn't feel great. I felt that we had to do it, and that was the best that was offered."

Q: Do you recall the first time you met him?

Katz: "In my office. It was prior to the (1984) draft. He was very overweight. He weighed around 280 at the time. We basically talked about that. He tells the story that he thought we didn't have room for him under the salary cap. Maybe he thought that, but we really did. He came in overweight and didn't want to get drafted, but that didn't sway me. I knew—I thought—he would be a very good player. Whether he weighed 280 or 290 or 270, we were going to draft him."

Q: Barkley has called you a cheapskate, among other things. I've never heard you respond, publicly . . .

Katz: "I never will. I don't play that game. I think the things Charles said are things he doesn't mean and he gets goaded or trapped into making those type statements. I know with me, one-on-one, I've never had one problem with him. I don't think he has a problem with me either, frankly."

Q: Wilt Chamberlain. Billy Cunningham. Julius Erving. Hal Greer. Bobby Jones. The Sixers retired their numbers. Will you hang Barkley's jersey alongside the others from the Spectrum rafters, after he retires?

Katz: "I would certainly consider it."

Q: Were you at the arena the night Barkley returned to Philly for his first game against the Sixers?

Katz: "No, I was in Florida."

March 28, 1993. As the arena went dark, the public address announcer spoke with a cheeriness that sounded canned. "And now . . ."

Displeased, even before the tip-off, spectators at the sold-out Spectrum gave the home team the kind of reception usually reserved for shady politicians and visiting teams. "Booooooo . . . here's the starting lineup . . . Boooooooo . . . for your . . ."

YOUR? That did it. "Booooooooooooo!" they cried, louder than ever . . . Phil-a-del-phia Seventy . . . BOOOOOOOOOOOOOOOO!!"

As the crowd drowned out the announcer, Barkley drank it all in, savoring the sweet malevolence. The bitter serenade was music to his ears.

"I'm not an evil person," he said the day before his homecoming in the city he still calls home. Barkley said he wished the Sixers players no ill will. He claimed he took no personal pleasure in the fact his former teammates were suffering through the club's worst season in 20 years.

Barkley had forecast disaster after his departure. But as he noted upon his return, trying not to gloat, "I'm not gonna say 'I told you so.' "

When Barkley was introduced, the crowd of 18,169 gave him a hero's welcome. He looked around the arena. Fans were on their feet, applauding, waving, holding up signs. "Yo! Knucklehead. Welcome Back!" "Barkley MVP." For the NBC national telecast, one fan had written, "N(eed) B(ack) C(harles)."

The cheers were for him, and him alone. The boos were directed at the Sixers organization, and Katz in particular. The Sixers were 21–46 and 26 games out of first place in the Atlantic Division.

"Trade Katz for Barkley," one sign suggested. Another summed up the Sixers' season: "It's a Katz-astrophe."

Barkley scored 13 points in the first half. Then it began to happen. A 3-pointer from the corner. A rebound and a floor-length drive and layup. A high fall-away jumper over his 7-foot-7 friend, Manute Bol. As his points piled up, Barkley relaxed, and had fun. He laughed when Armon Gilliam traveled while trying to score on him inside. Barkley finished with 35 points, 15 in the fourth quarter in the Suns' 110–100 victory, and the ending couldn't have been better if he had scripted it himself.

With 51 seconds left, and Barkley at the foul line, a fan ran onto the court. He gave Barkley a pat on the back before arena security grabbed him and took him away.

"He told me, 'I'm probably going to get arrested, but I'm happy to meet you,' " Barkley said.

"You going to post bail?"

Barkley shook his head. "I'm going to keep my money. You never know when I might get arrested."

Now, 10 months later, he was back. "I'm ready to play," Barkley announced as he entered the locker room before the game. But he remained on the injured list. He was still recuperating from the injury he sustained in Minnesota three weeks earlier.

He was glad to be home. But it was different this time as he watched his 11th game in a row from the end of the Suns' bench. "Hey, Charles! Get out there!"

"Whatcha want on your hot dog!"

"Hey, Barkley," another fan cried. "Spit on me!"

Barkley turned to Frank Johnson. "Frank, I've never asked for anything. But I want two things. I want the championship and I want this game."

After the Suns' 108-105 victory, Barkley called the Sixers game "just another bump in the road," but he couldn't hide his satisfaction. "Anytime you get divorced in this business and the divorce isn't amicable, I don't think you want your ex to be happy all the time. Anybody who tells you that they do is a liar."

23

Clothes Horse

Charles Barkley and Kevin McHale are longtime friends. Over the eight years they competed in the NBA Eastern Conference, at Boston Garden and the Spectrum, Barkley grew to respect and admire the Celtics center. "Kevin McHale," Barkley says, "is the best player I ever played against."

So when the Celtics called and asked Barkley if he could attend a banquet honoring McHale he said yes. Of course he would come. When? Jan. 29. Perfect.

The day after the Suns beat the Sixers, Barkley flew from Philadelphia to Boston. His wife dropped him off at the airport. Barkley had packed a suit, a dress shirt and shoes, his outfit for the banquet.

"You sure you want to check that?" Maureen asked.

"They can't lose it," Barkley said. "It's only a 45-minute flight."

Famous last words. "If it was a difficult connection I could understand it," Barkley said, reciting the head-shaking lament of everyone who has experienced the misadventures associated with commercial airline travel. "But the flight was 45 minutes. Straight through. How can they lose a bag?"

In Boston, Barkley checked into the hotel and waited. And waited. He told himself he could attend the event dressed as he was. McHale would understand. But this was a special occasion. Charles Barkley wasn't going to show up for a $400-a-plate banquet, honoring one of the classiest athletes ever to play the game, wearing jeans.

The cocktail party began at 6 P.M. When a hotel bellman knocked on his door, Barkley's well-traveled garment bag in hand, it was 9 P.M. Too late.

Next day Barkley related his story to Bob Young, a reporter for *The Arizona Republic*. Young nodded sympathetically. Too bad. A shame, all right. But Young was curious. "Chuck, there's a mall right by the hotel. Why didn't you buy a suit?"

"Bob," Barkley replied. "I don't mall shop."

Barkley is a clothes horse. He made *People* magazine's Best Dressed List for 1993. He wears $1,000 suits, which he buys by the dozen. He has rows of them, lined up like soldiers in his closet. All colors. A variety of fabrics. Wools for winter in Philly and New York. Lightweight suits for Phoenix.

Now that he is "large," as Barkley calls himself, referring to his fame, not his size, he has his clothing made. He wouldn't think of buying off the rack. "You know how it is when you go into a store. They have 10 suits. They're exactly alike. They're just different sizes."

"So? What's wrong with that?" I asked.

"All 10 of them guys might show up together at the same place," Barkley said.

I never thought of that.

The business card says "Everett Hall. The Designers, Inc." Everett Hall, 34, and his brother Edwin, 31, own a clothing design store in Silver Springs, Md. Their motto: "Elegance Never Goes Unnoticed."

I met Barkley's tailors at a Suns-Bullets game. The Bullets play their home games in Landover, Md., at USAir Arena. The place is a gloomy dump. "You think it's bad tonight," Scotty Robertson drawled, as he stood in the hallway outside the locker room before the game. The Suns assistant coach had to raise his voice to be heard over a vocal group as it rehearsed the national anthem. "You oughta be here the night before the circus opens." Obviously, Robertson had. "Animals penned up. Straw and shit *ever*-where." Scotty shook his head and gave an oh-well shrug. "If we gotta follow the elephants, that's what we'll do."

Barkley met the Halls six years ago in Philadelphia after a Sixers-Pistons game. The tailors took his measurements, stretching the tape around his neck, his chest, his waist, across his back. One measured his sleeve length and inseam. The other recorded the dimensions in a ledger.

He telephones Everett Hall three or four times each year. "In typical Charles Barkley style," Hall said, "Charles will call and say, 'What are you bums doing? What you been up to?' Then he'll say, 'By the way, I'm going to be interviewed by *People* magazine, or I'm doing this or that. For the fall I need 10 suits, 10 pairs of pants, 10 matching shirts . . .'"

Barkley doesn't select the fabric or the colors. He leaves those decisions to Hall and his brother. "That's one of the good things about working with Charles," Hall said. "He gives you a chance to do your own thing."

Barkley needed a wardrobe for the Barcelona Olympics. Hall sent him boxloads of garments. Cotton walking shorts and matching shirts. Linen pants. Golf wear. Three suits. Two sport coats and coordinated slacks. Barkley never wore the same garment twice. "Charles," Hall said, "doesn't like to be repetitive in his wardrobe."

Italian wools. Cashmere. Raw silk. Hall selects only the finest.

Price is no object. Charles wears the top of the line. "Our haute couture." If Hall knows Barkley is going to appear on a nationally televised talk show he will express-mail or personally deliver a new garment. He can fill an order in a week or less.

"I look good and I feel good!" Barkley often announces when he arrives at an arena on the night of a game. Always the last player to change into his uniform, he sits in front of his cubicle, chatting with reporters, most of whom he views as slobs.

One night he noticed a small stain on his gray trousers. "Look at that," he said. "That's what happens when you wear fine material like this and get something on it. It leaves a spot. It's not like that polyester crap you guys wear. Everything washes out."

Barkley is observant. Very little misses his eye. "Hey, how come you're so dressed up?" he asked one day. He was sitting in a chair in front of a mirror, shaving his head.

"I'm not, really," I said, and pointed to my waist. "I forgot my belt."

Barkley shrugged. "Doesn't matter," he said above the droning buzz of his electric clippers. He smiled at his reflection. "You ain't never gonna look as good as me."

24

Stargazing

Feb. 9, 1994

On the night before the NBA All-Star break, Barkley met with Richard Emerson, the team doctor, in Paul Westphal's office. "Doc," Barkley said, "tell Paul I'm ready to go next week."

"We'll take a look at him next week," Emerson told the coach.

"Tell him I'm 100 percent," Barkley persisted. "I'm close to 90 percent for sure. I couldn't do *this* three weeks ago." Westphal and Emerson smiled as Barkley strutted around the coach's office, lifting one leg, then the other, waist high, high-stepping like a drum major in a marching band. He felt frisky. Barkley was growing antsy. He had missed 16 games in a row. In the practice gym, he tested his leg against Suns rookie Malcolm Mackey.

"Mackey beat your butt," Westphal said.

"I got tired," Barkley said in his defense.

"They're getting on me for not putting Mackey in the game," Westphal said. "If he can beat your butt, what are they gonna say if I put you in?"

"Let me tell you what Mackey said on the bench one night." Out of action, Barkley heard all the bench conversations and asides. "We're getting beat on the boards. We're getting killed. Mackey looks at me and says, 'Doesn't Paul know I'm the number five rebounder in ACC (Atlantic Coast Conference) history?'" Barkley likes Mackey, more than the coaches do.

Barkley left Westphal's office and strolled into the clubhouse where reporters were waiting for him. "I'm not talking," Barkley said. "Y'all can read." Suns publicist Julie Fie had prepared a typewritten statement and posted it at Barkley's dressing cubicle. It read:

As an answer to your question: Being selected as the leading vote getter of the All-Star Game was one of the highlights of my career. Unfortunately, due to my knee injury I will be unable to participate in the Game Sunday. I am not 100 percent and I do not want to jeopardize the rest of the season with the Phoenix Suns.

Barkley and the NBA All-Star Game are synonymous. He has been selected eight times. His likeness appeared on a cardboard ad promoting the 1995 All-Star Game, which will be played in Phoenix. "Baby Ruth is your ticket to the NBA All-Star Weekend! Charles Barkley wants to meet YOU!!" A teammate had drawn sideburns on Barkley's picture, and given him a widow's peak. Barkley looked like a cross between Elvis Presley and Eddie Munster.

Barkley thumbed through his mail. He looked at a creamy envelope and broke the seal. "Holy shit!" His eyes lit up. "I got invited to the Academy Awards!"

"Who's going to win best picture?" someone asked. Barkley, a frequent moviegoer, had seen most of the motion pictures nominated.

"Probably *Schindler's List. Philadelphia* disappointed me. It wasn't a bad movie. But a movie that gets that kind of press you expect it to be spectacular. Tom Hanks was terrific."

"About the All-Star Game . . ."

"I'm crushed," Barkley said facetiously. "Actually, I am disappointed. But my major obligation is to the Phoenix Suns. It's just an unfortunate thing. I don't think I'm healthy enough."

"But you are going. Right?"

"I'll be there. I got obligations . . ."

When they stepped off the plane and entered the terminal at the airport in Minneapolis–St. Paul, Kevin Johnson couldn't believe what he saw. "It was like a frenzy," KJ, Barkley's fellow All-Star, said. "People were running up to him. Calling his name. Little old ladies with walkers"—Johnson broke into a cracked falsetto—'Oh, Charles! Charles! Can I have your autograph!?' That's what it's like. Charles is like a rock star. Being on a team with a guy who is that popular, it's exciting to me.

"We were on the plane and Charles was reading *USA Today*. He always reads the sports, but I saw him reading every section of the paper. Then it dawned on me what he was doing. He was getting his material for the interviews. Now that's a true professional."

The most popular All-Star at the media interview was the one who couldn't play. For almost an hour, Barkley held court at a table in a hotel ballroom. Reporters from all over the world pressed in around him, five deep. Microphones hovered overhead, like construction cranes. Photographers jostled and climbed up on chairs, each hoping to take a Pulitzer prize–winning photo of a bald man's shining head. The attention amused him.

"Y'all know I'm going to say something profound and intellectually stimulating," Barkley began, greeting the first media wave. "I'm really what people want to be. Everybody wants to do their own thing, speak their mind. Most people can't do that. You can't do what you want. You gotta kiss your boss's ass. I don't have to do that. Even people who don't like me respect the fact that I'm in control of my own life. I make my own decisions and speak my mind. Deep down, I think everybody wants to be like that."

"Charles . . .

"Hey, man. You need to put some bass in your voice if you want to be successful. Talk louder."

"How do you feel about expansion?"

"I think any time you dilute the talent pool, that's not good. I've never been a big fan of expansion in any sport. The fans get screwed. They're paying to see a bad team play, and I've never liked that idea."

"Do you think the talent pool is . . ."

"It's diluted. It's as low as it can go now. We got a lot of teams that aren't that good. I feel sorry for the fans. They pay a lot of money. They should get to see good teams play. If the Suns lose a player, it ain't gonna affect us. Same for Seattle. You're just adding a couple of bad teams."

"Have you talked to David Stern about it?"

"No," Barkley said. "Me and David don't talk. I don't like matzo balls and he don't like chili. We could never get together on the meal."

"Charles, who's your MVP?"

"Didn't y'all give it to Hakeem (Olajuwon) about three months ago? Why don't you let the players decide that at the end of the season. That's the only thing that pisses me off. You gave it to Hakeem, and now you want to give it to David (Robinson). They start losing and you'll want to give it to somebody else. Let's wait until the end of the season before we decide that."

"Is Seattle the best team in the league right now?"

"I consider us the best team in the league."

"Who are some of the rookies out there that encourage you and make you think there really is a lot of good talent out there?"

Barkley blinked. "Rookies don't matter. There are some other players who aren't rookies who are gonna be the men."

"Like who?"

"Shaq. Alonzo Mourning. David Robinson. Hakeem's still there. Rookies, they haven't had 20 good games. That don't mean nothin'."

"Charles, do you think because of the long-term contracts things have gotten out of hand? Guys aren't working as hard?"

"Yeah. No question. Guys don't work hard anymore. The league has changed. Now every time they score a basket, they turn around and stare in your face. They make a lot of money, but they don't play hard all the time. The league has deteriorated, as far as that goes."

"Are you saying there's too much trash-talking?"

"It's different. When we talked trash to each other back in the good old days, you were talking to have fun. Now guys have a vindictiveness in their voice when they talk trash. Larry Bird would say I couldn't stop him and I'd say he couldn't stop me. We'd go back and forth. It was a funny thing. Now it's like an evil thing."

"Why do you think that is?"

"I just think the players are making all this money and have these long-term guaranteed contracts and they turn into assholes."

"Charles, does it bother you not to be able to play Sunday?"

"No."

Gary Payton, the Seattle guard, stuck his head through the crowd. "How ya doing, Charles?"

"Are you from Seattle?" Barkley asked.

"Yeah," Payton said. "What's up?"

Barkley's eyes grew, a look of instant recognition. "Oh, it's GARY PAYTON! Hold on. Can I have your autograph? Somebody gimme some paper. Y'all are playing pretty good up there."

"Y'all are playing pretty good, too, without you," Payton said.

"We're .500 without me. I've told people we're just wasting the season. We should play you all in the Western Conference finals and the Bulls and Knicks play for the Eastern Conference finals. Let's start next week, and we can get to the golf course sooner. Peace, man . . ."

"Charles," a reporter said, "you're talking about dilution of talent and David Stern is talking about going into Europe and expanding internationally . . ."

"He's speaking in dollars. I'm speaking in basketball talent. There's a difference. I'm not concerned about making money. I want the fans to see the best product available."

Greg Boeck, who had interviewed Madonna for a question-answer feature in *USA Today*, told Barkley that the singer said that if she were an NBA owner she wouldn't want Charles on her team.

"She wouldn't?" Barkley and Madonna are friends.

"She said you'd cost too much money and be too much trouble," Boeck said. "Maybe she was kidding."

"I *know* she was kidding."

Barkley stared at a bearded, curly-haired fellow peering through a video camera. "Who are you? Aw, I thought you were Steven Spielberg. You look like him. I was gonna get your autograph."

"Charles, are you serious about running for governor of Alabama?"

"Yeah. I'm running in 1998."

"Do you think Alabama is ready to elect a black governor?"

"I think the South has changed a lot."

"You think it's changed *that* much?"

"Being from Alabama, I don't think any city, state in this country should talk about racism. Alabama and the South get a bad rap, but the rest of the country ain't that far behind."

"Charles, you're injured and yet you showed up here . . ."

"I'm getting paid to be here. If I wasn't getting paid, I wouldn't be here. I'd rather be in Phoenix playing golf."

"The centers this year. Are they as good as any centers since you've been following basketball?"

"I think you'd have to throw some names out there for me to answer that question."

"Shaq, Robinson, Olajuwon, Ewing . . ."

"Compared to who?" Barkley asked.

"Russell, Wilt Chamberlain, Jabbar . . ."

"No. The guys now aren't as good as those guys."

"Because . . ."

"Because they're not as fucking good. Wilt Chamberlain is the greatest player who ever played. Kareem is probably the second best player to ever play. Bill Russell was unbelievable. Nate Thurmond was one of the most underrated guys. No, you can't compare them."

"Are you going to cuss as much at press conferences when you're running for governor of Alabama?"

"How many cuss words have I said? Three."

"The question still stands."

"I'm gonna be my own man. My own person. I'm like that. I've earned that right."

"Is it a little disappointing not to play in this, if it turns out to be the end for you?"

"I just want to make sure I am 100 percent for the Phoenix Suns when we make a run for the world championship. This is a great chance for us this year. That's my number one priority, to win a world championship. All-Star games are fun. This is my eighth one. But I'm playing for one reason."

"Charles, how strange is it to be here, without Michael?"

"I never thought about it 'til you just asked me. You're the only person that's asked me that."

"Does it feel differently?"

"No, it don't feel different at all. Michael is one of my best friends, but I don't think people sit around thinking, 'Oh, Michael's not here.' We don't think like that as players. That's what you guys think. You know what kills me? When they have women on ESPN and "The NBA Today" talking about sports." Barkley looked at *Boston Globe* writer Jackie MacMullan, who also works for ESPN, pretending he hadn't seen her. "Oh, sorry Jackie."

"Play in the game, and maybe you'll get some (air) time," Mac-

Mullan shot back.

"Hey, they forget you quick," Barkley said, grinning. "I'm like an owl. Charles WHOOOO?"

"Charles, Kevin McHale said that in five years people are going to be asking, 'Michael who?' Do you agree with that?"

"Kevin needs to sober up when he makes statements like that."

"Karl Malone is kind of getting into the frame of mind you had in Philadelphia. The Jazz are a little over .500. He feels like the time he has to win a championship is running out."

"It's tough when you're losing."

"What are you going to do after you retire?"

"I'm just going to chill out a little bit. I'm going to be a black multimillionaire. Not many black people have money, but I'm gonna be one of 'em."

"Charles, can we talk a little bit about Canadian teams coming into the NBA? This is for Canadian television." As the camera rolled, the TV guy pasted on a big smile. "First of all, Vancouver. Because it's a West Coast town it would be a natural rivalry with Phoenix."

"First of all," Barkley replied, "y'all ain't gonna be no rivalry for nobody. Y'all are gonna get beat like a drum for a long time." The TV guy's face fell. "Nobody has a rivalry with an expansion team. You're just a sure win along the way."

"Charles, how good are the guys playing in the rookie game?"

"There are some good young players."

"How far are they away from being *the* All-Star Game?"

"A long way. You guys make everybody good right away. You know, in the good old days you had to have some good years before good things happened for you. Now you come into the league and have a good month and you're an All-Star. I don't think I got accepted as a great player until six or seven years in the league. Now a guy comes in and has two good games a week and one good year and you make him a superstar. I know the league is trying to make players popular because Michael is gone and I'm on my way out, but they should play their way into becoming great players."

"Does it feel strange sitting here, even though you know you're not going to be playing?"

"No. Nothing's strange to me. I'm a strange person."

"Charles, the new movie *Blue Chips*, which Shaquille is in, deals with the issue of college recruiting. Do you think the college players should be paid?"

"Yes."

"Why?"

"Because they're making a lot of money for the schools. Big money. Notre Dame is making big money. I see the SEC (Southeastern Conference) is going to sign a $100 million package. If they are going to make that kind of money, the players should get some of it."

"Were you offered money in the recruiting process . . . ?"

"I . . . I . . . I don't remember back that far." Barkley considered his lame answer and smiled. "The statute of limitations has run out, hasn't it?"

A fellow shoved his way to the front. "Hey, guys, we're gonna do one quick segment for MTV."

Barkley flared, as he often does when he feels he is being ordered to do something. "Hold on, man. What makes you think I'm gonna do that? You know, Abe Lincoln freed me. I have a choice what I can do now. Give me one good reason why I should do that, without getting paid?"

"I'm sorry."

"That's okay."

"Charles, can you say some words to Chinese audience? You have many fans in Chinese audience."

"I never been to China. But I tell you what. Why don't you set it up where I get a free trip there and I'll come speak to 'em personally? Can you help me out?"

"Sure. Of course. Thank you very much."

"You're welcome."

"Charles, how do you like Minneapolis?"

"Nice city. Terrible weather."

"Charles, will it be tough watching your teammates play Sunday?"

"No. I'll just be sobering up by then."

"Charles, I am from Romania . . ."

"Ro-MANE-ia?! Damn! I have friends in Romania? I never been to Romania. I'd love to visit Romania sometime. I have heard a lot about the country. Send me a ticket. First-class."

Barkley stood at courtside in the Target Center and spoke with Channel 12, the NBC affiliate in Phoenix. "I'm making my coaching debut today," he told Arizona viewers. Barkley looked into the camera and spoke directly to his coach, who was at home watching on television. "Coach Westphal, you can learn a lot today."

After the game, in the locker room, Barkley went to comical lengths to distance himself from the Western Conference's 127–118 defeat. He did not coach, he said, nor did he play. When Matt Winick of the NBA handed him his check for $5,000, Barkley argued that technically he wasn't on the losing team and therefore should not be paid loser's wages. "Why should I be penalized for their poor performance?" he asked in a loud voice. The winning team received $7,000. The way Barkley saw it, the NBA owed him $2,000.

25

Green Light

Feb. 14, 1994

Five weeks after hobbling off the court in Minneapolis, he plopped down on the green padded seat of the Hydra Fitness machine.

Five weeks. Or was it five months? Over the last five weeks the Dallas Cowboys beat the Buffalo Bills in Super Bowl XXVIII. Emmitt Smith, the MVP, went to Disney World. The Cardinals fired Joe Bugel and hired Buddy Ryan. The Black Coaches Association threatened to boycott NCAA basketball games. The Washington Redskins hired Norv Turner. Steve Carlton was voted into the Baseball Hall of Fame. Major league baseball owners announced plans to realign the divisions. NASCAR driver Neil Bonnett died in a crash at Daytona. The Winter Olympics, featuring Nancy Kerrigan and Tonya Harding, began in Lillehammer, Norway.

What was it Tonya called herself? "The Charles Barkley of figure skating."

"I was going to sue her for defamation of character," Barkley joked, "but then I realized I had no character."

Five weeks. President Clinton delivered his State of the Union Address. Michael Jackson settled out of court with a 14-year-old boy who had accused him of sexually molesting him. The U.S. lifted its trade embargo with Vietnam. Lorena Bobbitt was acquitted after cutting off her husband's penis.

"Know what I saw in your newspaper?" Barkley said one day.

"No, Charles," I said. "What?"

"An ad for penile enlargement." The one-column ad in the sports section of *The Arizona Republic*—for "MEN ONLY" the ad read, which seemed odd—claimed that after the one-hour surgery most patients appear as if they had doubled in size. "I told my doctor it *can't* be true," Barkley said. "She told me . . ."

"She?"

"Yeah. She said what they do is . . ."

Five weeks. Without Barkley, the Suns were severely average. They won eight games. They lost nine, including three of four games during a trip to some of Barkley's favorite cities—New York, Atlanta, Philly and Boston. Barkley couldn't play but he had fun. He has fun wherever he goes.

In New York, he teased Herb Williams as they rode an elevator in Madison Square Garden. "Herb, are you all Team Turmoil?" Williams stared at his feet and smiled. "Team Turmoil. That's what the headlines say," Barkley said. That day the *New York Daily News* ran a story quoting unnamed Knicks players complaining that coach Pat Riley relied too much upon Patrick Ewing. The elevator door opened. Williams got off. The door closed. "The Knicks are overrated," Barkley said. "They're the fourth best team in the league."

At the Omni, in Atlanta, Barkley went one-on-one against a youngster in a pregame workout. He playfully taunted the kid the way he did Barney on "Saturday Night Live." "You know who I am? . . . Don't you get cable? . . . Miss? Miss is a lady's name. I don't miss . . . Boy, you better respect my jumper. . . If you're scared, get a Rottweiler."

Paul Westphal walked by. "Coach," Barkley called out, "I know this isn't much competition, but I think I'm close to coming back." To demonstrate how well he felt, Barkley dunked the ball. "That's off the left leg," Westphal said.

"Yeah," Barkley said. "I don't know if I'm ready to do it on the right one . . ."

Five weeks. Seventeen games in street clothes. When reporters asked him about retirement Barkley repeated his standard line, which always drew a laugh. "I feel like I'm retired already. It's fun doing nothing every day. I'm getting pretty good at it."

In truth, Barkley was tired of sitting, watching, waiting. The day after the All-Star Game he pressed his spine against the backrest of the Hydra Fitness machine. His right leg didn't have to be as strong as his left. The target was 90 percent. Barkley extended his right leg and looked at the digital screen. Ninety-one percent. Good enough.

Like a teacher on the last day of school, Dr. Emerson watched, smiling, as Barkley bounded down the stairs of the athletic club and skipped down the hallway, windmilling his arms, a picture of pure joy. "I can play! I can play! I can play!"

26

Easy Money

He sat in front of the full-length mirror and moved the electric clippers across the vast curvature of his head. Side to side. Front to back. Back and forth. Barkley went to the slick look several years ago as a pre-emptive strike against premature baldness.

"Ready?" Robin Pound asked over the mosquito buzz. Pound is the Suns' strength and conditioning coach. It was time for their workout.

"Let's do it after the scouting report," Charles said, his eyes fixed on his reflected image.

"Why?" Pound asked.

"I want to make sure I look good."

Pound looked at him quizzically. "For the *scouting report?*"

"No," Barkley said. "I gotta do that thing in L.A. today."

Pound left and went to get a frozen yogurt, or some bean sprouts. Pound is a fitness nut. The Suns assigned him to help get Barkley in shape, and encourage him to follow an exercise regimen prescribed by the trainers and doctors. It's a full-time job.

"What's in L.A.?" I asked.

"I'm playing some Japanese guys in a two-on-two game this afternoon."

"You serious?"

"Yep." Barkley put down the clippers. He picked up a plastic bottle and squirted a stream of rubbing alcohol onto a towel and rubbed the towel vigorously over his shaved scalp. After repeating the process, he picked up the clippers and flipped the switch. The shears came alive with a droning *bzzzzzzz.*

"Who are they?"

"I dunno. Some Japanese guys called my agent and they want me to play a game with 'em. It's only for like an hour. They got a plane waiting for me at the airport. It's somewhere in L.A."

I told Barkley it sounded like one of those outings PGA Tour pros play with business executives on the Monday after a tournament. He nodded. "That's exactly what it is."

"Good money?"

"Forty thousand."

"Really? That's unreal."

"You think *that* is," Barkley said. *Bzzzzzzzz.* "I was talking to Michael. This was before he went into baseball. He said a couple of Japanese guys offered him like $5 million to go over there and play a round of golf with them."

"Did he go?"

"No," Barkley said.

"What, did he have something *better* to do that day?"

"No. I just think when you have as much money as Michael it doesn't matter. I told Michael he should give me the job. For $5 million, the Chuckster couldn't have got to Japan fast enough."

27

Tin Star

"There's a new sheriff in town!" Charles Barkley shouted.

Buddy Ryan, head coach of the Arizona Cardinals, laughed as they shook hands in the Suns clubhouse. Sheriff. The Law. Buddy liked the greeting. The title had a nice ring. It suited him.

"Charles, you know Clyde," Ryan told Barkley, introducing Clyde Simmons, the 6-foot-6, 280-pound defensive end with the Philadelphia Eagles. Ryan was courting the Eagles' free agent the way a college coach courts a blue-chip prospect on a recruiting visit. Difference is, in the NFL the money is on the table, not under it. NCAA rules don't apply. Ryan and Simmons had attended the Suns game. Afterward, they stopped by to say hello.

Barkley knows Simmons. He also knows Seth Joyner, another Eagle defensive star whom Ryan hoped to sign.

"I'll tell you what I told Seth," Barkley said to Simmons. "This is the greatest place in the world. Great weather. Great fans." Barkley turned to Ryan. "I know you'll be kicking ass, and I'll be right there. I'm buying season tickets." Buddy beamed.

They are kindred spirits. Barkley played eight years in Philadelphia. Ryan coached the Eagles from 1986–90. Barkley wanted out. Ryan was kicked out, fired, despite a 43–35 record. Both are outspoken. Opinionated. Competitive. Caustic. Controversial. Ryan and Barkley are like anchovies. You like them or you don't.

"I liked him and he liked me," Ryan said of their friendship, which dated back to their Philadelphia days when Barkley occasionally attended Eagles practices. "We both wanted to win. We both knew what it took to win." Ryan laughed. "A lot of faint hearts didn't care for either one of us."

In Arizona, Barkley is big. He is as big as the picture of himself painted on the side of city buses. On the cover of the 1993–94 Suns media guide, trick photography gives Barkley the appearance of being giant-like, towering over downtown Phoenix like the unfortunate victim of a plutonium explosion in the 1957 science-fiction movie *The Amazing Colossal Man*.

But Ryan is just as large in popularity. Barkley gave the Phoenix

Suns a national identity. Ryan does the same for the Cardinals. On Feb. 3, 1994, the day Bill Bidwill hired Ryan to replace Joe Bugel, Barkley joined in the public celebration. "Yes! My man got the job. Phoenix has finally arrived in the 1990s in sports . . . The Cardinals fans deserve something like this. He's going to win. He's won every place he's been.

"The media and the owners didn't like him in Philadelphia because he told the truth and didn't kiss any butt," Barkley said. "I've played for coaches who told me one thing, the owner another thing and the media something else. Buddy's a straight shooter . . . This tells me the Cardinals really want to win."

After Ryan was hired, Barkley began his recruiting mission. He telephoned Joyner. The All-Pro linebacker was familiar with the Phoenix area. He had visited friend Roy Green, the former Cardinals receiver who finished his career with the Eagles. "Even before Buddy got the job, Charles told me this is the place for me to be. When Buddy got the job, Charles was like, 'You've *got* to come out here now. There's no other place you should go.' He said it's the Cardinals' time. Charles had some insights into the city, having played here a couple of years. I took what he told me into consideration."

On March 17, the Cardinals signed Simmons to a five-year, $15 million contract. One month later, Joyner agreed to a similar deal. Within four months after Ryan became head coach, Cardinals season tickets doubled, to 48,000.

28

Franchise, Junior

On March 4th, the Suns played their favorite team, the Minnesota Timberwolves, and beat them for the 20th time in a row. Charles Barkley looked at his numbers in the box score. FGA, field goals attempted: 14; FGM, field goals made: 4.

"I was strokin' that jumper, wasn't I?" he said facetiously, referring to his 11 points, half his average. "You know some nights when you shoot it, the rim looks THIS big." Barkley locked his fingers and made a circle with his arms. "Like a big old hoop. Tonight it looked like one of them little Slinkies . . ."

"Yeah," someone said. "But you won."

"That's the only thing that matters," Barkley said. "That and today is KJ's birthday. We're going out to celebrate." Barkley raised his voice, so all his teammates would hear. "Tonight is a national holiday in Phoenix. As the future governor of Alabama, I PROCLAIM TONIGHT KEVIN JOHNSON NIGHT!"

Johnson asked, "Can I be your lieutenant governor?"

"Yes."

"Thank you," KJ said.

"We can't be responsible for our actions," Barkley continued. He was on a roll. "We're starting out at Majerle's, then we're going to P.F. Chang's and eventually we'll end up at Stixx. I was so pissed off on my birthday I stayed in the house. I was embarrassed because we had gotten humiliated (losing at Portland by 21 points). But that's not the case tonight. All the beautiful people will be there. If you don't look good, don't come."

Kevin Johnson was going out to celebrate his 28th birthday. Intentionally or not, Barkley made it sound as if he had organized the party and was in charge. He has a way of seizing the moment, grabbing the limelight, taking over. Even when Barkley tries to turn the attention from himself to his teammates, he upstages them.

Before a practice in Miami, Barkley took a seat beneath one basket in the empty arena. The TV mini-cams surrounded him. "Don't you all have anything better to do than follow me around?" he asked, leaning back, legs crossed. Barkley pointed toward the court. "There's a bunch of guys out there you can talk to. That's Kevin Johnson. He was on the All-Star team. There's Dan Majerle. He made Dream Team II. That guy over there used to be Frank Johnson. Lionel Hollins, our assistant coach, he used to play in the NBA. He was a defensive specialist, which means he couldn't score in a phone booth." Barkley nodded toward the solemn presence of Jerrod Mustaf. The 6-foot-10 forward, who wears No. 0, isn't one of Barkley's favorites. "That guy there," Charles announced, "is Jerrod Mustaf. I don't know *what* we got him for . . ."

It was Johnson's birthday, and Barkley's show. *That's just Chuck*, KJ said to himself, as he often does,

Before Barkley, Johnson was the focal point of the Phoenix offense. The Suns were, and still are, KJ's team, but not like before. The chemistry, the personality of the club changed when Barkley arrived, like a brass band, assumed the role of spokesman, and named Kevin "Franchise, Jr."

"Mind it? No, not at all," Johnson said of the nickname, which only Barkley uses. "That's just Charles. That's his way of saying I'm valuable to this team. 'I'm the second-most valuable player.' I'm a franchise player, but now I'm the second franchise player. Not many other people would put a 'junior' on the back of my name."

Johnson went through an adjustment period when Barkley joined the team. "Wherever Charles goes, *everybody* has to make an adjustment. That's reality. Jerry Colangelo had to make an adjustment. He had to be more lenient as it relates to things he wants to accomplish, on and off the court. I remember we were in training camp in Charles' first year with the Suns. We had a gym full of kids watching us. Charles is cursing up a storm, and I'm thinking, 'Oh, man . . .' We're scrimmaging and the training camp ref makes a bad call. Charles yells out, real loud, 'MERRY F-ing CHRISTMAS!' How can you screw up Merry Christmas? That day it all came clear. I realized then there is nothing you can do. Jerry heard about it and he was thinking, 'Oh, my gosh.' At some point Jerry approached Charles. I know this. I don't know what Charles said, but Jerry realized that Charles is going to be Charles, and Jerry can't control that.

"Charles is probably the best teammate I've ever had as far as potential on the court. He's got the biggest heart. His language is something you accept as part of him. One night after a game, Charles took my mom and my brother out to eat. I went home. I told my brother, 'Ronnie, when you're with Charles, every time he curses, put your hands over your ears.' Ronnie told me later that if he had put his hands over his ears every time Charles cursed, he never would have gotten to eat.

"Everybody has to adjust. Paul Westphal had to make an adjustment by allowing Charles to be himself, which means giving him a lot of leeway. As a player, it's no different. I was used to running the show. Doing everything I wanted on the court. The ball always had to be in my hands, and we won or lost depending upon what I did. And we won 60-70 percent of the time. Our first year together I realized that for our relationship and our success to be harmonious I was the one who had to make the biggest adjustment. Looking back, I think I overcompensated. Part of it was being a little apprehensive. I was much more reserved. I lost my personality a little bit. I tried to be too unselfish. The only other time I did that was when I played for Cleveland, when I was a rookie. I was young. All the guys were veterans. I didn't know the tricks of the trade, the business. I sacrificed part of my personality. When I got traded to Phoenix, I vowed I would never do that again."

One incident during their first season together bothered Johnson. The Suns were playing Detroit, at home. With two minutes left and the Suns leading by 20 points, Pistons center Bill Laimbeer hit KJ as he drove to the basket, sending him sprawling. The official called a flagrant technical foul.

Westphal was angry. "Laimbeer's a dirty player and should be suspended for throwing Kevin down. There's no place in basketball for that." Barkley downplayed the foul. "Kevin's a little dude. It's easy to knock him on his ass. I don't think (Laimbeer) intentionally tried to hurt him."

"Charles didn't take my side," Johnson recalled. "It bothered me for a lot of reasons, mainly because it was Bill Laimbeer, a guy I know Charles hates."

But there is no rift between them, no unsettled score. Johnson contends he treats Barkley no better or worse than his other teammates who stand before him in Kangaroo Court.

During the preseason, on their flight home from Munich, the Suns held a team meeting. "We decided we needed to hold everyone accountable," Johnson said, and by everyone he included a certain bald player who isn't known for his punctuality. The players agreed upon a list of rules. For a 10 A.M. practice, rookies and the younger players are required to show up at 9:30. The veterans must report by 9:50, or face a $50 fine for every minute they are late, unless they are receiving medical treatment. Standard fines range from $20 to $50. The maximum fine is $500.

"And you're the judge?" I asked KJ.

"I am the Chief Justice, the Chief of Police. I'm K. Edgar Hoover. Darrell Gates. I'm whoever I need to be. I've got my black book. Heidi Fleiss has hers and I have mine." Johnson produced a small spiral notebook. The name of each player was listed, along with the nature of his transgression and the fine he owed. "It's a fun way to challenge each other to be accountable, and to remind us that no one person is bigger, or more important, than the rules."

"Can you appeal a fine?" I asked.

"Definitely," KJ said. "I document everything. You appeal to me and then we bring the whole Kangaroo Court together and vote on it. Say you owe $20. If you lose your appeal your fine is increased by half. You would owe $30."

"Are coaches subject to being fined?"

"Oh, yeah. Train (Lionel Hollins) owes. Here's what we do. I'm a fair man. Very reasonable. Say Train owes $20. If he wants to go double or nothing he can shoot a three-pointer. I will allow you that opportunity. But only with certain people. People who rub me the right way. If I'm in a good mood, I'll even allow you two chances. I'm very flexible."

"Flexible?" Mark West shook his head. "You ever heard of Judge Roy Bean?"

"Some people are gamblers at heart," Johnson said. "So I can't allow them to go double or nothing. It's not in their best interest. Once a month I post the fines. Everybody has a week period to pay. If you don't pay, there's a 10 percent late fee."

I told Danny Ainge it all sounded a bit draconian. "There really isn't any justice because it's basically a dictatorship," Ainge said. "It's a waste of time to appeal. If you appeal and lose, the penalties are too great. It's a lost cause."

"Does Barkley get fined much?"

"Oh, yeah," Ainge said, smiling. "Charles has been fined probably twice as much as everybody else combined. I'll give you an example of how he is. One day he showed up five minutes before practice. Charles claimed he was getting therapy. He said he got a shot. First of all, a shot is not considered therapy. Second, I checked and he didn't get a shot. But he did take an aspirin."

"The hardest guys to catch are Mark West, Joe Kleine and Frank Johnson," Judge Johnson said. "Charles gets mad. He calls the Kangaroo Court the Rodney King jury. He says guys will turn him in in a heartbeat."

"I like Kevin," Barkley said. "He's a nice guy. I'd just like to see him become a little friendlier with the other players. I've been here two years and I don't know if I've ever been out to dinner with him.

"When I leave here, it's going to be Kevin's team. If you're not really, really close to the guys and talk to them every day you can't expect them to follow you. I don't think you can. You've got to go out and have a beer with them every now and then, even if you don't drink. You've got to have dinner with them every now and then. Go to a movie, whatever.

"I don't think you can just see guys in practice every day and then, when you get into a war, expect them to follow you. The other night, at his birthday, was the first time I've ever been out with Kevin, ever. I had a great time. We *both* had a great time. I'd just like to see a little more of that. I don't think the other guys really know him."

(Clockwise from left) Sir Charles is escorted through Marienplatz Square Munich, Germany during the McDonald's Open '93. • Barkley and Suns teammate Cedric Ceballos teach the art of giving a "high five" to German children during a shoot-around in the Sporthalle at the Olympic Park. If the German public had not heard of Charles Barkley, they were soon aware of his presence on and off the basketball court in Munich. • The international competition also was impressed —Real Madrid forward Jose Cargol (left) never saw Barkley fly through the air and dunk the ball. The Phoenix Suns won the tournament.

(Previous page)
Phoenix Suns star forward Charles Barkley looks to the basket as Houston Rockets center Hakeem Olajuwon tries to block the shot. *(Photos by Rob Schumacher)*

ockwise from left) Charles Barkley was jumping mad at referee Hank Armstrong after being called for locking foul. • Referee Ken Mauer gives his side of the story to Sir Charles following the ejections of eral Suns players in Chicago. • NBA referees get no peace even when Barkley, yelling at the officials game at Atlanta, is on the sidelines. *(Photos by Rob Schumacher)*

(Clockwise from top) 1994 NBA West All-Star team with top vote getter Barkley, who did not suit up because of a back injury. • All-Star forward Karl Malone keeps company with teammate Barkley. • Sir Charles holds court at '94 All-Star game in Minneapolis. • Philadelphia 76er Manute Bol hugs his former teammate. • Barkley steps onto the court at 199_ All-Star Game in Salt Lake City. *(Photos by Rob Schumacher)*

...kley puts his foot down . . . and Harold Ellis of the Los Angeles Clippers gets a close-up look at the bottom ...arkley's basketball shoe. *(Photo by Rob Schumacher)*

A superstars Michael Jordan and Charles Barkley laugh during a break in shooting for a Nike shoe commercial. *to by Rob Schumacher)*

(Top left) A fan at a preseason game in Madison Square Garden tries to get Barkley's attention with a special message. (Middle) Heckler Robin Ficker, an attorney from Maryland, makes Barkley laugh with his sign before a Washington Bullets game at USAir Arena. *(Photos by Rob Schumacher)*

right) A young fan at the Omni in Atlanta performs a dance for Barkley and his teammates that brought pregame shoot-around to a standstill. **(Bottom)** Autograph seekers wave and yell as Barkley boards the s team bus outside Market Square Arena in Indianapolis. *(Photos by Rob Schumacher)*

(Clockwise from top) As Barkley falls to the floor, he concentrates on finding a teammate during a game against Seattle. • Barkley and teammate Danny Ainge relax in the Suns locker room before the start of a game in Boston. • Plagued by a lower-back injury, Barkley is consoled by Suns head coach Paul Westph as he heads for the bench.

(Following page) In Game 7 of the '94 Western Conference Semifinals against the Houston Rockets, the Suns could not overcome the Rockets' offense or Barkley's severe groin pain. *(Photos by Rob Schumacher)*

(Counter-clockwise from top) Hundreds of autograph seekers flock to Charles Barkley during the '94 Michael Jordan Celebrity Golf Classic in Woodridge, Illinois. • Barkley played in and hosted the charity tournament for friend Michael Jordan, who was playing baseball for the Class AA Birmingham Barons. • Tucker and Benjamin Quayle get their caps adjusted by Barkley as they follow dad— former Vice President Dan Quayle— around the golf course during Jordan's annual charity event.
(Photos by Rob Schumacher)

(Left) Danny Ainge and Charles Barkley were found on the links after Barkley announced that he was returning for another season, saying that Ainge talked him out of retirement. *(Photo by Suzanne Starr)*

(Top) Barkley with his
daughter Christiana.
*(Photo courtesy of Andrew D.
Bernstein/NBA Photos)*

(Right) Former Junior
Flyweight Champion
Michael Carbajal uses
help from Suns center
Oliver Miller to spar
with Barkley during a
charity event in Phoenix,
April 1994.
*(Photo courtesy of Dana
Leonard/Phoenix Gazette)*

29

Fasten Your Seatbelts

March 7, 1994

The Boeing 737 with "1993 Western Conference Champions" painted on the side bounced as it climbed through the rain clouds. The Suns coaches sat in the front of the plane; players spread out in seats behind them, seat belts pulled tight. The plane bucked, like a rodeo bronco. Malcolm Mackey grinned at Elliot Perry and playfully crossed himself.

"Syrup!" Barkley was in the aisle, walking toward the back of the plane. "I need syrup for my pancakes!"

The Suns were embarking on their longest trip of the season. Over the next 10 days, they would zigzag across the NBA landscape like a pencil point connecting the dots on a picture puzzle. Phoenix to Charlotte to Washington to Miami to Orlando to Cleveland to Indianapolis. The team could relate to the bumpy takeoff. They were going through a rough stretch, and this trip was worrisome.

The Suns weren't playing well. Barkley was himself in name only since he returned to the lineup in mid-February. On Feb. 19, in Houston, he scored 15 points, with only four rebounds. During a timeout, as the Suns were on their way to an 18-point loss, the 1993 NBA's most valuable player removed his mouthpiece and turned to reporters seated at courtside. "I used to be Charles Barkley," he said.

On March 4, Barkley scored 11 points against the Minnesota Timberwolves. He heard the catcalls from the home crowd. "For Christ sake, wake up!" . . . "Hey, Chuck! If you don't feel good, siddown!"

Barkley didn't feel good. "I don't feel well at all," he said, glumly. "It's tough for me right now. I can't score because I don't have any power. Teams haven't been doubling me because I don't have the strength and quickness to move on those guys. I don't think I've ever been through a period when I haven't been able to jump. If I can't jump I'm just another 6-4 guy who is in the way.

"I'll be the first to admit I haven't played well. The last few weeks have been the most frustrating time in my career. Even when I was in

Philadelphia and was on a bad team I could play well. There's nothing worse for me than playing bad.

"I had a long talk with Paul. He said I've got to do better. Maybe not play better but he challenged me as a leader. He said last year I was more vocal. I was harder on guys. If I'm playing great, I will get on a guy's ass if he needs it. But I haven't played well enough to criticize other guys, and that's the bottom line.

"I'm caught between a rock and a hard place. But I've got to find a way to get it done. It's like Malcolm X said. You've got to get it done, by any means necessary. You have to find a way to make yourself successful . . ."

During the flight, Danny Ainge sat down next to Barkley. They talked, in whispered tones, for 20 minutes. "I told Charles that if this is really his last season, he shouldn't go out with any regrets," Ainge said. "He needs to give it everything he has. I told him to stop worrying. Beginning with this trip, let's get ourselves ready and prepared for the playoffs."

Barkley also visited with his coach. "Charles was kind of down," Westphal said. "I just wanted him to enjoy things more. Stop analyzing so much. Go ahead and play. Push himself. He needed to see how much he had, rather than assuming he wasn't ready to do stuff. He thought when he came back from his knee injury he would be Charles Barkley right away. It didn't happen. He wasn't physically able to be quick and jump. It depressed him and changed his personality toward the other players. He couldn't be the brash guy. He couldn't lead the team because he wasn't sure about himself. He was out six weeks in the middle of the season. He lost his conditioning. His legs were weak. You don't come back and be Charles Barkley the second you step on the floor."

Cotton Fitzsimmons: "The thing that frightens Charles is when he can't do something he used to do. The best example is if you go back to the film from last year. The Suns are playing Charlotte. They need the ball. If they don't get it, they don't win the game. Charles goes up between Larry Johnson and Alonzo Mourning and he takes it away from them. Sometimes this year there's been a look on his face that's a bit wary. Like, 'I didn't get it. I always used to get that ball.' "

This wasn't the same Barkley who picked up the ringing phone one day at the practice court and said, without identifying himself, "Don't you know we're having practice!" A grin spread across Barkley's face as he listened to the voice on the line. He put his hand over the receiver and called out to assistant coach Lionel Hollins, "Oh, Traaaaaaainnn. It's your wife. She's got you on a short leash."

This wasn't the same guy who strutted out of the clubhouse the night of the grand opening of Planet Hollywood in Phoenix. "I got a feeling it could be a bad night for me tonight," Barkley said. "I'm going to be hangin' out with Rocky and the Terminator. Jean-Claude Van Damme, Arnold (Schwarzenegger), Sylvester (Stallone) and the Chuckster, all in the same place. I wish you all were somebody," he told reporters, "so you could go too."

This wasn't the same fellow who, when told there was a shortage of hotel rooms in San Antonio because of a national urologists convention, held up his index finger. "Urologist? Is that the guy who sticks his . . ." No, Charles, that's a *proctologist.*

The Charles Barkley his teammates knew was confident, feisty, combative. "You didn't do nothing in eight years in Philly," Cedric Ceballos told him one day. "All you got to show for it is a bad back and bad elbows."

"And $15 million," Barkley shot back, laughing.

That Charles Barkley was missing.

With its two star players, Johnson and Mourning, sidelined with injury, the Charlotte Hornets had lost 16 of 17 games, eight in a row. A local preacher didn't come right out and ask for divine intervention but he hinted at it in his pregame prayer. "Lord," the minister intoned, his voice rising, filling the arena at One Hive Drive, "bless the Hornets and the Suns tonight, *in that order* if it so pleases . . ."

Westphal, a Christian, may have said a prayer, too. The trip hadn't started off well. When the Suns landed in Charlotte, the bus wasn't at the airport. Before the game, assistant coach Scotty Robertson cut his finger while opening a soft drink can. He didn't know he was bleeding when he reached into his shirt pocket. A bright red stain appeared on his chest. Scotty looked as if he taken a slug from a .38. Kevin Johnson nursed a deep thigh bruise. Ainge was playing with a badly swollen left ankle. Dan Majerle was in a shooting slump. And Barkley faced the prospects of a tough night in the paint as Mourning, the Hornets' 6-10 center, returned to the starting lineup.

It was tough, all right. Barkley missed his first five shots, and 11 of his first 12. He didn't go to the foul line until the third quarter. The Suns, the NBA's top-scoring team, shot only 37 percent. Mourning scored 24 points and grabbed 15 rebounds in the Hornets' 97–89 victory.

Barkley, for one of the few times in his career, was at a loss for words. "We haven't . . . we're not . . ." He stared at his knees, wrapped in ice, and shook his head. He looked tired. Sad. Concerned. Discouraged. The long march was just beginning. The itinerary read:

7:30 P.M. Phoenix at Charlotte. After game, bus to airport.

10:30 P.M. Depart Charlotte

11:50 P.M. Arrive Baltimore—bus to hotel.

30

Number One Fan

He didn't register at the hotel under his own name. He rarely does. For this trip, Charles Barkley was Nick Faldo, the British golf champion. Sometimes he is Tom Kite. Newspaper reporters who cover the Suns respect Barkley's privacy, but in the event they need to call him in his hotel room and don't know his alias, the best way to find him would be to go down the names on the PGA Tour's Top 10 money list.

I asked Barkley if, in his next life, he would like to come back as a professional golfer, expecting him to say yes.

He said no. "I want to be a woman."

"You want to be reincarnated as a *woman?*"

"Yeah," Barkley said. "I'd marry a rich guy and get divorced."

The Suns arrived at the BWI Marriott after midnight. Ten minutes later a young man who had driven two hours from his home in Manassas, Va., jumped out of his car and ran into the hotel lobby. He discovered, to his dismay, that he was too late. The Suns already had checked in and gone to bed.

Bill Osborne, 21, calls himself "the biggest Charles Barkley fan in the world." I met him the next day in the lobby. He wore a purple Suns jersey with "BARKLEY" spelled out on the back and he looked a little disheveled. Rather than drive home the night before, he slept in his car in the hotel parking lot. Osborne said he planned to camp out in the lobby, all day, if necessary, until Barkley appeared. He wanted the Suns star to sign his jersey, which his girlfriend had given him for his birthday.

"How long have you been down here?" I asked.

"Since six-thirty," Osborne said.

It was almost noon.

Osborne began following Barkley's career when Barkley played in Philadelphia. Last year, when the Suns came to Washington, Osborne had his picture taken with his favorite player. Osborne pulled out his wallet and showed me the snapshot. In the photo, Osborne stood alongside Barkley, all smiles. "I carry it with me everywhere I go," he said.

They are in every NBA city. They wait beside the bus outside the hotel. They gather at the team entrance to the arena. Many wear No. 34 jerseys. Others may claim to be Barkley's No. 1 fan but I cannot imagine anyone being more enamored with the Suns player than Osborne is. "I have a poster of him at home," he said, "and all his (trading) cards, except his rookie card."

"What do you like about him?" I like Barkley, too. But I wouldn't sleep in my car for the chance to meet the pope.

"It's his personality," Osborne said. "He came from a strong background, with his mother and grandmother bringing him up. He has strong family values. He's not afraid to speak his mind. He makes a lot of sense. Charles Barkley is the real thing, the link back to the old days of the NBA with Magic and Michael Jordan and Bird."

Osborne had tickets to the Suns-Bullets game that night. But he wanted Charles to sign his jersey before he left for the game, which Barkley did, as he walked through the lobby before boarding the 5:30 P.M. bus to the arena.

"When I die," Osborne said, "I want to be buried in this jersey."

I started to tell him if he should meet Charles in the next life, be careful. She's nothing but a golddigger.

31

Vegetable Plate

As the Suns trotted onto the court for their pregame warmup, a curly-haired man wearing a blue plastic hat rose from his front-row seat. Back ramrod straight, he raised a small megaphone to his lips. "Charles Barkley!" he shouted in the lecturing tone of a Victorian schoolmaster. "You are not eating your vegetables! Charles, you are not a role model. DO YOU HEAR ME, CHARLES BARKLEY!!"

Of course he heard him. He pretended not to, for the moment, but Barkley and his teammates couldn't tune out the familiar and annoying voice of Robin Ficker. The 51-year-old Maryland lawyer, who jokingly claims to be Barkley's attorney—"We have filed a case in the U.S. Court of Appeals, where Charles will be suing himself for libel because he was misquoted in his autobiography"—is a Washington Bullets season ticket holder. A former Maryland legislator, Ficker has attended every Bullets home game for 10 years, a testimony to his resiliency. Champion of the U.S. Constitution and the First Amendment, he sits directly behind the opponents' bench at Bullets home games and heckles the enemy.

Ficker isn't vulgar. He doesn't use profanity, or make racial or sexual comments. But he is grating and repetitive. This night his Barkley shtick involved bad puns and edible props, which he purchased at a grocery store before the game and carried into USAir Arena in a plastic garbage bag.

"Charles Barkley!" Ficker shouted.

Barkley dropped in a layup.

"Charles Barkley!"

Barkley swished a 17-foot jumper.

"CHARLES BARKLEY!"

Barkley glanced toward the sideline.

Ficker was staring at him and holding up a head of lettuce. "CHARLES BARKLEY, HERE ARE YOUR VEGETABLES!"

Because of his pyrotechnic personality and image as a villain, because he enjoys playing to the crowd more than any other NBA star, Barkley is a target in every arena. Fans taunt him. "Hey, Barkley! Spit on any little girls lately?" They rattle his cage, shouting insults, hoping to provoke some volcanic response. They often succeed. Barkley has more put-downs than a lounge comic working a tough room. His comebacks both shock and delight the crowd. One night on the road a fan started in on Barkley. He never let up. Finally, Barkley removed his mouthpiece and said to his tormentor, "I have a message from the NBA. Shut the fuck up!"

"It's a game," Barkley said. "You can cheer or boo. The only thing that bothers me is when they start abusing me. That's not right. There's no need to say things about your family, things like that. If somebody says something to me that's rude, I'm probably going to say something back."

Barkley is Ficker's favorite NBA player. "I love the guy. I've enjoyed his repartee more than anyone else's over the years. When he played in Philly he used to tell me that George Bush and I were the two biggest jerks in Washington, only he didn't use the word jerks. One time I told him, 'Michael Adams (a Bullets guard) should be on the Olympic team instead of you.' He said, 'Yeah, as the water boy.' "

It was rumored Barkley arranged for Ficker to sit behind the Chicago Bulls' bench for Games 1 and 2 of the 1993 NBA Finals at America West Arena. Barkley pleads not guilty. Armed with playing cards and dice, Ficker targeted Michael Jordan, whose gambling episodes then were national news. He razzed Jordan unmercifully. "HEY MICHAEL," Ficker bawled, "HOW MUCH YOU BET-TING ON THIS GAME?!"

That did it. Horace Balmer, vice president of NBA security, who was seated nearby, gestured with his thumb, like an umpire sending a hot-headed manager to the showers. Arena security told the heckler to leave. Ficker picks up the story: "I asked 'Why?' All I was doing was talking about gambling, which was a sensitive issue. Then the police came over. Being an attorney, I'm not going to argue with a policeman. You might get whacked on the head, or who knows what. They said I was ejected from the game."

Ficker left the arena and walked down the street to Majerle's, where he watched the remainder of the game on television. Ficker had left his Barkley poster and several signs beneath his arena seat. "So I went back after the game and tried to get back in. The security guy said, 'Once you leave you can't get back in.' I said 'Well, I left my posters under my seat.' So I went down to get them. As soon as I got there, the police and the director of security at the arena, which I now call the America *Arrest* Arena, told me I was under arrest. They put me in the holding tank. Then I was taken to the police station and put in the drunk tank. I don't drink alcohol at any of the games. I was charged with trespassing. Bail was like $160. I had over $1,000 in my pocket, but they wouldn't let me pay the bail right away. I ended up getting out of there at 1:45 in the morning."

Ficker went to trial in Phoenix in August 1993 on a trespassing charge. "This man is an absolute disruption to the game," prosecutor Kent McCarthy said. The judge, however, ruled that Ficker did not interfere with the June 11 game and cleared him of the charge.

The Bullets' most vocal fan teased Barkley and other Suns players, nonstop, throughout the Bullets game. He heckled Kevin Johnson. "Kevin, what was that George Karl called you?" During the 1993 playoffs, Karl, the Seattle coach, suggested the Suns point guard whined too much. He called KJ a "princess."

Ficker yelled at Dan Majerle: "Hey, Spock ears! Spock ears Majerle!"

To assistant coach Lionel Hollins: "I know what happened to that weight Oliver Miller lost. You look fat, flabby and forty!"

During a Suns timeout, Ficker turned up the volume. Paul Westphal had to yell instructions to his players to keep from being drowned out by the pest who stood behind him, his chest thrown out like a Marine drill instructor as he barked into the bullhorn.

The Suns scored 44 points in the first quarter and won, 142–106. But Ficker never gave up, even though the Bullets did. The loudmouth spared no one. He targeted No. 34, whose diet—Barkley doesn't like vegetables—was the theme of his courtside routine.

"Charles Barkley! Are you going to TURN-UP tonight?" Ficker produced a stalk of turnips. Each time he called Barkley's name and made a bad pun, he held up the corresponding vegetable.

"Charles! Where have you BEAN?!"

"Are you going to LEEK us some plays, Barkley?!"

"Are you going to cause a RHUBARB?"

"The Bullets are going to SQUASH you!"

On and on and on . . .

"Here's your team vegetable, Charles Barkley! The ARTI-CHOKE!"

"Charles, you look RADISHING tonight!"

Radishing.

Barkley looked at Ficker and cracked up.

32

Governor Barkley

I don't know if Charles would make a very good politician. First of all, the word politician means you have diplomacy. One of the things he lacks, one of the criticisms about him, is that he has no diplomacy. Stranger things have happened, but I don't think he's qualified at the moment to run for a very high office, like governor. I think that's far-fetched.
—Harold Katz, 76ers owner

If I'm going to screw up, it might as well be in a big office.
—Charles Barkley

Will Rogers said, "Be a politician. No training necessary." Barkley plans to follow that advice once his basketball days are over. Question is, can an outspoken black Republican who has never run for political office be elected governor of Alabama in 1998?

Opinions are mixed. Some political observers say Barkley may have a future in state politics. Others chuckle at the thought of Barkley kissing babies and cutting ribbons and stumping on the campaign trail.

"I would never underestimate Charles Barkley," said Dr. Wayne Flynt, a professor and historian at Auburn University. "He has universal name recognition. He might do very well in a race for a congressional seat. But I doubt he is electable as governor. Race still plays a very great part in Alabama politics. Since Reconstruction, only one black has been elected to a statewide office. About 25 percent of voters in Alabama are black. For Charles Barkley to be elected he would have to get the vote of about one in three whites, and most Republicans in Alabama are white-flight ex-Democrats. I don't think he could win a Republican primary.

"Charles would be attractive to white liberals. But they would want to know how he feels about poverty and child issues and health care. He would have to have a cerebral agenda."

J. L. Chestnut, a 64-year-old Selma, Ala., attorney and author of

Black In Selma, marched with the late Dr. Martin Luther King, Jr., during civil rights demonstrations in Alabama in the 1960s. "Alabama has come a long way, but it has a long long way to go. Remember, this is George Wallace country," Chestnut said. "The race card is played hard, often and with great skill in this state. I don't know what Mr. Barkley's politics are, but if he is of the Republican persuasion, his natural political base, if he has one, and I mean blacks, could evaporate. There aren't enough black Republicans in Alabama to shake a stick at.

"I don't know that Mr. Barkley is a Republican, but if he is I'd say he would be assured of Clarence Thomas's vote and that's about it. If he announces he's a Republican, it's over for him."

Bob Ingram, veteran political columnist for *The Montgomery* (Ala.) *Advertiser,* wrote: "The suggestion that (Barkley) might be a serious candidate . . . is worth a laugh. But only that."

The Mobile Press-Register took Barkley seriously enough to commission a poll on Barkley's chances of being elected to Congress. The newspaper reported that only 19 percent of those polled said they would support Barkley, while 49 percent said they would not. Thirty-two percent said they didn't know enough about him to make a decision.

The Birmingham News endorsed Barkley in a tongue-in-cheek editorial: "Charles Barkley . . . says he may come home to Alabama and go into politics. This is great news. Our state, long plagued by a dearth of leadership, could suddenly become a one-man leadership glut. This man battled Godzilla. He took on Michael Jordan. He's beaten up a couple of guys in bars. Surely he won't shy away from foes like crime and ailing schools and government waste. What's more, he's already got the perfect slogan: 'I'm a politician. Not a role model.' "

In December 1993, when Barkley began talking about plans to seek the state's highest office, he said he would not affiliate with any political party. "I'm independent, baby." He has since said he would run as a Republican, even though a majority of the registered black voters in Alabama are Democrats.

"The Democratic Party is the worst thing that ever happened to poor people, especially black people," Barkley said. "They put out all these social programs. If you're on welfare, they give you just enough to make ends meet and you spend your whole life in poverty. They perpetuate the problem. We need to take money and put it into employment and academics. The most important thing is we've got to do something with the public school system.

"The school system has deteriorated. Education builds self-esteem. Everyone needs an education in some field. When I'm governor I want to make some schools trade schools. You can learn to be an electrician. Or a plumber. Or a carpenter. Not every kid is going to learn algebra, but he might learn some kind of trade."

Barkley listens to Jesse Jackson. He also listens to Rush Limbaugh, the popular conservative talk-show host who is a devoted Suns fan and a friend of Phoenix coach Paul Westphal. "Rush has some great things to say. Jesse has some great things to say," Barkley said. "I don't agree with everything Jesse says, and I don't agree with everything Rush says."

Limbaugh likes much of what he has heard Barkley say. On his television show, Limbaugh related a dinner conversation he and Westphal had about Barkley playing in Arizona, a conservative state. He quoted the coach as saying that Barkley "has done it his way, on his own terms."

"Isn't that what conservatism is all about?" Limbaugh said. "I think that's a great story. It's a tremendously instructive story, because the assumption was that because Barkley's a black guy, he's not going to be comfortable around conservatives. Don't forget, Barkley is the guy who said, in response to Jesse Jackson's desire that black athletes give some money back and pay attention to the plight of blacks in the front office, 'Well, I would play for the KKK if they paid me what I wanted.' So you got to love the guy. You absolutely have to love the guy."

(A Barkley quote I heard referring to the KKK was in response to whether he would work for the Philadelphia 76ers after he retired. "I can be bought," Barkley said. "If they paid me enough, I'd work for the Klan.")

Candidate Barkley would have to choose his words more carefully. The Suns got a lesson in political correctness during their long road trip. In Miami, Dan Majerle made six of nine shots from behind the three-point line. Three were buzzer-beaters. After the Suns' victory, Westphal said of Majerle, "If he was in a Western, he'd be the guy with the long rifle who shoots the Indian off his horse from a mile away. It's not luck. Sometimes he's better from out there than from eight feet."

Westphal's characterization drew an angry response from Benjamin Chee of the Native American Heritage Preservation Coalition:

We as Native Americans take offense to this callous remark. I am sad to see that the archaic views of racism raises its head in the world of local sports. The quote which states your impression of (Majerle's) three-point shooting . . . demonstrates present-day insensitivity to Native Americans.

To equate the sport of basketball to the killing of Indians is an abomination. If this remark had been directed toward any other race, there would have been an overwhelming cry of indignation . . . A public insult demands a public apology.

"That's one thing that's wrong with our society," Barkley said. "Obviously, Paul said that in jest. People have to decipher what is said to be hurtful and what is said in jest. It's like the movie *White Men Can't Jump*. I was talking to one of my friends, who is white. We were talking about racism. He asked me why he shouldn't be offended by that. The movie title wasn't meant to be offensive.

"I don't think calling Washington the Redskins is a reason to picket. Black people use the 'N' word. I don't like that because blacks will say it to each other but get offended when a white person says it. Black people use it all the time. I was watching Oprah one day and Indians were saying they were offended when you use the expression 'low man on the totem pole.' I can't understand how that would offend anybody. But we live in a society where every little thing is dissected. Every little thing."

Suns 142, Bullets 106. "Chuck," Scotty Robertson said, "this is Senator Bob Kerrey. He would like to get a picture with you and talk politics."

"Did you enjoy the game tonight?" Barkley asked as he shook hands with the Democratic senator from Nebraska. "It's the first good game we had in two weeks. We might have to start carrying you with us."

"I hear you like politics," Kerrey said.

"I can't wait," Barkley replied. "I really am looking forward to it. I think it'll be a good thing for me. I'm moving back to Alabama in '96 and running in '98. It's something I really really want to do."

"Just tell the truth," Kerrey advised.

"That's it," Barkley said.

"I signed up on your team," Kerrey said, "the day you said, 'If you don't like the way I'm playing, you can kiss my big black ass.'"

33

Chuck and Mike

Charles and I talked about retiring at the same time, but it's a little different scenario for him. I've already accomplished a lot. He still has things he wants to achieve. I've been standing in his way.
—Michael Jordan, Oct. 6, 1993, the day he retired from the NBA

Bottom of the eighth. Two outs. Runner on third. The public address announcer's voice crackled over the speakers at Ed Smith Stadium in Sarasota, Fla.

"Now batting for the White Sox, Number 45 . . ."

When Michael Jordan, 0-for-13 in spring training, stepped to the plate the sellout crowd of 7,454 joined together and made a wish. *C'mon, Michael. Good eye. Wait for your pitch. Relax. Hang tough. You can do it.* Busloads of kids—1,200 schoolchildren—pressed against the railing, fingers crossed, chanting his name—"Mich-ael! Mich-ael!"—pleading for a hit.

At 6-6 he looks too tall to play baseball. In his uniform, he appears to be all legs, a marsh bird in pinstripes. He lacks power. His strike zone is as big as his bank account.

Inside, ball one. The crowd cheered. The windup, the next pitch. Swing and a miss. The little ballpark groaned like an old mattress.

"BAG IT, MICHAEL!" That was the headline on the cover of the March 14, 1994, issue of *Sports Illustrated*. The story, titled "Err Jordan," characterized Jordan's spring training tryout as a charade and called him an embarrassment to baseball. The magazine sarcastically chastised the White Sox for feeding Jordan's delusion—"Become a Major Leaguer in Just Six Weeks!"

The count at one and one. Jordan swung. The ball bounced deep into the hole at shortstop. The White Sox rightfielder sprinted down the line, his long legs flying. Jordan and the ball arrived at the first-base bag at the same time, a bang-bang play. Umpire Drew Coble punched the air with a theatrical flourish. Out!

"Michael got screwed," Barkley said, echoing the biased opinion of the ballpark crowd. Barkley, who was in nearby Orlando with the Suns, saw the replay on TV. With spring training in full swing, he followed the White Sox closely. He checked the box score every day to see if Jordan played, and if he did, how he fared at the plate. Jordan is his friend. "Michael Jordan may be my best friend in the world."

They were born in the same year, the same month, Jordan on Feb. 17, 1963; Barkley on Feb. 20. They met when they were in college, Barkley at Auburn and Jordan at North Carolina. "We played against each other in the Pan American trials," Jordan recalled. "He was guarding me and I was guarding him. You know," Jordan said, smiling, "*that* was a mismatch."

"Yeah," Barkley cracked, "but he got better."

Jordan was the third pick in the 1984 NBA draft. Barkley was the fifth pick. "It just developed into a great relationship," Jordan said. "We have similar personalities and yet we're different. We respect each other and see eye to eye on a lot of things. I'm there to support him as much as he's there to support me. I think that's what friends are for."

Barkley: "When I was in Philadelphia, Michael could relate to me because his first few years in Chicago he played on bad teams. He played hard. He tried hard. So did I. That's what we respect about each other. Michael Jordan is the only person I've met in my life who wanted to win as bad as I do. . . . I've got a lot of friends in the league. Karl Malone and I were roommates in 1983 at the World University Games. We are still friends, but not as close as me and Michael. Because Karl lives in Salt Lake City, he really has to walk a tight rope. Some people consider my personality way out there. So Karl has distanced himself from me a little. Not Michael. He's not afraid of that."

Barkley's loyalty to his friend is unwavering. When Jordan was criticized for gambling in Atlantic City during the 1993 Eastern Conference finals, Barkley came to his defense. "Michael Jordan didn't get to be as good as Michael Jordan by abusing his body." As for Jordan possibly being tired, Barkley posed the question: "What's the difference if a player goes out on the town, or stays in his room and has sex all night?"

Barkley likes to gamble, too. The Mirage in Las Vegas. Trump Palace in Atlantic City. "I love to play craps. As long as you gamble within your means I don't think there's anything wrong with it. Most people who gamble don't know their limit. If I lose $10,000 or $25,000, that's it for me. I don't ask for a line of credit. I don't want a line of credit. I'm done."

Barkley bets on golf. A $500 loss is nothing to him. "Monopoly money." He bets on football, and himself. On the practice court,

Barkley, ball in hand, will call out to Ainge, "Five hundred I make it." Ainge keeps a tab of Barkley's debt.

I asked Barkley if he thought he could turn a profit betting on the NBA.

"Number one, you can't bet," Barkley said. "Even if I could, just because you play in the league doesn't mean you know the teams. I don't have time to keep up with them. Besides, you never know how a team is going to play. There are nights when you're really tired and you play great. Those are the nights that surprise you. It's too unpredictable."

Their competitiveness is the tie that binds Barkley and Jordan. During the 1993 NBA Finals they traded points, and good-natured barbs. After Game 3 Jordan treated Barkley to dinner at Michael Jordan's restaurant. Between bites, Barkley told his friend the Suns were a team of destiny. "I told him it was his last supper," Jordan said.

One of Jordan's cars is a black Ferrari Testarossa. Barkley saw it parked outside Chicago Stadium. "I can afford a Testarossa," he said of his friend's Italian Batmobile. "How much is it, $100,000? $240,000?" Then the playful zinger, a reference to Jordan's gambling losses, "That's just a couple rounds of golf . . ."

The night the Bulls won their third NBA championship, Barkley embraced Jordan after the game. They were the portraits of victory and defeat. In the visitors' clubhouse, Jordan, who averaged 41 points and was named the Most Valuable Player in the Finals for the third year in a row, swilled champagne from the bottle and waved a cigar the size of a track baton. Down the hallway, Barkley sat at his locker, physically and emotionally spent. Elbows on his knees, head bowed, he spoke just above a whisper.

Barkley lost a championship. Two months later, Jordan experienced a much greater loss. The same week Barkley and Jordan played golf together in California, Jordan received news that his missing father, James Jordan, had been found. He had been murdered, shot, his body dumped in a creek.

"It was like a death in my family," Barkley said.

They are there, for each other, through good times and bad. The morning after the Suns lost to the Lakers in the 1993–94 season opener, the phone rang at Barkley's home. Michael was on the line. "He told me, 'Hey, man you looked tight as a drum.' He said everybody was trying to make me the man since he retired. He told me to forget that and just go out and relax and play basketball."

Barkley looked at the *SI* issue and did a slow burn. The cover photo showed Jordan swinging and missing a pitch. Another photo pictured Jordan booting a fly ball.

"That pisses me off," Barkley said. "*Sports Illustrated* has made a lot of money off Michael. He's been on the cover 30 times. Embarrassing baseball? I look at it differently. If a guy risks everything he has accomplished in his life, his pride and his ego, to try something else, what's wrong with that? It's amazing to me how many people are envious and jealous of you. How many people want you to fail.

"When a guy puts everything on the line to try something different, you've got to say this guy is special. There aren't that many people who would take an ego bashing like that. I don't know that I could. He opened himself up to unbelievable scrutiny. I have more respect for him now than ever before. 'Friends' is an overused word. 'Friends' and 'I love you' are the most overused words in the English language. When people tell other people 'I love you,' a lot of time it's a crock. But I consider Michael a true friend of mine. I can count on him. I don't say that about many people I know."

34

Back on Track

During March, the Suns never knew which Charles Barkley would show up. Neither did he. Barkley's inconsistent play brought to mind the Marx Brothers skit in which Groucho answers the telephone at the law firm of Schwartz, Schwartz & Schwartz.

"Mr. Schwartz, please," the caller says.

"Schwartz is out of town."

"How about Schwartz?"

"He's at lunch."

"Is Schwartz there?"

"Speaking," Groucho replies, his eyebrows doing pushups.

Barkley didn't know how he might perform against Orlando, but this was his kind of game. Sunday afternoon. National TV. Shaquille O'Neal. It was a playoff atmosphere as the *Orlando Sentinel* blimp floated overhead and Magic dancers in blue sequined costumes shimmied full-tilt-boogie to the theme from *Phantom of the Opera*. A sellout crowd risked permanent hearing loss when the public address announcer welcomed everyone to "today's game between the Phoenix Suns"—booooooooo—"and YOUR Or-lan-dooooooooooooo Maaaaaaaaa-gic!!!"

The night before the game, Joe Kleine mapped out his strategy with fellow center Mark West. "Daddy, you've got Shaq," Kleine said. "I'll take Tree."

Wayne "Tree" Rollins was the backup center for the Magic. Tree started the season as an assistant coach. Since re-enlisting as a player, he averaged seven minutes and two points per game. Rollins was 38 years old.

Kleine was joking, sort of. He knew the Suns needed West and himself, playing alternately, plus all the help Barkley and others could give to guard O'Neal, the 7-foot-1 man/child.

O'Neal got his points in the Suns' 100-93 victory. Shaq scored 39—16 came in the first quarter when he made his first seven shots. My notes looked like this: "Shaq gets tip-off. Spins, shoots over West. Over West again. Over West. Over Majerle. Can't stop him. Majerle falls back, staggers under Shaq's weight."

O'Neal's swooping dunk off Dennis Scott's above-the-rim pass was the slam du jour. No one person, or two, or three, could have stopped him on that one. "Big son of a bitch," Barkley called O'Neal. Indeed. Once, while diving for a loose ball, the Magic center slid face-down out of bounds. Kleine turned to the patrons seated nearby. "The whole floor is wet! Bring out the Zamboni!"

The Suns defended O'Neal as well as they could. West and Kleine made O'Neal take most of his shots away from the basket. They kept Shaq off the free-throw line for the first 30 minutes. Kleine deserved overtime pay for the 29 minutes he toiled beneath the basket, pushing and shoving, his hand pressed into the back of the Magic's immovable force. It was hard work, manual labor. Sweat poured off Kleine's face and dripped from his nose.

After the game, West nursed a bruised thigh. Kleine winced as he twisted and stretched. "My back hurts," he said, but he was smiling. It was a good hurt, if there is such a thing, honestly earned.

Barkley was smiling, too. The Suns won their third in a row on the road and Barkley played his best game since Christmas, with 30 points and 20 rebounds. Paul Westphal said, "That's the first game since he came back he's looked like Charles Barkley."

But there was one scary moment. Late in the third quarter, Barkley collided with O'Neal. Barkley dropped like a steer hit with a sledge hammer. As play continued, Barkley lay on his back. For several seconds he didn't move. "I gave up any thoughts about becoming a boxer today," Barkley said later. "I know now why those guys stutter so much." Barkley said he was "stunned" by the blow.

"You all right?" Joe Proski asked after Barkley returned to the bench, still woozy. The Suns trainer looked into Barkley's eyes and tried to determine the level of his awareness. "How many fouls do you have?" Proski asked.

Barkley gave the correct answer.

He held up one finger.

His middle one.

35

Give and Take

You don't play mind games with Charles. You just tell him.
What I was telling him that night was to stop babying himself
and forget about his (physical) troubles and go play. That's all it
was. Maybe he needed to get a little mad. Maybe to prove me
wrong. I don't know. I don't care. I thought he responded well.
—Paul Westphal

The coach knew he wouldn't like it. "I didn't *want* him to like it." The
night of March 22, Westphal benched Barkley for the start of the second half against Miami. He didn't sit long, and the Suns won in overtime. But after the game Barkley was steamed.

Charles, did you elevate your game in the second half? "My game
is always elevated," Barkley snapped. "Don't you have cable?"

You didn't start the second half . . .

"He didn't think I was playing hard in the first half," Barkley said,
referring to Westphal in the impersonal third person. "I may not have
been playing well, but I don't agree I wasn't playing *hard.*

"He's the coach. He does his thing. I do mine. But I didn't think I
deserved to get benched. When other players are struggling, we don't
bench them. If he is consistent, that's fine. But just to do it out of the
blue, I didn't like that. I didn't like it at all. I don't mind being criticized if I'm not doing the job. But he has to have the same criteria
with everybody."

Barkley dropped the subject, then picked it up. "In my old age, I've
mellowed a little bit. A few years ago I would have cursed him out. I
would have gone off on him. I would have lit into his ass like it was
Christmas. I don't think he benched any other guys for not playing.
That pisses me off.

"You can't treat one kid better than the other. That's what my
mama said. She always treated me and my two brothers the same. I
don't ever get into arguments with the coaches. Their jobs are on the
line. They make their own decisions. But I think you've always got to
be consistent. The next time somebody is struggling I expect them to

121

get benched. That's all I'm going to say . . ."

Barkley didn't speak on the issue again. Westphal chose to ignore the inflammatory remarks rather than respond through the media. The flame was extinguished before it became a brush fire.

Westphal is often asked how he coaches Barkley. His standard line—"It's easy, I let him do whatever he wants"—always draws a laugh.

"It's really not that far from the truth," Westphal said. "In a lot of ways I do let him do whatever he wants. You can't do that with very many people, but Charles is a special case. A coach's job is to help your players get into a position where they are able to do their best. You have to help people bring out their strengths and hide their weaknesses. You have to beat some players over the head to get them to hide their weaknesses and play to their strengths. Charles isn't like that. He knows what he is capable of doing. Since he is the focal point of our offense, my job is to get the other players to know what he is best at, and feed off that."

"Is there anything you can teach him?" I asked.

"There's really very little you can teach him. Charles is a great student of the game. You can remind him of things. Or you can say, 'Maybe you're not seeing this. This is what we need to do and why.' I don't know if that is teaching, but it is definitely coaching. Charles is receptive to that. I think it's important to let him have his say and, after that, he is willing to do whatever is decided upon. He doesn't feel like he has to tell everybody how it has to be. He just wants to be heard."

Westphal and Barkley hit it off from day one. "He was exactly what we thought he would be and I hoped he would be," the coach said of their first meeting. "You didn't know for sure, because he had a crazy reputation. But sitting down and talking to him he had very realistic expectations about what he could do for us. How he could do it. How his career had gone. What changes needed to be made. He's somebody I never worry about, as far as what he has to do to be successful, because he is."

Barkley is correct. Westphal doesn't treat every player on the team the same. The coach makes allowances for his star player. "He's a special case, all the way around. You have to understand that. The bus is an example. If we're supposed to leave the hotel at 5:45 P.M., Charles is never going to be there before 5:44. But he will never be there past 5:47 either.

"He wants to be the last person on the bus. Why? There may be anywhere from 10 to 100 people waiting for him. So if he walks out of the hotel early he is hounded for autographs. That's not how you want to prepare for a game. So he works it where he is the last person on the bus. He walks through the crowd and says, 'I'm sorry, I don't have time. I've got to get on the bus. We're leaving.' If he came down 20 minutes late we would be gone. We wouldn't wait. But I'll wait an extra two minutes for Charles Barkley."

"When you're drawing up a play, does he ever say, 'I want the ball?'" One popular T-shirt pictures Barkley with the caption, "Just gimme the #@%*& ball!"

"Sometimes," Westphal said. "He makes his feelings known. Most of the time we're trying to get a play that involves him anyway. We don't go toe-to-toe over something like that. But if he has a specific idea of how he can be the most effective, I want to hear it."

"Do you agree with him that only a few players want the ball at the end of a close game?"

"I think that's true. There's a lot of responsibility if you fail. You have to answer all those questions. Near the end of the game, if you shoot there's a good chance you're going to get fouled and not have it called. A lot of guys are not good enough to overcome those things. When you have a player who wants the ball like Charles does, you've really got something. I learned about guys like him from John Havlicek, who I played with in Boston when I came into the league. Havlicek said he felt if he took the last shot, as opposed to someone else on the team, he wouldn't be crushed if he missed it. He wasn't afraid to fail. He knew if he failed it wasn't because he choked. It's just that everybody misses sometimes. Everybody's makeup isn't like that. Some guys are very fragile. They can't stand that specter of defeat hanging over them. Get a guy who is not afraid to fail, you have a guy who will be at his best with the game on the line."

A quote from Detroit Tigers manager Sparky Anderson hangs on a wall in Westphal's office: "If you've got a group that wants to win, you've gotta let them." Translation—don't over-coach; don't stand in your team's way. One criticism of Westphal is that he is too laid-back, that he needs to be tougher, more demanding.

Danny Ainge disagrees: "When I think of Paul, laid back doesn't come to mind. He has gotten on some players individually. He's gotten on all of us at one time or another. There's not a guy in our clubhouse he hasn't pointed out for not doing their job. His first year, there was no need to yell and scream. We were on such an emotional high. This season there's been a lot of adversity. I think he senses, as we all have, there really hasn't been the same fire, night in and night out, we had last year when we went to the Finals. I don't think anybody can say the emotion is there this year that was there last year. Paul has felt more of a need to make people accountable, and that includes everybody."

Barkley likes Westphal's style. "I've never played for a bad coach.

They all were different personalities. My first coach, Billy Cunningham, was a tough son of a bitch. Tough as nails. I'd go to war with him anytime. Matt Goukas was a good coach, a nice guy. Jimmy Lynam was a guy you always could count on. I think Paul is the perfect veteran coach. He doesn't try to work you to death. We are all very successful, and we're going to be successful because we want to be. It's not like he has to force us to work hard. The most important thing for a coach is to treat your players like people first. They'll play harder for you."

Barkley has thought about coaching—for about two seconds. The only college job he would consider is Auburn, his alma mater. The NBA? Barkley says no. "I'd probably fight my players."

"He knows the game well enough to coach," Westphal said.

"But would he make a good coach?" I asked.

"I don't think so. He wouldn't need the aggravation. I can't imagine him wanting to put himself through what an NBA coach has to go through. Charles doesn't have the patience to deal with guys who have less heart than he does. As a coach, I've seen a lot of guys who have a lot less heart than he does. It's incomprehensible to him that some guys don't care. Coaching would be very hard on him."

"What if he could coach five Barkleys?"

Westphal laughed. "If he can coach five Charles Barkleys, he's a better man than I am. There's only room for one."

36

Christiana

The little girl with black eyebrows asked with upturned eyes, "Why does everybody call you Charles Barkley?"

"Well," her father replied, amused by her curiosity and innocent smile, "when Daddy is playing basketball he *is* Charles Barkley."

The child replied, "You're my *daddy* when you're playing basketball."

Christiana Barkley is the light of her father's life. Photos of the 5-year-old grace his dressing area in the Suns clubhouse. Christiana in front of the family Christmas tree. Christiana sitting primly on the bottom step of a staircase. Christiana and her father, heads together, their faces filling the frame, sharing a happy moment, all smiles.

"She loves school, which makes me wonder if she's my daughter," Barkley jokes. Then he looks at her, and sees himself in her, a pure reflection. There is no doubt. He knows, as she does, who her daddy is. "She looks just like me. She's beautiful."

"I wanted to name her Morgan," Maureen Barkley said. "But Charles was with me at the hospital the whole time, and I thought, 'You know, it's his first child. She's a picture of him.' I said, 'Charles, you can name her if you want.' When we got married, Charles and I eloped. We had to drive to this place in Maryland. We passed a mall called the Christiana Mall. Charles was kidding around that we were going to name our daughter after this mall because I was at a mall all the time.

"Two weeks later, after we got married, he met a little girl named Christiana. Charles said she was the cutest little thing. He said if we had a little girl, he would like to name her Christiana."

During the basketball season, he is Charles Barkley, first, and a husband and father, second. "My number one priority is basketball. So I put my family on the back burner. I try to spend quality time with her, and let her know I love her. I tell her, 'Daddy is trying to work so he can make life better for you.' Maybe she doesn't understand now but she will when she gets older. When she's able to go to college, and have anything she wants."

Barkley grew up without a father's love. He understands how

important it is for a child to be in a loving, supportive environment, which his mother and grandmother provided for him. "The experience Charles had with his father I think will only make him a much better and loving father," said Charcey Glenn, Barkley's mother, who shares the same birthday as her granddaughter. "He would not want to do to his children what his father did to him. He's a father now, but he will be an excellent daddy when he has the real time to spend with his daughter. I know this. She *loves* her daddy."

Barkley is at his best around children. "Kids are the best part of my job, by far." At heart, he is a kid himself. After home games, he ducks into the Suns' family room where his teammates' kids are playing. After a loss at home to Utah, Barkley sat in the clubhouse, simmering. Paul Westphal had accused the Suns of "spectating." Barkley was struggling physically. His legs were dead. He was doubting his body for the first time in his career.

"This ain't one of those rides you can get off," he told the media, although that night he sounded as if he wished he could. He wasn't in a mood to chat, and said so. When one reporter ignored the storm warnings and returned to ask a question, Barkley flared. "I told you now's not the time to be messing with me . . . I 'd like to slug somebody."

As the clubhouse began to clear, Jeff Hornacek's sons walked in. Barkley recognized them. A towel wrapped around his waist, Barkley walked over and glared down at them. "I'M IN A BAD MOOD!" he boomed in his best beanstalk giant voice.

The boys peered wide-eyed at the bald ogre, their daddy's friend, and giggled.

Barkley scowled at Ryan, age 5. "I want to bite somebody's head off. HOW ABOUT YOU!!!"

"No!" Ryan shrieked.

Barkley turned to the boy's 3-year-old brother. "DO YOU WANT ME TO EAT YOU?!!!" Tyler pointed a small finger up at Barkley, and turned the game around. "I'm going to eat YOU!" Barkley's brow smoothed and a grin spread across his face. The thunderstorm passed.

Barkley and Maureen have talked about having more children. Adoption is one option. But for now they are content caring and providing for a little girl who goes to school in Phoenix and spends her summer in Philadelphia, and who doesn't care whether the man on the basketball court they call Charles Barkley scores three points or 30.

He wishes she were older, old enough to appreciate how good he is at what he does. Before Game 3 of the 1993 NBA Finals in Chicago, Barkley couldn't raise his right arm above his head. Dr. Emerson drained fluid from his elbow before tipoff. Sore and bandaged, Barkley scored 24 points and grabbed 19 rebounds as the Suns beat the Bulls in a triple-overtime thriller.

Next morning, Barkley talked about his heroics. "In 25 years," he said, "I'll be telling my daughter"—here Charles slipped into his story-telling voice—" 'Darlin', they said my career was over. I couldn't move that night. What happened was, I had my arm ripped off in a tractor-trailer accident the night before the game. I had to have major surgery. They reattached my arm just before the game.

"The doctor said, 'Charles, you can't go out there. You could die.' I said, 'Doc, I gotta go out there. We're down, 0–2, and they need me to play.' The doctor said, 'Please, Charles, please don't do it.'

Barkley grinned. "Doc," he said, quoting himself, "I'm going out there. I'm playing. That's all there is to it."

Barkley doesn't need to embellish his accomplishments. "I just wish she could understand what it means to make an All-Star team. What it means to be on the Dream Team. What it's like to be in the NBA Finals. That's one thing I regret. I don't have any films of me playing. That's the first thing I'm going to do when I retire. I'm going to the NBA offices, go over my career and pick out about 20 games and put them on a videotape to save for her."

When she's older, the little girl can discover who Charles Barkley, the basketball player, was. She might learn even more about her father by watching another video, a black-and-white Nike ad in which Barkley solemnly recites a news account of a drive-by slaying of a Phoenix 4-year-old. Ashley Boss was in her living room when she was killed by a single shot to the head. A 16-year-old boy was arrested.

After Barkley heard of the tragedy, he urged Nike chief executive Phil Knight to produce the ad. The commercial, and another that features Barkley speaking about youth violence, promotes Nike's P.L.A.Y.—Participate in the Lives of America's Youth—a program designed to focus on the problems facing youngsters.

"It was devastating for me, as a father," Barkley said of the shooting. He thought of his own child, who painted her daddy's big toes with red nail polish before one game and made him a paper four-leaf clover for the playoffs.

"My little girl is the same age. It really struck a nerve in my heart. If somebody ever did something like that to my daughter, I wouldn't care what happened to me . . ."

37

Technical Foul

Charles Barkley tsi bi dahl tah.
　—Kenneth Maryboy, announcing a Phoenix Suns game
to radio listeners on the Navajo reservation in Window
Rock, Ariz. Translation: "Charles Barkley has been
ejected."

April 10, 1994

"**B**arkley Your Time Has Come and Gone."
　"WANTED: Minor League Bus Driver/Batboy. Call Michael."
　"Sir Chuck You Suck."
　Charles Barkley didn't see the welcome signs. He didn't hear the taunts from the sellout crowd at Seattle Center Coliseum. After the Suns blew a 17-point lead in the fourth quarter, after the Sonics had roared back to win and clinch the Pacific Division title, Barkley saw only the faces of the game officials as he approached them near midcourt.
　Barkley was angry. Angry the Suns had lost at Sacramento two nights earlier. "I felt like blowing up the plane," Barkley said. (He later dismissed the idea when he realized he would be on it.) He was angry the Suns couldn't hold their lead against the Sonics. The primary target of his wrath was referee Bill Spooner, a member of Joey Crawford's crew. With 6:19 left in the game, Spooner called Barkley for committing a flagrant foul against Shawn Kemp. When Barkley protested, Spooner hit him with a technical foul.
　After the final horn, Barkley went after Spooner. Crawford angrily waved Barkley away. Several Suns restrained Barkley and led him off the court.
　The Suns locker room was a tomb. Barkley sat in a folding chair and stared at the floor.
　"What did you say to the refs?" a reporter asked.
　"I'm not going to get into it about the refs. I don't want to answer any questions."

Another said, "Joey Crawford said he's going to take it up with the league."

Barkley's head jerked up. I had seen him like this before. On such occasions I think of those meteorologists tracking the eye of an approaching hurricane on radar and the TV footage of store owners boarding windows and emergency crews in slickers stacking sandbags as the first rain squalls move in.

"Hey, let me tell you something," Barkley said, his voice rising like the tide. "Fuck Joey Crawford. I don't want to hear that shit. I said I don't want to answer no questions about it." Barkley glared at the reporter. "You think you're gonna tell me what to do?"

"Charles, was it difficult seeing Seattle win the division?"

Barkley uncoiled, a little. "Not at all. We won it last year and didn't win anything. The playoffs dictate everything. We're playing for the world championship. That's all we play for."

"That flagrant foul . . ."

"That's private," Barkley snapped. "None of your business. It doesn't affect you in any way."

"Did it affect the game in any way?"

"It don't affect anybody except me and the refs. It don't affect nobody else."

"You don't think it helped the Sonics?"

Barkley gathered himself. The storm was dissipating. The worst was over. "Yeah, I think it helped them. But like I said, I'm not gonna answer any more questions about that." The NBA fined him $7,500 for failing to leave the court in a timely manner.

Barkley and the refs. It's part of the entertainment. Part of the show. Will Sir Charles behave tonight? Or will he lose his temper and his senses and go spinning off the track like an Indy car that hits an oil slick at 230 mph?

Fact is, Barkley rarely loses control. Usually when he receives a technical foul he has asked for it. He knows what he can say and do and get away with. Sometimes he pushes it to the limit.

"You're a pussy," he told a referee one night. Barkley already had received one technical foul. The official elaborately ignored him. "Did you hear me?" Barkley stared at the ref. "I just called you a pussy." Hands on his hips, Barkley cocked his head, as if to say, "What do you think about that?" The official didn't want to blow his whistle again. The fans had paid to watch Charles Barkley, superstar. Two technical fouls is an automatic ejection. The referee wasn't likely to kick him out of the game and Barkley knew it.

"Charles straddles the fence. He plays with matches," Kevin Johnson said. "He always knows what he's doing. He rarely lets his emotions get the best of him and cause him to do something he doesn't want to do. That to me is rare. That means, that within him, he's got a certain rudder. Something that slows things down. He's always able to process it and then react like no one I've ever seen."

Barkley crossed the line, once, in his first season with the Suns. He selected Madison Square Garden and a Martin Luther King, Jr., holiday crowd as the site and audience for one of his most theatrical performances. After the Suns' 106–103 loss to the Knicks, Barkley confronted the officiating crew of Joe Forte, Dan Crawford and Jimmy Clark.

"I told them they called a bad game, and they did," Barkley said.

At that point, Barkley said Clark told him, "That's going to cost you money," of which Barkley has plenty.

As the crew left the court, Barkley vaulted over the scorer's table, scattering chairs and knocking out power to a computer. He could have hurt someone, namely himself. Barkley tripped and fell, got up and pursued Clark down the runway toward the locker room, like a Doberman chasing a postman down the street. Cotton Fitzsimmons, who has seen it all, or nearly all, watched with fascination. The former Suns coach made a career sparring with officials. But Fitzsimmons never jumped over the scorer's table. "No," Cotton said, "but one time when I was coaching Buffalo (1978) I got thrown out of a game in New Orleans. Marvin Barnes carried me off the court on his hip, like a sack of potatoes. I went kicking and screaming all the way."

Paul Westphal acted as Barkley's defense attorney. "I don't know what he did that was so terrible, other than he wasn't very graceful going over the table."

But the New York media roasted Barkley. *New York Post* columnist Mark Kriegel wrote that he should be suspended without pay for two weeks and called him a "lunatic force of nature." George Vecsey of *The New York Times* described the incident as "a grubby way to end a day, any day," and said the NBA had no option but to suspend Barkley. The league did, for one game without pay, and fined him $10,000.

Barkley has his favorite referees. He likes Jake O'Donnell. He likes Crawford. He counts several as friends. "Here," Barkley said after a game, handing a ball boy a pair of his shoes, which Barkley autographed. "Take these to Jess." Jess is Jess Kersey, a veteran NBA ref.

One day the clubhouse conversation turned to officiating. "I can't believe that the NFL had instant replay and they gave it up," Danny Ainge said. "I say the less control the officials can have, the better."

"It's an ego thing," Barkley said. "The game is so fast for them they're gonna make mistakes. I can understand why they don't want instant replay."

"Is the officiating in the NBA better than in the NFL?" I asked.

"No," Barkley said. "It's bad. And it's gotten worse. They've gotten so powerful. You can't talk to them. If you say anything out of the way they curse you out."

"With three officials you get three different games," Ainge said.

"If you're at home," Barkley said, "and you've got a rowdy crowd and you make a run, the officials just go with you. That's why it's so hard to win on the road."

"You said officials curse players?"

"When I first got into the league a guy would say, 'Hey, I blew that one.' Now if you say something back to them they'll tell you to fuck off. Then you say something bad to them and they give you a 'T.' Most of them are good guys. Crawford. Jake. They just go out and do their job. You can talk to them. You can't talk to Mike Mathis."

Barkley and Mathis have a history, as they say. "It goes back a long way, and it's sad. We were in Atlanta. About six years ago. We said some things in a game to each other. And he hasn't forgotten about it. They ought to put us in a ring and let us go three rounds, for charity."

38

Nest Egg

Charles Barkley says he isn't motivated by money, but money is one of his favorite subjects. To wit:

"Baseball's a disgrace. They got guys hitting .230 today and making $3 million a year. You should reward players for playing well. I don't think you should reward players for being mediocre. But I like that arbitration thing. We need arbitration in basketball. I could meet with the arbitrator and throw out some numbers at him. That's what we should do. Tear up all the contracts in the NBA and arbitrate."

• • • •

"I wish I was young again. It disappoints me that all the young guys are making more money than the veteran guys. A guy like Larry Johnson is a proven commodity, but I don't think anybody coming in fresh off the streets should make more than I do. That's why I have a problem with the salaries of some of the rookies."

• • • •

"A lot of players now just play for the money. When I first got into the league guys didn't worry about contracts all the time. They didn't worry about who's making how much. Times have changed."

• • • •

"We teach our kids that you're not successful unless you make a lot of money. That's wrong. Doctors, teachers and policemen. Those are the people who have the important jobs."

• • • •

"The people who say money isn't the most important thing in the world, they've probably got it. You talk to people who don't have it and can't make ends meet, and they will tell you that's crap. If you don't have money you can't eat. You can't dress. You can't even have electricity. I've been poor and I've been rich and rich is a lot better."

• • • •

"I'm making $10 million this year. Around $10 million. Somewhere in that neighborhood. Good neighborhood, isn't it?"

• • • •

"I've got three years left on my contract, that I won't be able to collect if I retire. I won't be able to collect it because I tore my body up."

• • • •

"I'm making $10 million a year. If you live to be a hundred, you'll never make as much as what I make in one year. I'm happy with where I'm at. I'm not mad at anybody who makes more than me. I'm just trying to get my little egg. A basket of 'em."

• • • •

"Taxing rich people isn't going to hurt them. Let's don't kid ourselves. They'll just start laying people off. If you're in the 50 percent tax bracket, you're making some big money."

• • • •

"Fifty dollars? Oliver, I ain't betting no $50 dollars. Where I go, $50 won't get you a beer and a Caesar salad."

• • • •

"I don't see anything wrong with having money, if you earn it. There are 50 guys making more money than me. I know something is wrong with the salary cap. I go lower down the list every year. But I don't worry about money at this stage in my career, because I've got so much of it. But if I didn't, I'd be bitching every day."

39

Flies

NOTICE
Team dressing rooms must be opened to the media up to 45 minutes before the start of a game and no later than 10 minutes after a game.
    —David J. Stern, Commissioner, National Basketball Association

April 16, 1994

After the fast-finishing Suns beat David Robinson and the San Antonio Spurs in a 96-94 thriller in the Alamodome, NBC announcer Dan Hicks stood with the star of the game at courtside. "Charles, all year long your team has been a little bit inconsistent here and there. The local media in Phoenix has certainly let you know about that. But is this team really ready, finally, to be consistent, game in and game out?"

"Number one," Barkley began. Barkley often prefaces a remark by saying "First of all . . ." or "Number one . . ." when there is no "Secondly . . ." or "Number two . . ."

"As far as the media is concerned, they're assholes."

Barkley said the word on national TV.

He was in a sour mood. Barkley felt the media had been unfairly critical of the Suns after losses to Portland and the Sacramento Kings. In the locker room, after the Spurs game, Barkley groused about the negative reporting, which he does from time to time.

Barkley shares the view held by many coaches and athletes. The media is not qualified to judge or criticize an athlete's performance. "You may think you know what we go through," he once said, "but you don't. You don't have a clue."

Barkley's favorite synonym for the media begins with the letter *a*. He has several others. In his first season with the Suns, Barkley strolled into the locker room before the NBA All-Star Game in Salt

Lake City. "Hey, Paul," he shouted at Westphal, who was the coach of the Western Conference team. "GET THESE FLIES OUT OF HERE!" I checked the tray of cold cuts and fruit on a table nearby. No flies there. I looked around the room. Other than Barkley's teammates, there were two reporters in the clubhouse, and I was one of them. He was talking about me.

Barkley can be insulting, but most reporters who know him aren't offended. If anything, they are mildly amused. A sampling of his brand of humor:

"One day I'll be like you, old and useless."

• • • •

"How do I feel? I feel as bad as you look. I'm on my deathbed."

• • • •

"Unless you're a policeman, a doctor or a fireman, your life is cake. You guys are way down on the totem pole. You're right down there with TV evangelists."

• • • •

"Charles," a reporter asked, tossing Barkley a straight line, "what would you do if you retired?"

"If push came to shove," he said, "I could lose all self-respect and become a reporter."

• • • •

"You guys need to chill out and take a Valium."

• • • •

"You guys think too much. This ain't brain surgery."

• • • •

"You guys have no life."

• • • •

"The Philadelphia media could make Jesus Christ out to be bad. Like that deal at Stixx. Where they said I hit a guy. In Philadelphia, I'd already be convicted of murder."

• • • •

"Chris Webber's a star. Shaquille's a star. Shawn Kemp's a star. You guys make everybody a star. It pisses me off. . . . If you guys write that the world is flat, half the people would believe it by the end of the week."

• • • •

"A lot of people can do your job. I can count on one hand the people who can do my job." Barkley made a fist. "Come to think of it, there may not be *anybody* else."

• • • •

One night Barkley got into a playful discussion with reporters about how he has been treated by the media during his career.

Barkley contended that the press has unfairly portrayed him as a villain. "I'm not as bad as the media makes me out to be."

"Charles, you get great press," someone said.

Barkley disagreed. A reporter with an accent asked a question. "What country you from?" Barkley asked.

"France."

"They don't like me either," Barkley said.

"Charles, in France, they don't like anybody who's American. Except Jerry Lewis."

Everyone laughed.

The media is his audience. In Chicago, during the 1993 NBA Finals, Barkley was holding court at his cubicle when a cockroach scurried across the concrete floor toward his chair. "Damn, I'm back in Alabama!" he shouted. As reporters laughed and stepped back, Barkley stomped the roach with the sole of his polished dress shoe.

Barkley fell into a silent study of the reporters' footwear. Sam Smith of the *Chicago Tribune*, whom Barkley has known for years, was wearing round-toed saddle oxfords. "Ball boy! Hey, ball boy!" Summoning the youth, Barkley stood and draped an arm around the kid's shoulder, and pointed with a grin at Smith's shoes. "Son," Barkley announced, "you should be wearin' those, not that 50-year old man."

During Game 3 of the 1993 Suns-Lakers playoff series, a game the Suns had to win, Bob Young of *The Republic* sat at a courtside table behind the baseline in the Forum, head down, pounding out a story, deadline perched on his shoulder like a malevolent bird.

"Bob! Hey, Bob!" a voice called out.

Young kept typing, nose to the keyboard, fingers flying.

"BOB! BOB!"

A photographer seated beneath the basket turned and tapped Young on the arm. "Are you Bob?" he asked. When Young looked up and nodded, the photographer pointed toward the court.

Barkley was standing along the free-throw lane. "BOB, I'M TALKING TO YOU!" Barkley shouted, above the crowd noise. Charles was grinning. "Isn't this fun!"

For Barkley, half the fun of playing basketball is sparring with reporters and telling them how he won't miss them after he retires. But he will miss the exchanges, like the one he had during preseason with Yoko Narita, a Japanese reporter who was interviewing him for a feature story for a Tokyo magazine.

"How do you unwind yourself?" Yoko asked.

"I drink beer and have sex," Barkley replied.

"How many times?"

" 'Til it works."

"What will you do after you retire?"

"I have a lot of business opportunities."

"Will you miss basketball too much?" Yoko asked.

"You've got to give it up sometime."

"What is your best golf score?"

"I shot 80 a couple of times."

"How long you been playing?"

"Four years."

"That's very good."

"You're right," Barkley said.

Yoko asked Barkley about his Japanese TV commercial for instant noodles. "Do you have the noodles at your house?" Yoko asked.

"No."

"You don't eat them?"

"I didn't say that."

"Yes, but if you don't . . ."

"You asked me if had the noodles at my house. You didn't ask if I ate them. It's two different things."

"But . . ."

"You're turning it around. You didn't ask if I ate the noodles. It's two different things. I didn't say I don't eat them." Barkley scowled, but his eyes were smiling.

"Where you from?" he asked. "Philadelphia?"

40

In This Corner...

"**W**hat are you looking at, boy?"

Malcolm Mackey was staring.

"Do you want a shot at the title?" Charles Barkley looked at the Suns rookie the way prizefighters glare at one another as they stand face-to-poker-face, unblinking, in the center of the ring before the opening bell.

When Mackey didn't reply, Barkley lost interest and turned away. "I didn't think so."

He is the heavyweight champion of basketball, or that's how he likes to think of himself. On the court, when he puts in his mouth-piece and goes to work, he displays a fighter's mentality and temperament. He even looks the part. Norm Frauenheim, who covers boxing for *The Arizona Republic*, described the Suns forward as having Marvin Hagler's haircut, Joe Frazier's body and Muhammad Ali's mouth.

"Boxing is my favorite sport to watch," Barkley said. He ticked off the names of fighters he has seen in the ring. Mike Tyson. Larry Holmes. Carl "The Truth" Williams. Buster Douglas. "What's great about boxing is that a man can control his own destiny. He doesn't have to worry about teammates. If you have great talent and work hard you're going to be successful."

Barkley sat near ringside at the Nov. 6, 1993, heavyweight title fight between Evander Holyfield and Riddick Bowe. That night in Las Vegas a paraglider dropped out of the desert sky. It was like Red Buttons parachuting into the French village in the war movie *The Longest Day*. The intruder crashed into the ring ropes and tumbled backward onto the floor. Several ringsiders began punching him. One of Bowe's bodyguards clubbed the paraglider with a walkie-talkie. Barkley was unsympathetic. He thought the guy got what he deserved. The fellow is fortunate he didn't land in Barkley's lap.

"If a guy makes a move on you, you gotta hit him," Barkley said, stating Barkley's Law. Not surprisingly, Barkley defended Buddy Ryan after Ryan threw a punch at a fellow Houston Oiler assistant coach during an NFL game last season. Barkley said Kevin Gilbride provoked Ryan, and Buddy was within his rights to retaliate.

Barkley sees similarities between boxing and basketball, the way he plays it. "I don't really want to fight, but I'll push the intimidation to the limit, basketball-wise. Competition is about the will to win. That's why I love Joe Frazier. I always looked up to him as an overachiever. Bang. Bang. Bang. That's the way I play. I play basketball the way Joe Frazier boxed. He never quit."

On April 14, two weeks before the Suns began their playoff drive, Barkley made his ring debut in a one-round bout against Michael Carbajal, the 5-foot-5, 112-pound former IBF/WBC Junior flyweight world champion.

The event, which raised $60,000 for Carbajal's 9th Street Gym, was billed as "An Evening of Boxing," but this wasn't a typical Phoenix fight crowd. Mercedes, Cadillacs, Rolls Royces and stretch limos lined up outside the front entrance of the Ritz Carlton Hotel.

This was a black-tie event—$350 a plate. At the pre-fight cocktail party, waiters in white gloves served champagne and pâté. The four-course meal was hardly Golden Gloves fare: grilled Maine lobster with citrus saffron sauce, salad of haricots verts, crème fraîche with toasted almonds and pimientos, followed by the entree, an extra-thick grilled veal chop with roast baby artichokes. For dessert, a chocolate mascarpone cake with mocha sauce.

The 400 guests, which included Arizona Gov. Fife Symington, dined by candlelight in the hotel ballroom, where a boxing ring had been erected. The evening's entertainment included three sanctioned professional fights, featuring boxers with colorful names. Luis "Lethal Weapon" Rodriguez. Martin "Cobra" Ulloa. But the tuxedo crowd had come to watch Carbajal "box" one round each with Suns guard Dan Majerle and Sir Charles.

Jerry Colangelo, who sat near ringside, had only one concern, and the Suns president voiced it to his good friend Jimmy Walker, a local insurance executive who organized the event. "Jimmy," Colangelo playfully warned, "no one better get hurt."

There was little chance of that. Two leggy card girls paraded into the ballroom carrying serving trays. On each was a pair of gold Ever-last boxing gloves the size of pillows. Carbajal slipped them on. The gloves covered his elbows.

As Carbajal warmed up against Majerle, Barkley strolled into the dressing room, wisecracking as he often does before a big game. "I don't know why everybody keeps wishing me good luck," he said. "The guy weighs a hundred pounds!" His robe, with "SIR CHARLES" printed on the back, lay on a table, with his trunks. He picked up the trunks. Red, white and blue-striped and spangled with stars, they looked like the shorts Apollo Creed, the bombastic champion, wore in *Rocky.* "Isn't there supposed to be a cup, or a jock—something?" He looked around the room. "I need a big cup. Extra, extra large!"

After Carbajal and Majerle battled to a draw, Suns broadcaster Al McCoy, mike in hand, introduced the next challenger, who needed no introduction. "From Alabama . . . NOT making his first fight . . ." — the room howled— "Sir. . . CHARLES . . . BAAAAARK-LEY!"

The hood of his red satin robe covered his shaved head, but it couldn't conceal his grin as he entered the darkened ballroom, illuminated in a cone of light. Led by his "manager," Louis Gossett, Jr.,—Barkley placed his hands on the actor's shoulders, the way boxers do—Sir Charles made his way to the ring. He climbed through the padded ropes, washed in cheers.

Barkley bounced lightly on his toes, and scowled at his diminutive opponent. Carbajal, pound for pound one of the toughest fighters in the game, laughed as Barkley disrobed and did the Ali Shuffle. The crowd loved it.

Oliver Miller, the Suns center and the celebrity card's referee, called the fighters together. "No blows to the head," Miller warned Carbajal. Both looked at Barkley's shiny dome. Miller said, "It already looks bad enough."

Boxing is theater. Anything goes. Nothing is too silly. Muhammad Ali once stepped into the ring against a Japanese wrestler, Antonio Inoki. What transpired that night was one of the strangest sights in boxing history. When the bell rang, Mr. Inoki threw himself to the canvas and scooted around the ring on his rump, lashing out at Ali with wicked karate kicks. This went on for 15 rounds, with Inoki scrambling in circles like a crazed crab and Ali dancing and mugging, climbing the ropes, and occasionally kicking back. The bout ended in a draw. Houston sportswriter Mickey Herskowitz, who witnessed the spectacle on closed-circuit television at the Astrodome, suggested the decision couldn't have been more fair, or more poetic, unless they had put both fighters in jail.

The list of basketball players who have gone on to enjoy successful careers as boxers is a short one. Only one basketball star who had pugilistic ambitions comes to mind. Wilt Chamberlain once talked about fighting Ali, for real. The bout never took place. Wilt the Stilt arrived at a New York television studio, where he was to be interviewed by Howard Cosell. When Ali saw the 7-foot-2 Goliath, his eyes grew wide. *"Tiiiimmmmm-berrrr!"* Ali cried. Unamused, Chamberlain turned and walked out.

Barkley gave the crowd a show. At the clang of the bell, he ran across the ring and pinned Carbajal against the ropes, his powder-puff gloves flailing. Carbajal shed his giant gloves and held up his fists, exposing real gloves, the blood-red, 8-ounce tools of his trade. Barkley backed up, as if he had seen a rattlesnake.

Midway through the round, a white towel floated into the ring. The fighters ignored it. They clowned around, alternately laughing and punching, until the bell sounded. Miller stepped to the center of the ring and motioned the two fighters to his side.

"Judge What's-his-name scores it, 10–9," Miller announced.

"Judge Whoever-he-is scores it, 10–9.

"Judge I-forget-his-name scores it 10–9. The winner, by unanimous decision, Michael Carbajal!"

Charles Barkley, who said, "I'd fight my mother for the right price" but did this for fun, because it was for a good cause and because he is Charles Barkley, shook his head.

"Typical NBA officiating!" he told the referee.

41

Animal House

Charles Barkley pointed to the floor. "Look at that."

Like a scolded child, Malcolm Mackey gazed at the scraps of adhesive tape he had cut from his ankles and left on the clubhouse carpet.

Here it comes, Mackey thought. *The how long lecture.* "Mackey, let me ask you a question. How long would it take you to walk over and put that in the trash?" Barkley was pointing again, his voice growing louder. *Two seconds.* "It would take two seconds. You're just like Oliver. You just throw stuff everywhere."

Barkley shook his head and heaved a world-weary sigh. "I'M LIVING WITH ANIMALS!!"

Besides scoring and rebounding and selling Nike shoes, Barkley believes his obligation to society, his duty in life, is to impress upon Mackey and Oliver Miller and anyone else within the sound of his voice the importance of Picking Up After Themselves. Barkley believes cleanliness is next to godliness. Those who don't, in his view, have a serious character flaw.

Barkley can find it in his heart to forgive a player who misses free throws, or doesn't help out on defense or complains about not getting enough playing time. But he has no patience with teammates whose personal habits he equates with those of animals in a zoo. Tape or wet towels strewn on the clubhouse floor set him off. "How can anyone *live* like that!? . . ."

"I like to keep the place neat," said Rich Howell, the Suns equipment manager and owner Jerry Colangelo's son-in-law. "If Mr. Colangelo comes in, I don't want the place to look like . . ." Howell paused, searching for a description.

"A fraternity house?" I suggested.

"Yeah."

Howell, whose nickname is "Thurston" after Thurston Howell III, the millionaire in the TV series "Gilligan's Island," would award Barkley the *Good Housekeeping* Seal of Approval, if he had one to give. "If Charlie is the last one left in the locker room, he'll walk around picking up towels for me. Empty cans. You wouldn't think a guy like that would bother."

Barkley's habits are ingrained. "I taught our kids that whatever you had, you took care of," said his mother, Charcey Glenn. "I taught them to wash and clean and cook for themselves. It's important to learn how to do those things. When Charles was growing up, he cleaned our house as good as I can. He washed. He mopped. He would wax the linoleum floors. They were so shiny you could see yourself."

Barkley said, "It didn't make sense that my mother had to clean other people's houses all day and then come home and clean our house. So I told her, 'Mama, the house will always be clean. Except for the dishes.' I hated to do dishes. One of the first things I bought when I got to be a millionaire was a dishwasher."

Barkley passed the laundry detergent test during his freshman year at Auburn. "I thought when Charles went off to school there's no telling how his clothes would look," his mother recalled. She had this mental image of her son haphazardly tossing white and colored garments into the wash together, even though he knew better. "Charles came home, and I want you to know his white clothes were just as white as when he went down there. My other sons, they were taught the same way. But they throw underwear in with the other clothes. Not Charles. No, no, no, no, no. He's just like me. My mother used to get after me and say I was the washing-est person in the world. I can't stand dirty clothes in the hamper." Neither can her son.

Barkley's home in Paradise Valley, a fashionable Phoenix suburb, is spotless. "Charles is very neat," said his wife, Maureen. "I am, too. He has rubbed off on me." A poor sleeper, Barkley might be up at 2 A.M. wiping a refrigerator shelf or cleaning the bathroom glass. He cannot abide fingerprints on mirrors.

"Everything is perfect in my closet," Barkley said.

"How about your clothes drawers?" I asked.

"Of course," Barkley said.

"Socks?"

Barkley nodded. "All rolled up in little balls."

Leon Wood and Barkley roomed together as NBA rookies. Wood was Oscar Madison; Barkley, Felix Unger. "If you come into a room it takes two seconds to take your shoes off and put them together against the wall," Barkley said. "Leon didn't care. He'd walk in and just kick them across the room. Every time I came in one of his shoes would be over here, and another one would be over there. I'd tell him, 'Leon, when you take your shoes off it's just as easy to put them together against the wall.' He wouldn't do it. We were together a week, and we fought every day."

In Philadelphia, Barkley took in new players, like stray pets. "Back East, if you got an apartment, you had to sign a 12-month lease. So

I'd let guys who I didn't think would make the team move in for a while. Those were the good old days. Used to be, veterans made all the money and the rookies didn't make anything. Now the rookies make all the money and the veterans don't make any."

Players would stay for a week. A week became a month. "We never talked about this before we got married," Maureen said. "It was never planned that they would stay for as long as they did. Charles is not one to speak up, even though he acts like he is Mister Bad Guy. He doesn't want a confrontation. I didn't want to hurt their feelings, either. But after a while I was like, 'You guys need to go. You've been here six weeks. C'mon. You can find an apartment.' We don't get much privacy as it is."

Scott Brooks of the Houston Rockets was one of his boarders. The 5-foot-11 guard, who claims to be the only college athlete who was both a Horned Frog (Texas Christian) and an Anteater (University of California at Irvine), lived a month with the Barkleys, rent free. To hear Brooks describe his stay, it was like living in a hotel. Each day he returned from practice to find his bed made. His dirty towels had been replaced with clean ones, neatly folded. Barkley did everything but leave Brooks a mint on his pillow at night.

"You could eat off the floors," Brooks said. "If I'd leave clothes on the floor he'd get upset. I'd tell him, 'Charles, give me a break. I'm living out of a suitcase.' He said that was no excuse. You should have seen the refrigerator. It was spotless. You know how when you spill a drop of punch on the refrigerator shelf? Me, I'd just leave it there. Like a normal person. Not Charles. He'd rather be late for practice than leave a messy house.

"He would make a great maid."

42

Higher Education

All men by nature desire knowledge.
—Aristotle

We were swapping stories about snap courses in college. Bob Cohn, a sportswriter at *The Arizona Republic,* said when he attended George Washington University he took a full-credit course titled, "History of the Movie Musical." "All we did was watch Fred Astaire and Ginger Rogers movies," Cohn said, "and write one paper."

I recall reading about a course offered at the University of Oklahoma called "Communications 2010: Apprehension Reduction." Students lay on the floor of a darkened classroom and learn to relax through mental imagery. Indiana University offers, or did at one time, "Geology 103: Earth Science—Materials and Processes." Also known as "Rocks for Jocks."

Bob Young, the Suns beat writer, piped up. "When I was at Arizona State I took a human sexuality course."

"Charles, how about you?" I asked. "What was your major?"

"Music Appreciation," Barkley lied. He leaned back in his chair, grinning. "It was great. I went to this class and they played music. After class I told the teacher, 'I *appreciate* that!' I got an A."

Barkley makes light of his educational experience at Auburn. Asked why he didn't stay in school and get his degree, he joked, "I had to leave after three years. We were over the salary cap." He left college after his junior season to play in the NBA and doesn't regret the decision.

Barkley knows some people will see him as being hypocritical for encouraging young people to stay in school, when he quit college. Nevertheless, he preaches the sermon of reality at every opportunity.

"Hey, I love you guys," Barkley will tell kids who attend his summer basketball camp. "Let's be positive a second. Then let's be realistic. There are 800 of you here. Say 300 of you make it to the NBA. That's every job in the NBA. You get all of them. That means 500 of you still have to go out and find work somewhere else. But 300 of you aren't going to make it. Because I've got one of those jobs. Karl Malone's got one. Kevin Johnson's got one. You need to get an education . . ."

"I hate it," Barkley said, "when I meet parents and they say, 'My kid's gonna be playing against you someday.' First of all, they don't know that. Second, they shouldn't be telling their kids that. They should be telling them to make good grades, in case something happens. Even if your son's a great player he could tear up his knee tomorrow. And even if he does make it he can only play basketball X number of years. You're still going to have a majority of your life to live."

In 1989, the NBA and the NBA Players Association created the Stay in School program to address the nation's critical high school dropout problem. All 27 NBA teams participate. Hall of Famer Bob Lanier, the national chairman of the program, has visited more than 500 schools nationwide. In his speeches, Lanier challenges kids to take PRIDE in themselves: P for Positive mental attitude; R for Respect; I for Intelligent choice making; D for Dreaming dreams and goal setting; and E for Effort in education.

Each year as part of the All-Star weekend, students in the host city who meet goals of attitude, attendance and achievement during the fall semester are invited to attend the "NBA All-Star Stay in School CELEBRATION." Celebrities, entertainers and NBA players attend.

Barkley says the NBA doesn't do nearly enough. "I don't think you can have one public gathering once a year for kids who do well in school. The kids just want to come and meet the celebrities.

"Just saying 'Stay in School' doesn't mean anything. Stay in school for what? You're going to be poor all your life, but stay in school and get your high school diploma and spend the rest of your life in the ghetto because you can't afford to go to college? That's what it means to me. You've got to give them opportunities. You've got to give money.

"We have so much money at our disposal. When we had our players association meeting, it was mind-boggling the dollar figures that were thrown around. You got $125 million per expansion team that the owners get to divide. The licensing is a $3.8 billion business and the players don't get any of that. There's something fundamentally wrong with the system.

"People say athletes make so much money. Number one, they should make it because they are creating the money. They're not selling posters of the owners. My picture is part of a bonanza. The players should get that money. But if they don't, it should go into some kind of scholarship fund.

"I was watching "Geraldo." There were all these gang members on there. They said they had no other choice than to steal or kill or whatever. Geraldo said, 'I was born poor and I'm from the ghetto.' And this girl said, 'Yeah, but you're one in a thousand and I don't think I'm that one in a thousand.' For every Geraldo there are 999 kids who have no shot because they are uneducated by the system and, even if they do make good grades, they are not lucky enough to get a scholarship. A lot of kids want to go to school but they can't afford it. If it wasn't for basketball, I couldn't have gone to college.

"The NBA should make every team give X number of dollars a year to kids so they can get scholarships. If you're an NBA player and you are making over $500,000, you should have to give one kid a scholarship during your career. If you make over a million, you give a kid a scholarship every year.

"I think the NBA is hypocritical. When we are on NBC the league puts those 'Stay In School' signs on the backs of the seats. Why don't they have them on there every game?"

43

A Great Day

April 26, 1994

JOHANNESBURG, South Africa (AP)—Black South Africans made history Tuesday, voting by the tens of thousands to take control of their country for the first time since whites arrived 342 years ago.

Refusing to be cowed by a wave of deadly bombings, the elderly and infirm came in droves from squatter settlements and thatched villages to mark a simple cross on a piece of paper. Some literally crawled and others were pushed to the polls in wheelbarrows. Many broke down in tears after making their mark.

"This is like Christmas," said homemaker Charlotte Jerom, 52, a black voting for the first time. "We finally feel like human beings. We are free. We are free!"

"**F**rank, this is a great day. A great day! They're letting people in South Africa vote for the first time. This is one of the greatest days in my life."

Frank Johnson, who was shaving the back of his teammate's head, ignores about half of Barkley's pronouncements, but Johnson was in a playful mood and felt like sparring. "Chuck," he replied, "you can bullshit with the best of them. You know that?"

"That's typical of you, Frank," Barkley shot back. "You don't care about the rest of the world. I was watching this documentary on TV last night and . . ."

"Oh, get outta here."

"See," Barkley announced, his voice rising, filling the clubhouse. "That's typical of the black man, not concerned about other black people. Frank, they had this documentary on last night and it said that 75 percent of the people over there are black and they don't even get to vote because of the apartheid system. They had these white people on there—and I really felt bad for them—they took them to meet black people for the first time. These white people started crying when they saw how bad they treated black people there. It was unbelievable."

Mark West walked by.

"Daddy, they're lettin' people vote in South Africa today! It's a great day."

"A new day," West said.

"See, Frank," Barkley said in a lecturing tone. "Daddy knows about that. Me and Daddy worry about things like that. Frank don't care about nothing."

Johnson rolled his eyes. "Yeah, right."

"Hey, Daddy. Did you see "Nightline" last night? When they took those white people to see black people for the first time. Aw, man . . ."

"Chuck," Johnson said, clippers in hand. "Keep your head still."

"Frank," Barkley said, "these people had never seen black people before. They lived in these little tin sheds. Hundreds of them. Out in the middle of a field. It's just a great day. A great day."

"You need some new clippers. You make all this money and you got the cheapest clippers around."

"Just do your job," Barkley said. "Or we're gonna waive you. You ain't gonna get no playoff cut."

"I can do this after retirement," Johnson said, determined to have the last word, and, for once, getting it. "You can make a lot of money cutting Charles Barkley's hair."

44

Well Heeled

Charles Barkley strolled into the Suns clubhouse, as bouncy as Br'er Rabbit, that sassy, long-eared character in the children's storybook. "Gonna be fun," he announced, in full voice. The message: *Relax. Lighten up. Enjoy.* "Everybody don't get invited to the big dance. Only 16 teams. Ain't *no* better place to be than the playoffs!"

A new season, the second season, the only season that matters. For the past couple weeks, as time crept by, Barkley said, over and over, like a broken record, "I just want to get the regular season over . . ." He lives for the playoffs, and now, at last, they were almost here. Phoenix vs. Golden State. Barkley was excited, anxious, wound up, recharged, eager to get started.

He glanced at the clock.

Six thirty-five.

"We *still* got an hour to go?"

Barkley unbuttoned his shirt. A religious pendant, the likeness of the face of Jesus, His forehead ringed by a crown of thorns, hung from the chain around his neck. Barkley unclasped the chain and put it away. Dr. Danny Ainge, wearing a stethoscope, rushed up to Barkley and placed the instrument against his teammate's chest. "That's one thing," Barkley told Ainge, "you don't have to worry about."

Six-forty P.M. Barkley removed a pair of size 16 sneakers from his top shelf.

"Hey, Ced!"

Cedric Ceballos looked up.

Grinning, Barkley held out the black footwear as if to say "See what I got?" and called out in a sing-song voice, "It's t-i-m-e!"

Barkley was breaking out his new line of basketball shoes. He had been waiting for the playoffs to unveil them. The new model sounds like something that would carry a nuclear warhead. Nike Air Max^2 CB. Ceballos could look at them. He could hold them. Barkley might even autograph a pair and give them to him as a keepsake. But wear them? Barkley shook his head. "Nobody wears these bad boys except me."

Ceballos has played in almost every other sneaker made. "Nike, adidas, Puma . . ." Ceballos ticked off the manufacturers. The Suns forward, who has had foot problems, wore five brands of athletic shoes and 23 different models during the season, which may be a record. Ceballos is the Imelda Marcos of the NBA.

Times change. When Paul Westphal joined the Boston Celtics in 1972, NBA players wore adidas or Converse. "White or black," Westphal recalled. "And the Celtics took one choice away. We wore black, so they didn't have to wash them. My rookie year, I was glad to get a free pair. Saved me $20. At the end of my fourth year, when I played for the Suns, guys from Nike came to our hotel. I had never heard of Nike. They said, 'C'mon down to our room and we'll make a mold of your foot and make you some shoes, plus we'll pay you to wear them.' That was an offer I couldn't refuse. It was the first time I'd heard of making decent money for wearing shoes."

Back then, shoes were simply shoes. Asked to describe Barkley's new footwear, and the changes made to improve them, Peter Ruppe, Nike's basketball business director, sounded like a NASA engineer. He talked about "air technology" and "high- and low-pressure chambers" and "gas molecules" and "pounds per square inch."

Barkley was sitting in front of the Suns' big-screen TV one day—he will watch almost any sport, except drag racing—when someone asked about his new Nikes. What was so special about them? "I can't describe it. I gotta show you." Barkley put down a plate of barbecue ribs and walked to his locker, as 20 reporters followed. Shoe in hand, he pointed out the new advanced eyelet-locking lacing system, and other high-tech features.

Ric Bucher of the *San Jose Mercury News* was impressed. "Nike did that especially for you?" he asked.

"I'm pretty large, little fella," Barkley reminded. "They'll do *anything* for me."

Colleen Doerrhoefer and her sister, Barbara, had finished their workout out at the Phoenix Suns Athletic Club, which is adjacent to America West Arena. Colleen was standing at the front desk. When she turned around, there was Charles Barkley.

"Hey, you have my shoes on," she said.

Barkley looked at his feet. "You have these shoes?" he asked.

Colleen is a mother of three. "All my kids have them, too. *Several* pair. Thanks a lot for coming out with the new ones," she said facetiously. "What kind of car did I help buy you?"

"A Mercedes 600 SL."

"You're welcome," Colleen said.

"Wanna go for a ride?" Barkley asked suddenly. He loves to surprise people.

Colleen blinked.

"C'mon, let's take a ride."

"Oh, no, no." The woman laughed and shook her head.

"Let's go," Barkley said.

"No. Really. No, I couldn't . . ."

Barbara gave her sister a nudge. "Colleen, go ON!"

Barkley began walking toward the door. He glanced over his shoulder. "You coming or not?"

A ride. Around town. With Charles Barkley. He dropped the top on the black convertible, and mashed the accelerator. As they sped away, the wind blowing through her hair, she laughed to herself and thought, "The kids will *never* believe this . . ."

45

The Genie

His shaved head gleams in the light. His arched eyebrows are so black, so pronounced, they look as if they were penciled by a cartoonist's hand.

He looks like . . .

"The Genie." Casey, our 7-year-old, pointed a small finger at the picture in the storybook. In the wonder of a child's eyes, there is a resemblance. Dress Barkley in silk harem pants and he could be that friendly apparition who magically appears in a cloud of smoke from the spout of Aladdin's lamp.

The Suns made a wish for Game 1 of the playoffs. They wished for Charles Barkley. Not the guy with the bad back, but the man who led them to the NBA Finals the year before, the player known for his remarkable ability to elevate his game in big games and carry his team.

Their wish was his command.

Barkley scored 18 points and grabbed 11 rebounds—in the first *quarter.* Playing like he was 21, the age of Warriors rookie Chris Webber, Barkley scored 36 points and had 19 boards in the Suns' 111-104 victory. Webber couldn't guard him. Neither could Chris Gatling, Byron Houston or Jeff Grayer. The Suns had seen him play like this before, but this was something special. Unexpected. Almost magical.

"Surprise me? It did surprise me, to be honest," Danny Ainge said. "I was just amazed. Charles was so explosive. He jumped up in the air like he did last year. He bumped guys with his chest. He finished off three-point plays. He blocked a big shot. He made a big steal in transition. He sprinted back on defense. He looked like last year.

"I was jacked up just watching him. I thought, 'He *is* back! He really *can* do it. He really can walk through the regular season and turn it on.' I was hoping he could, but now I know he can. I never questioned whether he thought he could, or whether he wanted to. I just questioned whether he was able to, with the bad leg he had, and the bad back. I never questioned his heart. When you think about Charles and his career, we probably shouldn't be surprised, but I've played with a lot of great players and seen them not able to come back.

"I saw Larry (Bird) start tailing off. He wanted to do it and he found ways to win, but he couldn't still do it the way he once did. Charles did it the way he has always done it. With his raw power."

Barkley was everywhere. He did everything, his way, including making the biggest play of the game, when he tipped in Kevin Johnson's missed free throw with 16 seconds left, giving the Suns a five-point lead.

"Every time we needed a basket, he was there," KJ said. Like Ainge, the Suns point guard said he felt like a spectator. "It wouldn't have mattered which team he played on. Just to be there, on the court and to say I'm playing with one of the most unbelievable players ever to play the game. He's had big games. But this was a little bigger than a big game. He didn't do anything wrong. It was a flawless performance."

Barkley believes what separates good players from great ones isn't physical talent. One night, over Peking ravioli and orange peel chicken at P.F. Chang's in Scottsdale, Barkley talked about the mental game. "Confidence. It's *everything*," he said. "People don't have any idea how important it is. Isn't that right, Roy?"

Roy Green, a former NFL receiver, played for the Cardinals from 1979–90. He still holds team records for career receptions and total receiving yards, among others.

"There are receivers in the NFL who will have a great game," Green said. "But it's like a surprise to them. They're not sure they can do it again. They're not that confident. They doubt themselves."

I asked Ainge who is the best player he ever played with, or against. "I'd put Larry Bird number one," he said, "and close behind I'd put Charles." Ainge ticked off other names. Kevin McHale. Dennis Johnson. Kevin Johnson. Clyde Drexler.

"Charles has unbelievable confidence. No one had more confidence than Larry. I'll give you an example. Larry and I used to play 'horse' for money. One night we're playing the Knicks. Before the game Larry and I are out on the court, shooting threes. Larry is *banking* in threes. The Knicks trainer comes over and says, 'Larry, I'll bet you $10 you don't make one of those in the game tonight.' Larry told him, 'Okay, you're on.' The game was a blowout. We're up by 20 at the end of the third quarter. Our starters are sitting on the bench. Their trainer looks down to our bench during a timeout and says, 'Larry, you owe me 10 bucks.' Larry had forgotten the bet.

"In the fourth quarter, the Knicks cut it to eight. Our coach, K.C. Jones, puts all the starters back in. First possession, Larry catches the ball and banks in a three-pointer. New York calls time. Larry runs by their bench and points at their trainer. That's what I mean. That's the kind of extra confidence he had. The great players have that.

"I could tell Bird stories all day. We were in a playoff game, in Milwaukee, and the Celtics are down by two. K.C. calls a play for Kevin McHale to score. This is a big game, and we're behind and we're taking the ball out of bounds. Fourteen seconds left. I'm supposed to set a pick for McHale. Larry is supposed to dump the ball into Kevin. So Larry catches the ball in the wing and I cut through to set the pick. McHale comes into the post. Now there's eight seconds left on the clock. I look and Larry's *pump-faking*. I'm thinking, 'Oh my gosh, he's going to shoot a three!' Sidney Moncrief's guarding him, crouched down low. Larry stepped back, shot the three and we went on to win the game."

Barkley's performance was a tonic for the Suns' confidence. He erased any doubts that he might not be equal to the challenge against a young, cocky, athletic opponent. He also silenced critics. "A guy on CNN said my numbers are down this year. Well, it's kind of hard to play on one leg and a bad back. If I'm good enough to play on one leg and a bad back and finish in the top 10 in scoring and rebounding, miss 20 games and my team has one of the five best records in the league, I'll take that."

The game over, Reggie White, the All-Pro lineman with the Green Bay Packers, walked into the Suns happy clubhouse. He was looking for Barkley.

"Hey, man!" Charles called out.

White found the star of the game sitting neck-deep in the bubbling waters of the whirlpool, tending to old aches and new ones and wearing a big grin. "This is what happens," Barkley, 31, told White, 33, "when you get old."

46

Fifty-six Points

People pay to see certain guys do special stuff. That's why we get paid so much money. If they pay me $3 million a year I'm not supposed to get 12 points and 10 rebounds. I'm supposed to do something special. Make them say "Wow!"

His first shot went in. So did the second. So did the third and the fourth and the fifth. The sixth one dropped. Seventh, a three-pointer, swish. Eighth, slam dunk. Barkley from 15 feet, yes.

Another three. Oh, my. And *another!*

This wasn't happening. Was it? Floating on air, Barkley raised his arms overhead, like a football referee signaling a touchdown and cut his eyes toward the Suns bench. His teammates were on their feet, cheering, shaking their heads, writhing in laughter. Joe Kleine made a circle with his arms, as if to indicate the rim was the size of a hula hoop. Barkley was pitching pennies into a wishing well. He himself couldn't explain the first quarter—11 in a row, no misses, 27 points— although he would look back on Game 3 of the Suns-Warriors play- off series and say of his performance, one of the greatest shooting sprees in NBA history, "It was like God was letting me do it . . ."

The Warriors' Byron Houston: "You couldn't do anything. He was hitting everything he threw up." Chris Mullin felt helpless, too. "It was like 'That's a bad shot.' It went in. 'That's another bad shot.' It went in. It just kept going all night . . ."

Yes it did.

FIRST QUARTER

Time	Shot	Points	Score
11:45	18 feet	2	2-0
10:33	15 feet	4	4-7
9:48	15 feet	6	6-9
9:36	2 free throws	8	8-9
7:56	16 feet	10	10-15
7:25	18 feet	12	12-15

Time	Shot	Points	Score
5:59	15 feet	14	18-20
4:18	3-pointer	17	26-29
3:59	dunk	19	28-29
2:28	15 feet	21	32-34
2:15	3-pointer	24	35-34
1:40	3-pointer	27	8-36

SECOND QUARTER

11:19	layup	29	44-44
10:46	tip-in	31	46-46
7:22	free throw	32	54-60
3:46	2 free throws	34	66-63
1:07	layup	36	72-69
:42	15 feet	38	74-71

THIRD QUARTER

10:43	dunk	40	80-77
9:09	free throw	41	85-83
8:38	layup	43	87-85

FOURTH QUARTER

10:26	17 feet	45	114-111
9:58	16 feet	47	120-112
7:35	layup, free throw	50	124-117
5:28	15 feet	52	128-122
4:11	8 feet	54	130-124
2:08	layup	56	133-129

Fifty-six points. Barkley felt it. The ball was his oxygen, his insulin. He waved his arms, demanding it. When he drilled in a flat-trajectory jumper over Chris Gatling, the Suns star turned to the Warriors cheerleaders huddled under the basket. His grin said, "You can't stop me. Not tonight."

Rudy Tomjanovich saw the game on TV in a hotel in Portland, site of the Houston-Portland first-round series. He quit watching when Barkley reached 40 points. "I'd seen enough," the Rockets coach said. "The guy is a great player. He goes outside. He drives. He posts up. He does the dirty work and grabs it off the boards. I had my scouting report. Inside. Outside. Left side. Right side . . ."

Before they headed west for Game 3, Suns players were told to pack for a nine-day trip. If Phoenix, up 2–0, lost Game 3 and won Game 4 to advance to the Western Conference semifinals, they would go directly to Houston. Barkley brought one change of clothes.

"Amazing," Suns owner Jerry Colangelo said after the 140–133 victory, a Suns sweep. "Charles had his mind made up that he was going home."

Paul Westphal called the game "NBA basketball at its best." The halftime score—Suns 74, Warriors 73—sounded like the final of a Knicks game. "The Knicks couldn't score 100 points," Barkley said, "if you locked them in a gym all night."

Don Nelson's strategy was not to double-team Barkley. The Warriors coach stayed with that questionable game plan, to the bitter end. "Nellie thought Charles was hurt," Westphal said. "He didn't believe he could hold up the whole game. Charles gave a superhuman effort. I can't say what he did surprised me that much. It was more of a validation. It was like, 'Well, that's him. There he goes.' It was amazing, but it wasn't like I didn't think he had it in him. Some guys do that and you can't believe what you're seeing. With Charles, it was awesome, but not unbelievable."

At the post-game press conference, Nelson gave Barkley his due. "He had one of the most spectacular games I've ever witnessed, as a player or a coach."

Barkley listened from the back of the interview room.

"Hey, when does the LSD wear off?" I whispered.

Barkley shook his head.

"I was just making a lot of shots," Barkley told the media. "I think they kind of forced the issue by not doubling me. When I'm making shots from 12–15 feet my game's a lot stronger. It was a good series for us. Three tough games. The first one was rough. The second game was rougher, and the third one was the roughest of them all. We expected to win because we think we have a better team. Our goal is to win the world championship. We said that from day one. We're not going to jump around and get all excited. It's just one round down."

"Charles," a reporter asked, "how about the trash talking?"

"I don't want to get into who called me a punk the other day, but I really didn't like it that much."

"Are you insulted they didn't double you?"

"Am I insulted?" Barkley asked. "Well, I think what happened is, people got a false sense of security about my skills during the regular season. Teams didn't double me as much. If I'm healthy, teams are gonna have to double me. But I hope not. I kinda like it. I'd rather shoot the ball than pass it anyway."

It was 10:45 P.M. when he returned to the Suns locker room. His teammates had dressed and left. "What's that Hammer says? It's all good!" Barkley shouted. Someone had put a strip of adhesive tape above his locker. "CB 56 MVP."

"Man," he told the trainers. "Y'all got some work to do on my back."

"Hurt?" I asked.

"Yeah. It's real sore." Barkley winced. "I'm just glad I got a couple days off."

Fifty-six points. "It's an unbelievable feeling. When you're shooting it, and they all go in. Everybody was telling me how many points I got. Somebody said, 'You need one more. You need one more.' I didn't know what they were talking about. Somebody said I needed one more point to break some kind of record. Man, I don't care about records. I was trying to *win.*"

"You kept asking for the ball."

"Because the game wasn't over. We went three or four times when I didn't touch the ball and they scored and got back into the game. I was pissed, because I was feeling it. To say the least."

"When did you know you were on?"

"When I hit my first five or six shots. I was feeling good. It was like 'oh' 'oh' 'oh,'" Barkley said, imitating the groans by the Warriors crowd with each basket. "We knew if we could keep it close we had the advantage, because when you take a shot with the end of the season near that basket gets *small.*

"Don Nelson was giving me shots. Wasn't doubling. He made up his mind. If he wants to be stubborn, fine. When he didn't make an adjustment, I said, 'Just keep it going.' Hey, what did I tell you before the game, Train?" Barkley looked at assistant coach Lionel Hollins. "Don't hold me back. Just give it to me."

A Bay Area reporter asked, "Is this your last game here?"

"This is it."

"Any regrets?"

"Yeah," Barkley replied. "I didn't get 60."

47

Point, Counterpoint

May 14, 1994

"**C**harles, we're putting together a media playoff outing tonight. We'd like you to join us. Our treat. You'll be the guest of honor."

"Where you going?" Barkley asked.

"You like catfish?" I asked.

"I like fried catfish."

We were going to a place in Pasadena, Tex., called Sudie's (all you can eat for $8.75). Afterward, we might stop for a beverage at one of Houston's gentlemen's clubs. Judging by the newspaper ads, Houston has several hundred. According to *The Houston Chronicle*, Ms. Busty Brittany was performing at Baby Dolls. If Barkley preferred, we could take him to the Century restaurant/cabaret, which featured Miss Nude Sweden. It sounded like a once-in-a-lifetime opportunity.

"What makes you think I'd want to go to a place like that?" Barkley said. He was smiling.

Just a guess, I said.

Barkley said he didn't think he could make it but thanked us for the invitation. We agreed to postpone Barkley/Media Night until June. Either in Chicago or New York.

The Suns, barring disaster, were returning to the NBA Finals. Phoenix won the first two games of the Western Conference semifinals on Houston's home court. In the opener, the Suns rallied from an 18-point deficit, winning 91–87, before 3,000 empty seats. Rockets guard Vernon Maxwell, angered by the lack of support, called Houston fans "the worst."

Rockets management reminded that the game was played on Mother's Day. In fairness, Mother's Day probably did hurt attendance, more so than if the game had been played on, say, Lincoln's birthday or Groundhog Day. Not everyone has a groundhog, but everyone has a mother.

After Game 1, the Houston media suggested the Rockets had something lodged in their throats. After Game 2, the *Chronicle* and

The Houston Post were sure of it. CHOKE CITY, the giant headlines screamed.

Depending upon one's perspective, Game 2 was the Greatest Comeback in NBA Playoff History or an El Foldo like no other. In Houston, insurmountable lead is an oxymoron. The Houston Oilers led the Buffalo Bills, 35–3, in the third quarter of an NFL playoff game in 1992. The Oilers lost in overtime. In Game 5 of the 1980 National League championship, the Houston Astros led the Philadelphia Phillies by two runs and were six outs from going to the World Series, and Nolan Ryan, baseball's all-time strikeout king, was on the mound. The Phillies won.

In Game 2, the Rockets led by 20 points with 9:57 left. Houston scored eight points in the fourth quarter, and lost, 124–117. Joe Kleine, who was ejected in the third period after arguing two quick foul calls against him, couldn't believe what he was seeing as he watched the comeback on TV in the visitors' clubhouse.

"Were you in there by yourself?" I asked.

"Just me," Kleine said happily, "and Miller Lite."

Barkley continued to lead the Suns' playoff march, with 34 points and 15 rebounds. His three-point basket with two minutes left in overtime was the dagger in Houston's heart. Down 0–2, the Rockets looked dead as Napoleon, if not more so.

"If they don't win Game 3, it's over," Barkley said. "When you're down 3-0, you ain't coming back. You can forget it. It's gone. There ain't nothing a coach can say to you. Get down three-zip, and whatever a coach says is just rah-rah."

"But Yogi Berra said it's not over 'til it's over," I reminded.

"He's right about that," Barkley said. "But baseball is different from basketball. Baseball is the only sport where you don't run out of time."

"So, if Yogi had been in the NBA, he wouldn't have said that?"

"That's right," Barkley said. "Time would have run out on him. If Yogi had been in the NBA, we never would have heard of him. He wouldn't have made it."

Everything was falling into place for the Suns. The day before the Houston opener, Barkley and his teammates gathered around the TV in the visitors' clubhouse. Denver led Seattle with less than a minute left in overtime in Game 5 of their first-round playoff series. The No. 8 seed was beating the No. 1 seed. The Suns were hanging on every possession, every shot. They laughed. Clapped. Hoped. Prayed. Cheered—"Mutombooooo!"

This can't be happening. That's what the face of George Karl said as the Seattle coach glanced nervously at the scoreboard clock and ran his fingers through his thinning hair. Seattle's season, its home-court advantage, its dreams of an NBA championship were going, going . . .

"They're done. DONE!" Barkley shouted.

There would be no Seattle-Phoenix rematch in the Western Conference finals. Assuming the Suns took care of the Rockets, they would have the home court edge against either Denver or Utah in the conference finals, and they felt confident they could beat either team. "Seattle has been talking all year about how they are going to beat us," Barkley said. "They put all their emphasis in the regular season on getting the home court. The home court doesn't mean anything unless you protect home. I feel bad for George. He's a good guy. But when you've got all those knuckleheads on your team that's what happens.

"It's obvious they didn't have a go-to guy." Barkley described himself when he said, "You've got to have a guy who says, 'The ball is coming to me. I either score or I get us wide-open shots.' Nobody wanted to shoot the ball for Seattle."

When TV crews entered the locker room, hoping to capture the Suns' celebration, Barkley stopped them in their tracks. "HEY, YOU GUYS TURN THEM CAMERAS OFF!" Barkley didn't want to give the public the appearance the Suns were dancing on the Sonics' grave. Yes, everything was going well. Very well.

Too well.

May 15, 1994

"It's all good!" The upbeat lyrics of the song by Hammer became the Suns playoff battle cry. Before Game 4 of the Houston series, someone wrote the following on the message board in the Suns clubhouse:

IT AIN'T ALL GOOD UNLESS:
1. We go to work
2. Leave all distractions outside
3. Focus on Rockets
4. Win home playoff games!!!
5. Have no excuses

After the game, Paul Westphal stood before the media and tried to sound positive and optimistic. The Suns, after winning two on the road, had lost two at home. Rockets guard Kenny Smith put his hands to his throat after Houston's 107–96 victory as if to say, "Who's choking now?" The series was even. The big question was: What's wrong with Barkley?

"He's running like he's hurt," Carl Herrera, the Rockets forward, said. "He seemed tired at the end. He wasn't looking for the ball." Barkley missed 27 of 43 shots during the Suns' lost weekend. With three minutes left in Game 4, Barkley attempted a dunk against Hakeem Olajuwon, who Barkley called "that monster in the middle."

Monsters usually don't faze Barkley. Ask Godzilla.

In real life, Barkley went up on dead legs. Olajuwon rose up to meet him, like a bad dream. Olajuwon's block was a signature play, and an ominous one for the Suns.

"Is Barkley hurt?" Westphal was asked.

"I don't know," he told the media. "If you can get him to answer that you're a better man than I am."

"In the middle of the playoffs, you don't want to give the other team any information," Westphal said after the season. "My opinion was he was hurt. He didn't necessarily want to announce it. If the other team knows you have a bad back, they'll hit you in the back. If they know you have a sore ankle, they may not double team you as much. My feeling is that anytime Charles goes 7-for-21 in a big game there was something wrong with him. But there really wasn't a whole lot I could say. We were in the middle of a battle. Number one, I don't want to make excuses. Number two, I don't want to give the opponent anything to attack. At the same time, it was obvious to me, by his lack of effectiveness by his standards, that something was wrong."

Barkley limped off the court, head bowed. He remained in the whirlpool until his teammates dressed and left. His interrogators camped out at his cubicle.

It was like sitting in a hospital waiting room. With nothing to do but wait, reporters idly surveyed Barkley's dressing space. There were photos of his daughter. A Texas Rangers cap. A Birmingham Barons sticker, his tribute to Michael Jordan. A stack of mail. A quotation from Theodore Roosevelt about dealing with criticism. A poem by Ralph Waldo Emerson titled "Success."

To laugh often and much
To win the respect of intelligent people and affection of children
To earn the appreciation of honest critics and endure the betrayal
of false friends
To appreciate beauty
To find the best in others
To leave the world a little bit better whether by a healthy child,
a garden patch or a redeemed social condition
To know even one life has breathed easier because you have lived
This is to have succeeded.

Barkley came out of the shower. The media huddle parted as he walked to his cubicle and sat down. He was tired. His back hurt, after four rugged battles against Otis Thorpe, who is 6-10, 240. "In this business," he said, "you go from the penthouse to the outhouse in a hurry. Right now, I guess you could say I'm definitely in the outhouse. I don't really know what to say, to be honest with you."

"How are you physically?" someone asked.

"Let's don't get into that. I'm not playing well. Leave it at that. I'm not playing well right now. That's the way you have to write it."

"Tired?"

"I'm playing bad."

"Who has the advantage now?"

"I'm not sure who has the advantage. When the series started, I felt like it would be 2–2. But I'm disappointed we didn't win at least one at home. I thought everybody on our team played pretty well, except myself. I've had bad games before, but it's still frustrating. When I let other players down, that disappoints me.

"I said before, if Houston is making those threes, there's nothing you can do. You've got to double Hakeem. They're a streaky team."

"Your back is okay at this point?"

Barkley lifted his eyes and fixed them on the questioner. "I just said I'm playing bad right now, my man."

His interview over, Barkley pulled himself to his feet. He walked into the bathroom and stood at the lavatory. "You're not going to say you're hurt, are you?" I asked as he brushed his teeth.

"Would I be wrong to say you're hurt?"

Barkley glanced at me in the mirror.

He continued brushing.

May 17, 1994

When Danny Ainge arrived at The Summit before Game 5, reporters were waiting. They wanted his reaction to being fined $5,000 for beaning Houston's Mario Elie with a point-blank, baseball-type throw in the closing seconds of Game 4. Ainge didn't want to comment.

Barkley did. "Hey, Ainge! If the motherfucker celebrates on our floor, he *deserves* to get hit in the head. If he does it again, hit him in the head again."

Barkley scored 30 points. Houston won Game 5, 109–86. "If we're scared," Barkley said of Game 6, "we won't show up. We'll skip it and fly to Hawaii for the weekend." The Suns showed up and won Game 6 handily, 103–89. But Barkley played with a strained groin muscle.

Thirty-five hours until tipoff.

May 20, 1994

The morning before Game 7, Dr. Emerson gave Barkley an anti-inflammatory injection in his groin. "I've had a lot of shots but never one there," Barkley said. "I don't ever want to have another one, either."

He spent the day and night hooked up to an electronic muscle stimulator, the control panel tucked inside the waistband of his shorts. A thin wire dangled between his legs. One can imagine the jokes, but it was no laughing matter. Barkley was hurt. The only cure was rest, and Barkley felt fairly certain the Rockets wouldn't agree to postpone the game to accommodate him.

"I'll be all right by tomorrow," he said.

"How bad was it?" I asked after the season.

"I was *done* after Game 6."

48

Lion Heart

He's got what you wish all players had and hardly any of them do. He has a lion heart to compete, and to not make excuses, and to try and find a way to win over any obstacle. Charles has that. He's got that to as great a degree as anyone I've known. I wasn't going to ask him if he thought he could play. To do that would be an insult to him. He was going to play.
—Paul Westphal

May 21, 1994

The game was over. I had a column to write. . . .

HOUSTON — Blood ran from A.C. Green's scalp. Kevin Johnson, clutching his elbow, doubled over in pain.

The saddest sight of all was the image of No. 34 limping like a soldier with a bullet in his leg, dragging himself along, trying to win, trying to keep the dream alive, trying to play the game he loves and doesn't want to leave, on guts alone.

This isn't the way it is supposed to end for Charles Barkley.

Barkley has no vision of how the last chapter of his remarkable basketball career is supposed to read, but he doesn't want to say goodbye. Not like this. Asked whether he tried to reach back for something extra as the clock ticked down in the fourth quarter, the game, the series, the Suns' season on the line, Barkley said it all with simple eloquence. "I didn't have anything to reach back for. I couldn't run. I couldn't jump . . . I wanted to make something happen. I couldn't do it physically."

It's over for the Suns. Last season they played 24 playoff games and came close enough to winning their first NBA championship that they vowed this would be the year.

"We started the season with one goal," Barkley reminded his teammates as they huddled before Game 6 of the Western Conference semifinals—their final victory.

But their playoff drive ended after 10 games Saturday as the quicker, more athletic and resilient Houston Rockets, led by Hakeem Olajuwon, prevailed, 104–94.

The Suns will be back next season. But will the man whose teammates jokingly, and respectfully, call "our fearless leader"—the man who carried this team the past two years—return?

"I can honestly say I don't know," Barkley said, his painful day, his unfulfilled season, done.

He wasn't being coy. He was being honest.

It isn't easy to make the right decision with all those voices talking at the same time. His heart tells him, "Don't quit. You can still play this game." His mind says, "True, listen to your heart." Then it turns around and says, "But you've done it all. You have nothing left to prove."

His body spoke the loudest on the day the season died. Knocked to the floor, it told him, "Stay down." A fighter, he pulled himself off the canvas and fought on.

When he took a charge under the basket and ended up with Rockets rookie Sam Cassell lying between his splayed legs, his aching groin cried, "Get off. Get off." The competitor in him said, "Okay, Doc," as he received one injection in his hip and another in his groin at halftime.

If this had been a regular-season game, he probably wouldn't have played. But this was a must-win game. The winners advance and the losers go home. Barkley was determined to play, to give whatever he had. About all he had left was want-to.

He wanted to score, and he did, 24 points. He wanted to rebound, and he grabbed 15 boards. He wanted to run the court, and he tried. But it was a painful thing to watch.

More than anything else he wanted to win, and when reality set in and it became obvious the Suns weren't going to win, he shoved Olajuwon in anger and frustration, and was ejected with seven seconds left.

Will we see him again in a Suns uniform? If major surgery is the only remedy for his back, the answer is no. But Barkley is hopeful, which is his nature. So are his teammates and Paul Westphal and Jerry Colangelo, who made the trade to get Barkley.

Has it really been two years? Seems like yesterday Barkley came to Phoenix. The memory brings to mind that classic final scene from *Casablanca* where Bogart, as Rick, puts his arm around Claude Rains, the French captain, as they walk into the mist. "Louie, this could be the start of a beautiful friendship."

49

In a Boat Alone

I believe Charles Barkley loves the game. He loves the limelight.
And what this is giving him is the platform to be Charles
Barkley. That all goes away when he quits playing. I think that
is the overriding factor that brings him back, regardless of what's
out there that has to be done. My gut instinct is that he will be
back. I've seen them come and go. A lot of great ones. It doesn't
take long to be forgotten. Retirement is permanent.
—Jerry Colangelo

May 26, 1994

Five days after the Suns season ended, he sat in the stands in America West Arena. The basketball floor was gone, replaced by artificial turf. The only sound in the empty arena was the slap of pads as the Arizona Rattlers, the local Arena Football League team coached by Danny White, the former Dallas Cowboys quarterback, practiced.

Barkley watched the workout in silence, staring out at the players in the copper-colored helmets, shining like new pennies.

"So what are you going to do?" I asked.

Surgery? A rehab program? Barkley shook his head. "I dunno. I've got to prove to myself I want to go through all this stuff. It's a big commitment. It might be the biggest commitment of my life. I've always dedicated myself to basketball, because I wanted to be good at it. But after 10 years in the NBA, do I want to go try the unknown? The doctors haven't said anything to make me think if I have surgery I'll be 100 percent. They said they might be able to make me feel better, but surgery also could make me worse. I can't honestly say I want to rehab three months on my back."

"Are you afraid of going through rehab and being disappointed with the result?"

"I worry that I won't perform well," Barkley said.

"What else?"

"If we don't win the world championship next year, I won't be happy I came back, if I do. All that stuff plays into it. But the bottom line is whether I am willing to take that chance at this stage in my life. . . .This is hard for me. I feel like I'm in a boat by myself. Because most people voicing an opinion have something to gain. I understand it. My agent has something to gain. Nike has something to gain . . ."

"Jerry Colangelo," I said.

"Jerry, too. The bottom line, realistically, is the most I could play is one more year. If I come back and we don't win the world championship, I'm gonna be pissed."

"Has the window of opportunity closed?"

"I don't believe that. We'll never know, if I was healthy, whether we could have won the Houston series. Everybody says our team is bad. But I think we lost to the team that will win the world championship. That's nothing to hold your head down about."

"Who do you lean on emotionally?" I asked.

"Who do I lean on?" Barkley thought a moment. "I'm pretty selfish. I bear everything myself. There are not that many people who can give me an unbiased opinion about what I should do. Everybody in life wants something from you, not always in a selfish way. Most of the time I try to sit back and figure things out for myself."

"How about Michael?"

"Nobody can tell me what to do. I've talked to Mario Lemieux. Larry Bird. Those are the only two guys I can think of who I know have been through back surgery. None of those guys were the same after surgery. They played but they were never the same. I think you need to get the opinion of people who have been through it."

"Is Oliver a factor in your decision?"

Barkley likes Miller even though he calls him "a pain in the ass." Like himself, Miller was overweight when he came out of college. He had a high opinion of himself, as Miller does. Dan Majerle recalls the first time he met the former University of Arkansas star whom the Suns drafted in the first round, the 22nd pick overall.

"Hi, I'm Dan Majerle," Majerle said, sticking out his hand.

"Big O," Miller said, shaking it.

Miller played in every Suns playoff game as a rookie. He helped save the Suns from elimination in Game 5 of the first-round series against the Lakers with seven blocks and nine of his 17 points in overtime. He is a gifted player, very mobile for his size, with long arms and great hands. But he battled his weight all year, and a back problem limited him, as well. A restricted free agent, Miller ended the season in the Suns doghouse.

"Oliver's a factor in what I do," Barkley said. "Oliver is really important to our team, but he's at the point he has to reach his potential. It's time for him to do it, now. He wasn't as good this year as he was last year. And as our team is structured, he's got to be the starting center. If you can't put your best player at each position out there against the other team's best player you can't win."

"But does he have the self-discipline to lose the weight?"

"It's one of those things he's got to prove. I'm from Missouri. I played with a lot of guys who learned and did it, and I played with a lot of guys who didn't. At this stage in Oliver's life, his weight should not be an issue. He gets losing weight and being in shape confused. People think you lose weight you're automatically in better shape. That isn't necessarily true.

"I had to learn that my first year in the league. I went from 290 to 270. I thought I was in good shape. I was still in terrible shape. Oliver's got to produce. He's not a bad kid. That's why I'd like to see him do it. But it's frustrating when we were trying to make a run for the championship and Oliver's into it with the coaches about his weight. Being in condition to a professional athlete should never be a question. Never. I mean, not just Oliver. Anybody. If you're not in shape, you can't help your team win. It's that simple.

"Oliver rebelled against the team this year. We as a team let it run its course and went to Mark West and Joe Kleine. Oliver has got to make the decision to lose the weight himself. You know, it's kinda funny."

"What?" I asked.

"If I do decide to go through all this crap," Barkley said, "it's a little scary knowing that I'm doing it with everything riding on Oliver."

As it turned out, Barkley's concerns about Miller became irrelevant. Over the summer, the Suns traded West to Detroit for two draft choices and said goodbye to Miller after Big O signed a four-year $10 million offer sheet with the Pistons. Colangelo added free-agent forwards Danny Manning and Wayman Tisdale.

50

Maureen

It's not easy being the wife of an NBA player. A lot of guys go through divorces because their wives can't handle it. They feel like they're second fiddle. When Maureen and I are out together, people push her out of the way trying to get close to me. I told her when we got married that's just part of it. I'm the luckiest man in the world.

Maureen Barkley was packing. The season over, she and her daughter were going to fly to Alabama the next morning, to visit Charles' mother. Barkley had an appointment in L.A. with a back specialist. He would meet his family in Leeds.

"We'll be going back and forth this summer," said Maureen. Back and forth meant Phoenix, Alabama and Philadelphia, her home. They met in Philly seven years ago, at a Friday's restaurant. The Barkleys still have a townhome in the suburbs, where they lived when he played for the 76ers and where Maureen and Christiana remained during Barkley's first season with the Suns.

A tall, slender, attractive woman, Maureen curled up on the carpet of their family room and leaned back against a black sectional sofa. The sofa is where her husband spends much of his time at home, feet propped up, hand on the channel selector, watching sports and movies on their big-screen TV. Christiana sat at the bar in the kitchen, bent over her coloring book.

Did you watch the last game?

"No," Maureen said. "I watched bits and pieces of it. I watched the first quarter completely and then I saw him kinda chugging along. I thought maybe he was just tired. Then in the second quarter, he kept pressing against his groin . . . the pain on his face . . . I would leave and come back to see what the score was. I was in tears. I'm not kidding."

He was hurting.

"When I saw him trying to run up the court, I said this is ridiculous. There is nothing in the world worth it to me. I hate to say this, and a lot of people are probably angry with me for saying this, but I'm glad it's over. I couldn't stand to see him play."

I don't think he could have played the next game, if they had won.

"I don't think he could have played the next round. The next two games, anyway. He's so hard-headed, though. He would have played."

He told me he feels like he's alone. Everybody wants him to keep playing . . .

"I told him last night, 'Charles, if you want to play for yourself, I'll support that. But please don't play because you feel obligated to the Suns. Because you feel obligated to Nike. Because you feel obligated to Glenn (Guthrie, his agent). Because you feel obligated to us to set up a better life for us. It's not worth it to me.' I can't have him walking around like that. We have plenty of money. We probably have more money than most people will make in three lifetimes."

The fans don't want him to quit.

"Somebody said something to me the other day like, 'Oh, I'm sorry the Suns lost.' I said 'Thank you. I appreciate that.' And this person asked me how I felt about it. I'm not going to lie to somebody. I said, quite honestly, 'I'm glad it's over with because I couldn't stand to see Charles in that pain.' They had the nerve to call me selfish. 'Oh, that's selfish.' And I'm thinking to myself, 'Where do you get off? You're not out there playing. It's not your body that's breaking down.' Charles is entitled to live a pain-free life as much as he can, as hard as he has worked. He has provided a good life for a lot of people. He's given a lot to a lot of people. He's entitled to enjoy it. And if he wants to give it one more shot to get the ring for himself, I say go ahead. But if he's doing it for financial reasons, I don't want that. Quite honestly, I don't think he should. I don't. Like I said, if he decides he wants to play, I won't be happy with it because I'll be scared he'll get hurt. But I want him to get the ring. It's kind of like there is good and bad to both."

He was taking those shots in the groin.

"That's got to hurt. And he's had so many shots. He's had too many, in my opinion. I'm not a doctor. I don't know a lot about it, but he's had them in his back, and his groin. I told him, 'Like what are you, Charles, some guinea pig?' "

The decision, it's weighing heavily on his mind.

"Last night I asked him if he had to choose right now, what would his answer be. He said, 'I can't really answer that.' He had his meeting today with Jerry (Colangelo). Charles told me if he had to answer, either way, he would be happy with his decision. I said, 'So, say I flipped a coin. Heads you play. Tails you retire. Whatever it landed on, you would feel comfortable with that?' He said yes. So I felt a little better with that. I don't envy him that he has to make that decision. I wish I could make it for him and help him with it. But I don't think I can."

I think people misread him when he says, win or lose, he's going to play golf the next day regardless. It's a great philosophy. But I know he hurts when he loses. He just doesn't want the public to see it. Does he bring that home?

"Especially, I think, if he feels responsible for the loss, which isn't really fair. I don't think any one person can win a game or lose a game for a team. It's a team sport. It's not one person, like boxing, golf. There are five guys out there on the court. I think it's unfortunate he takes it upon himself where he feels the need to carry the whole team. That's not fair. It's too much stress to live under. It's like if you mess up on your job, who sees? Your boss. If Charles misses a free throw at the end of the game and they lose by one point, he feels that it is his fault. And all of Phoenix sees it. If it's on TV, the whole viewing audience sees it. I don't think that's fair."

How is it for you, living in Arizona?

"Because of the people that we hang out with, we are surrounded by people in the same situation. So you feel accepted easier. Quicker, I should say. I can't quite get the feel for the city. Everything to me is beautiful here. The mountains are gorgeous. I'm a warm-weather person, and I love to exercise and you can do that every day here. And the weather is kind of bad back East, especially this past winter. But there's still something about home. Charles probably feels the same way about Alabama."

How long will you live here?

"I don't know, honestly. If Charles retires, I'm sure we'll stay here a little while but I don't think we'll make Phoenix our home. And that's probably another reason I've adapted to it easier. Knowing that it's only short-term."

I asked him what it's like being married to Charles Barkley. He said you told him that during the season he's a jerk.

"He's very focused. He can be kind of nasty, but I think most of the time he's thinking about the next game. Initially, it was hard for me, because I didn't know. I used to think, 'What did I do? He's upset. Did I do something wrong?' Charles is a very moody person, where I'm not. I'm pretty much the same, day in, day out, unless I'm sick or someone in my family is sick. But Charles, I guess because of his body being in so much pain, his moods can change like that. And I had never really been around anybody like that because my whole family is the same way I am. Just kind of go along with the punches. So I used to take it personally all the time. And now that I know him, I know the way he is. I know when to approach him. I know when not to. And I just let him do his own thing, really, on a game day. I mean he goes to practice, he comes home. He lays right there where you're sitting, and gets his pillow. I make myself invisible."

He says he is hyper on game days.

"He is. He doesn't sleep the night before. When you travel as much as he does, going from different time zones and playing games at night, he'll be wound up after the game. He can't go right to sleep because his adrenaline is going. Players will grab a bite to eat. Go have a beer or two. Whatever. Charles won't get to sleep before two o'clock, or two-thirty. Then he's up in the morning and it's the same thing."

Can you be Maureen, or are you always Mrs. Barkley?

"I think that goes with the territory. I think people who have known me all my life, hopefully, it doesn't matter to them who I'm married to. But when you are put in a situation where you are so sought after, it's hard to trust people. That's the thing that is not so pleasant. Because you never know if someone's being friendly because they want to or because they want to meet Charles, or because they want tickets to a game, or because they want to be in the scene, as they call it. I think that is hard. Lack of privacy is very hard. Especially where Christiana is concerned. We can't do things as a family that most people can."

Of the things you give up, privacy first comes to mind.

"It's ridiculous, isn't it."

Have you ever gotten accustomed to Charles being asked for his autograph when you're together in a restaurant?

"No. I get angry with that. I really do. I think people are entitled to, if they're excited, you kind of give them a little leeway because people act silly when they get excited to meet somebody. But there should be some common sense. Everybody is entitled to a meal. I don't care how excited I might be to see somebody, or meet somebody. I would never approach somebody while they're eating. That's just the way I am. Being married to Charles, I see what it's like being on the receiving end, through him. You know, I've had people come up to me and tell me stupid things, sometimes. Some woman came up to me the other day at the game and said to me, and she thought she was flattering me, or giving me a compliment, she said, 'You are the nicest wife.' I said, 'Thank you. I appreciate that.' Then she started talking badly about the other ones. That's so untrue, because everyone with the Suns is so nice here. I said, 'Do you know Amy Johnson, Frank's wife?' She said no. I said, 'Do you know Dana Kleine?' No. 'Elaina West?' No. 'JoAnn Fitzsimmons?' No. I said, 'Then how can you say that?' But in her mind she was so nervous to be talking to Charles Barkley's wife she was looking to say something that, I guess, would butter me up. It was stupid. But some people have no common sense when they get around so-called celebrities."

You get stared at, I would think.

"I think I'm used to that by now. Charles and I have been together for seven years. I don't really see it, now. I very rarely will make eye contact with somebody if I'm somewhere crowded. I'll just go where I need to go. If somebody says hello, I'll say hi back. Or if I happen to make eye contact, I will say hi. But sometimes you just need to be left alone and go out. Eat dinner. Go to a movie. Or hang out with our friends. Or play tennis. Whatever. Without being asked a million questions."

Can you become involved in a cause, or do you have to watch what you get involved with because you are Charles Barkley's wife?

"Yes. Are you talking about negative publicity or do you mean somebody using my name?"

Do you have to watch what you involve yourself in?

"Oh, definitely. I've done a lot of charity events this year. I let people know from the beginning that I'm not getting an autograph from Charles. I'm not asking anyone with the Suns to appear. I'm not asking anyone with the Suns for anything. If you want me to help you, I'm more than willing. It's not like people with the Suns are nasty and wouldn't do it. But he has enough people after him for autographs. Wanting him to speak here. It's for a good cause. He shouldn't have to come home to that with me. I think I'm the one person in the world who should alleviate that from him. I shouldn't enter into that picture. No way. I'm his wife."

When do you spend time together? Over dinner, after games?

"Pretty much. But we usually have other people with us. Charles and I are both very, I want to say, accommodating, for lack of a better word. Say when a team comes to town. Utah comes to town. Charles is going to invite Karl Malone out to dinner, just out of courtesy. And I'm sure when Charles is in Utah, Karl takes Charles out to dinner. The time we have is at night, when we come home after dinner. We watch TV for a few hours."

You mentioned going to movies.

"Yeah, Charles and I go, but it's a hassle. I run in and get the tickets and Charles waits outside. We run in when it's dark and we leave before the movie ends. It's so weird now because when I go to a movie with my friends, or I take Christiana to a movie, I find myself near the end of the movie getting that anxious feeling, like we need to get out of here before people start to bug us. So now it has kinda carried over into my life, too, even when I'm not with him."

Charles said he regularly changes your phone number. Is that because strangers get it?

"Yes. I have no idea how. About three months ago, somebody

called here. The guy sounded nice. He just called to wish Charles good luck. It was during the regular season. I said, 'Do you mind me asking where you got our phone number?' He said he got it from somebody in a gym. . . . I can't understand the obsession with celebrities. I really can't. Not to take away from them. They've worked hard and they are entitled to admiration but not to the point where it's kind of like they're a god."

What's your daily routine like?

"When Christiana's at school, I volunteer at Children's Hospital. I go there a few times a week. I work out every day. I'm always at her school doing field trips and things with them."

Does she like her school?

"She loves it. Yesterday was her last day."

She will grow up fast.

"She's smart. She said to me today, 'Mommy, I'm biracial. Right?' I said, 'What?' She said, 'I'm biracial. My daddy is black and my mommy is white. I'm both, right?' I said, 'Yes, you are.' I mean, 5 years old. Just out of the clear blue."

Are you concerned about how other kids will treat her?

"Kids tease kids. I was teased because I was skinny. Charles was probably teased because he was fat and because he was black. All kids tease kids. But it seems like when it comes to interracial children, they really go down hard on them. Even though Christiana is biracial, most people are going to see her as being black. I mean, it's just a fact. If you are one quarter black and three quarters white, you are considered black. I'm not saying I want to ship her to school somewhere in the middle of the inner city, so that she's around black people. I'd like her to be around more of a mixture because I don't think it would be fair to her. I don't want to deny her of anything. I can't teach her the black history because I don't know anything about it. I'm white. And Charles could teach her a little bit, but he's so far removed from it in this lifestyle. So I feel she needs to be around it to at least experience it a little bit. She deserves to know about both sides of her family."

Do you want her to grow up in Philadelphia?

"I think there are pluses and minuses. In Philly, the crime rate is so high and I don't really want her exposed to that. It's ridiculous there now. I don't know if it's died down since I left, eight or nine months ago. I doubt it. I would send her to a private school, right by our house. All kinds of people go there. They have Armenian children. White children. Black children. Oriental. A real good mixture. Every nation there. That I would like.

"But I don't know if it's a better place to raise an interracial family. It's something we need to seriously think about. For the time being, she's okay. Frank Johnson's kids are in her school. Frank's daughter is in her class. So she's not the only black person in there."

Before you married, you must have discussed how people would react to a biracial marriage. Has it been more difficult, or easier, than you expected?

"It doesn't bother Charles and me at all. I have no problem with it. When people say stuff to me, it doesn't hurt my feelings because I don't feel like they're insulting me. It bothers me because I feel like they're insulting Charles. Like people will call me an N-lover. Ooooooh. Please don't insult me that way. What a bad person I am to care for someone of a different color than me. I don't care. I figure if they say that, they're ignorant, and it doesn't even matter to me. The thing that concerns us the most is with her. Everything concerns us the most with her. But I think she's very well adjusted so far, for a 5-year-old."

He said you don't take Christiana to many games because all fans aren't nice. You don't want her to hear the stuff some people say.

"That's true. Plus there are sickos out there. About a month ago, some creep came running down the stands after us. She was with me. He kept trying to get down to us the whole game. The security guards had to rush us out of there. I didn't know what was going on, but it just frightened me so much. The whole time I'm at the game with her I don't relax at all. I'm looking around all the time."

In his book, Outrageous, *he talks about rumors regarding his private life. To test how fast rumors can spread, he told someone that the two of you were divorcing and the word got back to you before he could get home that same day.*

"Yeah. I don't go to him with every rumor that I hear. Otherwise, I would be talking to him every day. I've heard some crazy ones about myself."

Such as?

"I heard that I was on drugs. I've never done drugs. I've never smoked pot. I heard it after I had Christiana. I didn't gain a lot of weight with her and it didn't take me long to lose weight because I've always been in shape. I'm not saying I'm a stud, or anything. I work out. I'm not lazy about that. And I lost my weight after I had her probably within four weeks. But someone started a rumor that I was doing whatever drug that would make you lose weight. I guess cocaine or speed. Something that would make you hyper. There was another rumor going around in Philly that I was messing around with one of Charles' teammates. Listen to this one. Charles got tickets for us to go see Luther Vandross. We had six people all together. Three couples. But then Charles forgot he was supposed to go to a bachelor party that night. So he told Brian Oliver to go with me. Mind you, the concert was at the Spectrum where Charles plays. So Brian and I went with these four other people. Excuse me. Gimme a break. Would I be so stupid as to take the guy to where my husband is employed? Not to mention it was Charles' idea in the first place. So I've been on the receiving end of some crazy rumors. And I've heard some a lot crazier about me and a lot crazier about him. I just don't understand. I guess people have no life. That's how I look at it. They have no life, so they are obsessed with ours. And misery loves company. I hate to say that, but that is so true."

Is your daughter talking about wanting brothers and sisters?

"Yes. I want to have more kids, but I want to wait until Charles retires. We've talked about adopting, too. I'd like to have one or more of our own. Maybe a little boy. I'd like to adopt one or two children because we could provide them with such a life. But see, I don't want to raise them by myself. It's not the work that I mind. It's that he's not there. He can't really take a big part and I don't feel it's fair to the kids. She doesn't understand why. One time we were watching a TV show, and this really did it to me. These little kids were going trick or treating. The father was taking them out trick or treating and she looked at me, you know, not in a sad way, and she said, 'Daddies take their kids trick or treating?' It was just the way she said it. I thought, 'You know, in your world they don't.' Charles did not see her take her first step. He didn't hear her say her first words. He missed out on so much. I'd rather him be around to see it."

Christiana just had a birthday?

"Her birthday is the same day as Charles' mother's birthday. We have a lot of that in our family. My brother was born on my dad's birthday and his younger brother had a baby born on my birthday."

Did you have a party?

"No, we didn't because the Suns had a game that day and it was a noon game. She said she wanted to wait until she got back to Philly so all her cousins could be there, and her friends back there."

Do you envision the day when Charles will have time for you and your family?

"Especially more time to do stuff with Christiana and any of the other children we may have. Just to do stuff like a family. Miniature golfing, as an example. Something as minuscule as miniature golfing. Going to the zoo. We can't do any of that."

He's talking about running for governor of Alabama. Is there much difference between a famous basketball player's wife and a politician's wife?

"No, probably not. I know what you are saying about having a more normal life. To have some of this stuff die down. Do I look forward to that? Oh, yes. Yes. Yes I do."

51

Candles, Incense, Prayers

The man whose black business card says "Shamanistic Healer" pulled the drapes and instructed me to sit facing him, my back to the altar. The funky smell of incense fill the darkened room.

"This is what you would do for Charles?" I asked.

The man nodded. His wife and son sat on either side of him, hands folded in their laps.

"And it's not going to hurt?"

The healer, dressed in a green golf shirt, jeans and sneakers, smiled gently and assured that whatever he was about to do was painless and wouldn't take long. Afterward, he said, I would feel better.

The typewritten letter, accompanied by the black business card, was delivered by hand to my office. It was dated May 22, 1994, the day after the Rockets eliminated the Suns in the playoffs. The letter began:

My name is Robert Martinez and I am a healer. I have tried to get through to Charles Barkley to offer him a pain-free alternative to the medical treatment he is receiving, but the letters I have written to him or Jerry Colangelo have never gotten past their secretaries.

I have given people healing from all over the world. I do not want publicity or fame. What I want is to do what I do best, heal. There have been people with depression, lack of energy, migraines, back problems and every conceivable ache and pain known to man have come to me for help. They come after they have exhausted all other forms of traditional medical or psychiatric help. They come willingly or sometimes they come because they can no longer live with their pain no matter if healing seems to go against all the things they thought they knew or believed. . . .

"How did you get started?" I asked, before we did.

"I started many lifetimes ago," Martinez said. "Do you believe in reincarnation?"

"I dunno."

"In my past life, I was a healer from India. I've been to Tibet and Guatemalo in previous lives." In this life, Martinez said, he worked 30

179

years as a gardener for the city of Phoenix before he retired four years ago and went into the healing business full time. "I have a lot of dreams that come true."

"You were in a lot of them," Alva, his wife, said.

"I was?"

"Yes," she said. "We knew what kind of person you are before you came."

I do not advertise or go around telling people who I am or what I do. The people who come to me are through word of mouth from others that came and left without the pain many of them had experienced for years. In this case, I wish to make an exception for Charles Barkley. My admiration for him goes beyond his ability as a player . . . he is a warrior. Anyone with his guts and determination deserves to get what he has worked so hard for. Because you can't help anyone unless they are willing first to help themselves.

Time is running out for him if he makes an irreversible decision to have a back operation or go into retirement. It's not his time to quit and I swear, he has more playing time ahead of him if he will meet me face to face for a healing.

I do not expect you to put your reputation on the line for someone you've never met. If you suffer from aching shoulders, sleepless nights or anything that troubles you mentally or physically, I can prove my ability to you.

"We have helped people from all over," Martinez said. "South America. Belgium. Mexico. India. They don't even have to be here. We can heal them through pictures."

"You mean photos?"

Alva nodded. "We have a whole album of people we have helped."

"We can help not only Charles Barkley. We can help the entire team," Martinez said. "Dan Majerle, for instance. During the playoffs he lost his confidence. Kevin Johnson, he is always hurt. We can prevent injury by sending positive energy to the aura all the time."

"Is that's Barkley's problem? Energy?"

"His pain," the healer said, "is from negative energy in the body, that's all."

"You think so?"

"I know so. He has a lot of negative energy in his aura. We can get rid of that."

Alva said, "He wants to win the championship. As long as he is in this realm, it's going to bother him. It's a distraction to him. No matter what he says . . . We're not against doctors. They have their place, like everyone else. If you have a broken leg, you should go to a doctor. If people come here and they need to go to a doctor, we tell them to go see a doctor. We know we can help Charles Barkley. All he needs to do is come in one time."

The healer's wife said she literally felt Barkley's pain. "Even when he was denying he was in pain, or just not talking about it, I could feel it in my back. It was very painful. No matter what position I was sitting, or what I did, the pain wouldn't go away. And what I felt wasn't nearly as profound as what he feels."

"All he has to do is come in and have faith," the healer said. "That's not very much for a championship."

"If he does," I asked, "what do you want in return?"

"We just want him to be happy, and win the championship, not just for himself but for his soul."

The room fell silent. Martinez placed his hands above my head and slowly brought them down on either side of my face, drawing them down around my shoulders, not touching me, but gauging me, measuring my invisible emanation, my aura. Alva closed her eyes. Behind me, their son Andrew lit three white candles arranged in a triangle on the altar.

The healer picked up a brass dish, containing the smoldering incense, and held it under my nose. "I want you to take three deep breaths."

One, two, three.

Martinez took my hands in his and stared deeply into my eyes for a long time. Suddenly, his eyes rolled back and his eyelids fluttered. I thought he was having a seizure. The healer began reciting a prayer, in rapid Spanish. "In the name of the all powerful God, in the name of the Divine Spirit, in the name of Jesus Christ, in the name of the brothers and sisters . . . we ask all of you to rid this person of all sickness, diseases, visible and invisible, in all things natural and unnatural. . . . I Robert Martinez cleanse your body of all witches and warlocks . . ." On and on it went, with gibbering references to "Satanico" and "Christo."

The prayer over, the healer turned me around in the chair. A crucifix, three burning candles and three glasses filled with water were arranged on an altar.

"The water is like a filter," Martinez explained. "Whatever negative energy you have is removed and it goes through the water."

"How about the candles?" I asked.

"They're for energy."

As they say, talk is cheap. It's easy to promise all kinds of things and never deliver, but that's not how I work . . . Meeting you face to face would explain more about who I am and what I can do than all of the thoughts and words I can direct at you.

"Now," the healer announced, "I am going to throw my energy to you." Martinez held his hand over my head and began snapping his fingers rapidly, like the leader of a jazz band picking up the beat. He circled, snapping away. He gave me 25 seconds' worth before his hand tired. After the energy transfer, the healer repeated the Spanish prayer.

So I hope that you can arrange a meeting so that I can help Charles Barkley, not through all kinds of vague words and promises but through a healing. Afterward, he will definitely feel better.

"How do you feel?" Martinez asked.
I thought of soul singer James Brown. "I feel good."
"It will keep on working," the healer said, "for about 10 days."

52

Being the Man

He's one of those players who has never given me any respect.
He only gives the superstars like Michael, Magic, Isiah and
Larry credit and respect. That's his claim to fame. It's all a
front. He kisses their butts.

He walks around thinking he's the ambassador of the league, but
he's a phony person. He's a very good player, but you can't
compare yourself to Michael, Magic and Bird. Barkley won
MVP last year, but so what? They got the rings, and he doesn't.
Until he gets a ring, he's not the ambassador of the league. Until
then, I'm considering myself the ambassador.
—Scottie Pippen in *USA Today*, Feb. 27, 1994

So, he was asked everywhere he went, what do you think about what
Pippen said about you?

Barkley didn't take the bait. He held his tongue. A phony? An ass-
kisser? "That's his opinion," Barkley said airily. "Scottie Pippen is
entitled to say whatever he wants. It's not against the law. That's
what's great about America."

He knew why Pippen lashed out. His remarks stemmed from
Barkley's assessment of the post-Jordan Chicago Bulls. Early in the
season Barkley predicted the Bulls wouldn't repeat as champions. Not
without Michael Jordan. "Scottie Pippen and Horace Grant talk
about how good the Bulls are without Michael. There's no pressure
in January and February. In June, they'll be standing there with their
thumb up their ass."

Barkley didn't say anything when Chicago, after a strong start, lost
seven of 10 games, including six of eight at home. He didn't comment
when Pippen criticized fans at Chicago Stadium who booed him after
a loss to Cleveland. As he left the floor, Pippen made an obscene gesture to the crowd. He later said, "In my seven years here, I've never
seen a white guy booed in the Stadium. Toni Kukoc went 0 for whatever (0 for 9) and I never heard one fan get on him."

Barkley watched the Bulls-Knicks playoff series with special interest. In Game 3, Pippen refused to return to the game with 1.8 seconds left because he disagreed with his coach, Phil Jackson, on a play call. Pippen later apologized to his coach and teammates. The Bulls, like the Suns, were eliminated before reaching the NBA Finals.

"So why didn't you react to Pippen's insults?" I asked.

"The thing you have to understand is that I've been a star a long time," Barkley said. "I understand the responsibilities. That goes with it. It was very obvious that Scottie didn't know how to handle being the man. He went off on the fans. Talking that black-white stuff, talking about how they don't boo white guys. Then he went off in the playoffs.

"They all want to be stars. But it's unbelievable the responsibilities that go with being the man. Not many guys can handle it, which is why there aren't that many. People talk about how many superstars there are in the league. There are very few superstars who can make plays at the end of the game. Everybody talks that stuff, but there is a reason Scottie Pippen is not there in the fourth quarter. He's a great player, but he's not one of those guys who can make plays with the game on the line.

"Remember, when Paul (Westphal) benched me in the second half of that game? My first reaction was to go off. I voiced my opinion, but I felt I had an obligation not to make a scene. But for a guy like Scottie not to go back into a game? I couldn't do that. I wouldn't. Sometimes you just have to take it.

"Refusing to go into a game? Just because the play isn't called for you? You never hear of a really successful player doing stuff like that."

53

Margaritaville

June 10, 1994

As Hakeem Olajuwon and Patrick Ewing battled for a rebound on the television in the clubhouse bar, Charles Barkley peeled off a $20 bill.

"Here, Denise."

"What's this for?" she asked.

"For doing such a good job." Barkley happily sucked down his third frozen margarita, while the waitress headed to the bar to get his fourth. "And bring me a bigger straw! This little thing's giving me a hernia!"

Barkley appeared to be coping with life after the playoffs. Two weeks after the Suns' season ended he sat with friends around a table in the clubhouse bar at the Seven Bridges Golf Club in Woodridge, Ill., a Chicago suburb, site of the Michael Jordan/Ronald McDonald Children's Charities Celebrity Golf Classic. He still had to make a decision about his basketball future, but for the moment his only concern was his golf game, namely his putting. "I could have shot 85, easy. I missed eight straight par putts on the back. *Eight*," Barkley said. "I don't know what I did to piss off the golf gods."

Mike Eruzioni nodded sympathetically. Barkley shot 90 in the first round. Eruzioni, the captain of the 1980 U.S. Olympic hockey team that beat the Soviet Union's best and went on to win the gold medal, didn't fare much better. He trudged in with an 87, 15 over par.

"You won't believe what happened to me on No. 14," Eruzioni said. "I hit a good drive. I'm standing there with a wedge. I shank it straight right. I mean 40 yards to the right. And I hit Stan Mikita—my idol—right in the butt! I wore No. 21, Stan's number, my whole life. I took a nine on the hole. Then I double bogeyed the next hole, and the next one, too. I was upset because I shanked it. But then to hit *Stanley*, of all people . . ."

The tournament, which is staged in partnership with the Celebrity Golf Association, attracts some of the nation's top athletes, sports personalities and celebrities. Many of the contestants, like heartthrob Jack Wagner, star on the TV soap opera "General Hospital," are low-handicap or scratch players. Barkley and the actor are friends.

"What's wrong with your back?" Wagner asked on the practice tee.

"There's three things wrong," Barkley told him. "I've got a bulging disk and a congenital problem and something with a nerve. It hurts when I play basketball."

"Does it hurt playing golf?" Wagner asked.

"A little."

"How about sex?"

"I'm always on the bottom."

With Jordan playing baseball with the Class AA Birmingham Barons, Barkley filled in as host of the 54-hole tournament. "If Michael keeps hitting .200," Barkley cracked, "he'll be back (as host) next year." Barkley was paired with two good players, Houston Oilers placekicker Al Del Greco and former vice president Dan Quayle.

Barkley tells the story of the time his mother lectured him about the perils of voting for George Bush. "He's for the rich," she said.

"Mama," Barkley reminded, *"I'm rich."*

"If Charles decided to run for governor, I told him I would come in and campaign for him, or against him, whichever would help," Quayle said. "We both have a commitment to people. To strong values. To principles. To parents getting involved and giving certain direction to their children. We also have a strong commitment to putting our children first. We haven't talked about taxes, North Korea, things like that . . . But Charles is someone who takes life very seriously." Quayle described Barkley as a "tremendous individual" and "great human being." The former vice president didn't comment on Barkley as a golfer.

Barkley's fundamental flaw is his grip. His caddy, Dave O'Neal, a local club pro, looked at Barkley's grip and shook his head. Barkley turns his right hand far to the right. His palm is facing almost skyward, instead of toward the target.

"It's weird," Danny Ainge said on the practice tee as he gripped his driver à la Barkley. "Chuck, I feel like I'm riding a Harley."

Barkley tends to hook the ball, but his occasional wildness off the tee didn't keep the gallery away. Thousands of spectators followed him around the course. Barkley talked to himself throughout the round. "Great, right behind a tree . . . I could get arrested hitting some of the hooks I hit . . . My luck I'll hit the sprinkler head. I got buzzard's luck. Can't kill nothin' and nothin' won't die . . ."

At No. 15, a 162-yard par 3, he hooked his tee shot into the crowd. When he arrived at the green, a fan called out, "Charles, were you trying to hurt us?"

"Not 'us,' " he replied. *"You!"*

During the round, Barkley felt his back tightening. Why, if his back hurt, did he play golf? "Nobody bitched about me playing basketball when my back hurt so why do they complain because I play golf?" But the pain in his back reminded him he had a decision to make. His back was asking him, "What are you going to do?" Barkley ruled out surgery.

No one could tell Barkley what to do. Not his doctors. Not his teammates. Not his agent. Not even his friend and confidant. Michael Jordan flew in the morning of the second round, thanked everyone for supporting his tournament, hit a ceremonial ball off the first tee (into the water) and appeared at a press conference, Barkley seated at his side.

Michael, are you allowed to live a more normal life in Birmingham than in Chicago?

"The biggest difference is the weather and the traffic. The people are nice, respectful." Jordan looked at Barkley. "It's his home state."

What do you think about Barkley running for governor?

"He's got my vote."

Can he make it in politics?

"I think he's witty enough. He's opinionated enough. I think he's honest enough. I don't think he's corrupt enough." Jordan and Barkley laughed. "But I think he can do a good job."

Michael, do you think you'll regain your love for basketball, enough to play it again?

"I love the game. It wasn't that I lost the love. I lost the challenge. I'll play anytime you want to play. I just don't play organized. I'll play pickup any day."

Do you play now?

"Yeah. I play a little bit. I'm not as bad as you may think. I still think I can play the game."

What's your golf handicap?

"I dunno," Jordan said. "What's Charles' handicap?"

"I'm a 22." Barkley said.

"I give Charles 11 shots a round," Jordan said. "So I guess I'm an 11."

Do you have anything else to prove on the basketball court?

"No. No matter what I do in baseball, if I hit .100, nobody can take away what I've achieved in basketball. Some people may feel my basketball experience is tarnished by my baseball experience. That's their opinion. What I did on the basketball court nobody can challenge."

Is there anything in this world that would bring you back?

Charles answered before Michael could. "Yeah. A trade to the Phoenix Suns."

54

Babylon

Brad Cesmat, host of "Sportsline" on Phoenix radio station KTAR, didn't bring up the story. Barkley did. "I know there was some stuff written about me and my teammates," he said in a live interview on the sports talk show.

The stuff Barkley referred to was an exposé that appeared in the June 15 issue of *New Times*, a local weekly newspaper. The tabloid's front-page teaser read, "Police Report Lifts Veil on Suns' Sex Party." The reporter, Darrin Hostetler, detailed a "morbidly compelling story of arrogant, unchecked desires, of life inside basketball Babylon."

The night the Suns returned from Houston after being eliminated from the playoffs, Barkley and Suns teammates Cedric Ceballos and Oliver Miller went to Jetz, a popular Scottsdale nightclub. They invited several women they met at the bar to join them later at a party at Ceballos' home.

Cesmat: "Did that party happen?"

Barkley: "Did that party happen? It wasn't no wild sex party. You know what's amazing. There were 25 people there. There was no wild sex going on. First of all, if there's wild sex going on I'm pissed off because I wasn't involved. Seriously. That's unfair. To say there was a wild sex party going on. First of all, if you got 25 people there—that other stuff is not my business, because I don't know what happened—but to say we have 25 people at a teammate's house and there's wild sex going on everywhere, and there's only been one even mention of sex, I think that's really unfair to write an article: 'Suns' wild sex party.'

"The thing that pisses me off the most is they made me the focal point of the story because of who I was, because they knew it would bring media attention to the story. If an alleged rape happened the person who committed the alleged rape should have been the focal point of the story. But what they did, they knew they were wrong, but the fans don't understand that aspect of the media . . .

"People got to realize that athletes are human. We do stupid things. We do things wrong just like Joe Bob and Cindy Sue. . . . If people don't accept me for being human, I don't want to be around them. The day you stop doing things wrong you're going to be dead."

55

Commitment

Two sixty-seven. That's what the scales said. In five weeks since he last touched a basketball, Barkley had put on 15 pounds.

"Charles, I'll make you a bet," Howard Eskin said. "If you retire, I'll bet in six months you'll weigh 290."

Eskin, Barkley's golfing buddy, didn't want Charles to retire. Neither did Danny Ainge. They double-teamed their friend during a weekend Celebrity Golf Association tournament in Toronto.

Charles, they said, you're only 31. You're still a great player. Look what you did against Golden State in the playoffs. Sure, it's fun playing golf every day, but you can play golf for the next 40 years. The Suns still can win the NBA title. If you commit yourself to a rehab program, and come back in the best shape of your career, who knows how good you could be? Are you ready to give up on your dream of winning the championship? Do you really want to quit? If you do, you'll spend the rest of your life wondering. What if, what if . . .

On Monday, Barkley flew to Phoenix. He promised Suns owner Jerry Colangelo he would make a decision before the NBA draft, which was Wednesday. Tuesday morning, Ainge telephoned Barkley, and made one last plea. Eskin called too, at 10 A.M. "What are you going to do?"

"I don't know," Barkley said.

Colangelo thought he knew. "Based on all the information I had, I believed Charles was going to retire. We were already making plans to go on without him. We were working on a couple of trades, involving free agents."

At 11:30 A.M., Colangelo invited Barkley into his office. Barkley closed the door behind him. Before they sat down, Barkley blurted, "Well, I've decided I'm going to play . . ."

Colangelo was happy to hear the words. But they still had a lot to discuss. The owner told Barkley what he expected of him, in terms of rehab. He talked about leadership. "We're all products of the experiences we have had," Colangelo said. "People who have gone through this process, like Charles has, can really offer something positive to younger players in terms of leadership. I'm not sure Charles has ever been interested in that role. He just wanted to take care of his own business. But I would like to see that. I really would."

At 12:15 P.M. the Suns announced a press conference for 1 P.M. As media outlets rushed to America West Arena, 50 folding chairs were placed on the floor of the Suns practice court. The same court where Barkley once told Joe Kleine, who complained that he had been fouled, "Would you like some cheese with that whine?" The same court where Barkley clanged a three-pointer off the rim and shocked a visiting class of students from Adams Elementary by angrily knocking over a ball rack. The same court where Ainge accused him of dogging it one day in practice.

"Ainge, you can have me now," Barkley said, "or you can have me tomorrow at seven o'clock." Ainge opted for game time.

He had talked about retirement all year.

"I'm gone. It's time. I've made up my mind." . . . "I've accomplished everything I ever wanted to accomplish" . . . "I don't think about winning the championship every day but I think about my golf game every day." . . . "I don't want to play in pain." . . . "I'm serious." . . . "I'm tired of answering questions about it." . . . "I've told you what I'm going to do." . . . "Write whatever you want. I'm outta here. . . ."

His teammates dealt with the never-ending story with good humor. "Charles, next year we can win 55 games without you," Kevin Johnson said after a victory in December. "We'll pull you out of the bleachers when we get into the playoffs. What do you think? Same salary. Whatever you want."

Barkley brightened. "Let's see. Off October, November, December, January, February . . . Start working out in April. I *like* it. I'd be ready by May."

But he wasn't smiling as Colangelo stepped to the podium. Barkley was subdued. He appeared almost melancholy as he stared at the floor. Barkley had made the decision, but Colangelo had set the terms for his return during their 45-minute meeting.

"Charles informed me he has made his decision," Colangelo told the assembly, "and although he has wavered back and forth, his final decision is he will continue to play. The reason I personally feel excited about that is that the only way he can continue to play on a level that he is comfortable with, is with a commitment, a personal commitment to work and rehab, and come to camp in the best shape he has ever been in his life. He made that commitment to me. The important thing is, he knows, because of his pride, he is not going to come in here and just try to get through a season. That wouldn't be good for anyone. That's not his intent. He would have quit. Simple as that."

Barkley listened, head bowed.

"So the real encouragement is with the commitment that it will take. And I don't think Charles Barkley has ever let anyone down once he has given someone his word. With that kind of commitment we could look forward to a big year in Phoenix. Because it would take commitment"—the sixth time Colangelo used the word—"and work and dedication to fulfill that. He is prepared to do that. We're all excited about that. And now we can plan accordingly. So I'm going to turn it over to Charles . . ."

Two weeks earlier, I asked Barkley if he quit, what would he say? Mickey Mantle said goodbye after the pain in his legs and the pride in who he used to be won out. Mantle's farewell was brief, simple, eloquent. "I can't hit when I need to. I can't steal a base when I want to. I can't go from first to third when I have to. It's time to quit trying."

Barkley said he didn't know what he would say if he retired, but he knew the words wouldn't come easily, whatever decision he made.

"Up until the last 48 hours I was definitely going to retire," Barkley began. He paused. Swallowed. "Uh . . . the person I've got to thank for coming back—I hate to give him credit—is Danny Ainge.

"I had called Dr. Emerson last week and told him I was going to retire. I didn't feel like I wanted to go through the rehab. After spending the weekend with Ainge riding my back, he opened my eyes up to a lot of things about personal sacrifice. If I had retired it would have been because I would have been lazy and didn't want to do the effort it would have taken . . . . for me to let it all end, just because I didn't want to work out, I didn't think that would be right.

"After watching the NBA Finals—and congratulations to the Houston Rockets—I feel like if we were healthy we could have played with them. I still feel we have one of the five best teams in the NBA. If we're healthy and we tinker with our team just a small bit we can be title contenders."

Barkley flashed a nervous smile. "I know this is probably going to be the hardest thing I've ever done as far as rehab, but I look forward to it. Right now my hands are shaking a little bit because I'm not really sure, to be honest with you. This is one of those decisions you make that you're really not sure it's worth it until next summer.

"I've got a great coaching staff. A great owner. Great teammates. We're in a great city. The fans here are tremendous. So I want to try it. See what happens. I want to do my part, because I don't want to embarrass myself. I wasn't happy with the way our season ended. For me personally and for the team. I don't want my last game to be remembered limping around.

"I was kinda talking myself into retiring . . ."

It was true. At golf tournaments, fans called out, "Charles, don't retire!" Barkley's standard reply: "I know you don't want me to retire, but *your* back doesn't hurt . . ."

"Ainge challenged me. Danny was very positive. He said if you do what you're supposed to do you can be really good again. It was good for me. I guess I wanted someone to talk me into it, to be honest with you. It's really difficult to say you're not going to play anymore. I wanted to change my mind, but I couldn't do it myself. Once you make that decision, it's final. You don't want to be like a boxer who boxes and says he's retired and then comes back. I don't think that's the way you do it.

"Obviously not winning the championship has something to do with it. But I'm very happy with my career. If my career was over today, I could deal with that. I didn't want it to be over just because I didn't want to do the rehab. The bottom line is that I would have been kidding myself. And if I did retire I probably would have been pissed off forever. . .

"This year maybe I won't break down as much. If I do break down it won't be because I didn't do my rehab. I've got to think positively. If my legs don't go numb as much as they did this past season and take all my power in my legs away, I feel like I still will be able to play well. What frustrated me this year was I couldn't play well in back-to-back games. I want to play well in back-to-back games. I owe that to the fans. I just want to play. I love playing basketball . . ."

56

"Charles! Charles! Charles!"

8:30 A.M.
July 18, 1994

Danny Singleton, camp director, stood at the microphone and welcomed the group to the second annual Charles Barkley All-Star Basketball Camp.

"If you hear me," he said, "clap once."

Clap.

"If you're *listening,* clap twice!"

More than 500 youngsters answered with a rousing clap-clap. They were listening, all right. The boys and girls ages 8 through 17 sat on the edge of their seats in the auditorium at Gilbert High School. Many of them wore Barkley T-shirts or No. 34 Suns jerseys. All of them were excited about meeting Barkley and his co-host at the four-day camp, former NBA coach Chuck Daly.

"We promise you are going to have some up-close and personal time with Charles and Chuck," Singleton told the kids. "We *promise* you that you will get a signed autograph from both of them. We *promise* you that you will have an individual picture taken with Charles and Chuck TO-DAY! You will get an autograph of Charles and Chuck TO-DAY!"

The camp director's voice rose with each promise. His speech produced the desired result. The campers hardly could wait. Is he here? When is he coming?

Barkley had a full schedule. He planned to begin his eight-week rehab in San Francisco on July 25, but the Suns insisted he move up the starting date to the 17th, which was the same day his camp opened.

"The Suns asked me how I was going to do both," Barkley said. "I told them not to worry about it. I'll get it done. If push came to shove, I'd cancel the rehab before I skipped the camp." Registration fee for Barkley's camp is $350. "I don't think it's fair to the kids for me to make a token appearance. It's not right. I don't put my name on something, and that's it. I've got an obligation to them, too."

The camp director looked to the back of the auditorium. Not yet? "Most of you know that Charles has an injury," Singleton told the campers. "It's pretty significant. He's going to have to be gone part of the time to take care of his back. But he's going to be here lots. He's going to be with us all day today, and part of the day Tuesday and Wednesday. And he'll be with us all day on Thursday. We're excited for you."

The director got the cue. Barkley was here. "Charles, Charles, Charles," he said into the microphone.

Heads turned. Eyes widened. When they spotted him, the campers squealed with delight, and picked up the chant, "CHARLES! CHARLES! CHARLES! CHARLES!" Barkley walked down the aisle and climbed the steps to the stage. The camp director fell to his knees and began to raise and lower his arms, bowing in Barkley's presence. He looked like a Hindu on a prayer rug, doing the wave.

The camp director jumped up and grabbed the mike. "Ladies and gentlemen," he cried, meaning boys and girls, "Chaaaaaaaarles BARK-LEEEEEEEEEY!"

"Welcome," Barkley told the campers. "It's good to see everybody and be back in Phoenix. We're going to have a great time this week. The Suns are on my back about starting my back rehab. I'm going to get my back worked on, but I'll be here.

"We're here to have fun, but we're also here to talk to you about the things that are really important. We want to be open and honest with you. I want to talk to you about education. I want to talk about listening to your parents. Most of all, I want to talk to you about trying to be a good person."

After Barkley's welcoming speech, Daly joined Charles on stage. It was the first time I had seen them together since the Summer of '92. Daly was the coach of the U.S. Olympic team. Barkley was the Dream Team star.

"I thought Charles really blossomed as a personality that summer," Daly recalled. "Plus, people realized he was a much better player than anyone thought—at least I thought. Sometimes when you're on the other bench you appreciate another player, but you don't quite appreciate him the same way. My opinion of him went up dramatically at the Olympics.

"Talk about focused. He was terrific. There was no fooling around. There was no doubt why he was there. I knew Charles was a great player, but I didn't think he was that good. Charles Barkley is one of the top three, four, five best players in the league. In the *world.*"

• • • •

"So, anybody have a joke?" the camp director asked.

A small boy raised his hand. "If you're an American when you go into the bathroom and you're an American when you come out of the bathroom, what are you when you're in the bathroom?"

"I dunno. What?"

"European," the kid said.

POSTSCRIPT

So, they buried Richard Nixon today. You know I'm not saying any-thing against President Nixon. But when I go, I hope everybody says good things about me, no matter what I did. There is hope for me. In fact, I can't wait to die. When I die all these people who say bad things about me now will say, "Oh, Charles, he was just misunderstood. He had a great year, particularly with all the adversity he went through."

— Charles Wade Barkley
   April 27, 1994

ABOUT THE AUTHOR

David Casstevens is the Executive Sports Editor and columnist for *The Arizona Republic* in Phoenix. He joined the *Republic* staff in 1990 after working as a sports columnist for newspapers in Dallas and Houston. A native of Fort Worth, Texas, Casstevens holds a Bachelor of Journalism degree from the University of Texas at Austin. He has received numerous state and national awards during his 25 years of covering sports. His work has been published in *Sport* magazine and *Best Sports Stories,* an annual sports anthology.

Casstevens has covered the Olympic Games, Wimbledon, Super Bowls, World Cup soccer and other national and international events. He ranks a harrowing bus ride along a narrow, winding, icy road on a snowy night in the French Alps during the 1992 Winter Games as his "greatest sports thrill."

He and his wife, Sharon, live with their three children in Tempe, Arizona.